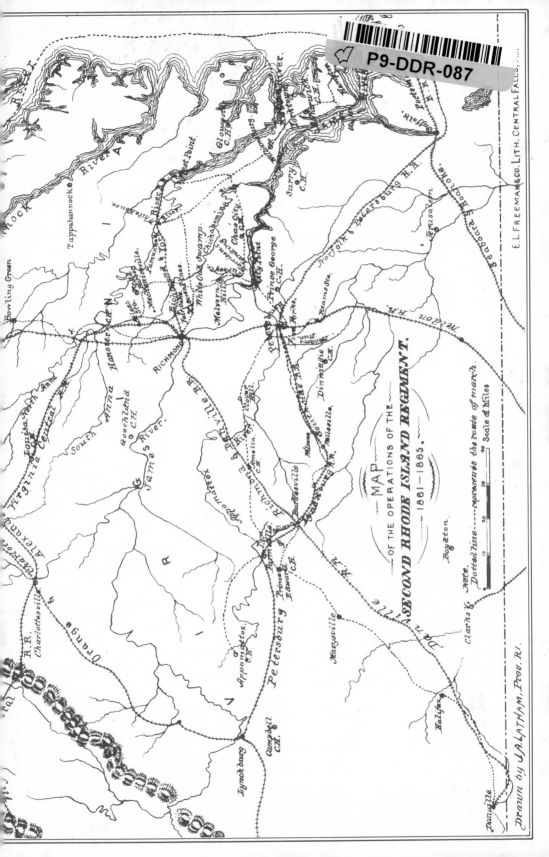

MAP
OF THE OPERATIONS OF THE
SECOND RHODE ISLAND REGIMENT.
1861—1865.

Note.
Dotted line ----- represents the route of march.
Scale of Miles

E.L.FREEMAN&CO.LITH.CENTRAL FALLS.

Drawn by J.A.LATHAM, Prov. R.I.

ALL FOR THE UNION

E. H. Rhodes

Colonel 2ⁿᵈ R.I.V. Inf'y.

ALL FOR THE UNION

The Civil War Diary and Letters of
Elisha Hunt Rhodes

Edited by
ROBERT HUNT RHODES
Foreword by
GEOFFREY C. WARD

Orion Books, New York

Published by Orion Books, a division of Crown Publishers, Inc.,
201 East 50th Street, New York, New York 10022.
Member of the Crown Publishing Group.

Originally published by Andrew Mowbray Incorporated in 1985.

ORION and colophon are trademarks of Crown Publishers, Inc.

Manufactured in the United States of America

Library of Congress Cataloging-in-Publication Data

Rhodes, Elisha Hunt, 1842–1917.
                    the Civil War diary and letters of Elisha
Hunt Rhodes / edited by Robert Hunt Rhodes.—1st Orion ed.
    p.   cm.
  Originally published: Lincoln, RI : A. Mowbray, © 1985.
  1. Rhodes. Elisha Hunt, 1842–1917—Diaries. 2. Rhodes,
Elisha Hunt, 1842–1917—Correspondence. 3. United States.
Army. Rhode Island Infantry Regiment, 2nd (1861–1865)—
Biography. 4. Rhode Island—History—Civil War, 1861–1865—
Personal narratives. 5. United States—History—Civil War.
1861–1865—Personal narratives. 6. Soldiers—Rhode Island—
Diaries. 7. Soldiers—Rhode Island—Correspondence.
I. Rhodes, Robert Hunt, 1937- II. Title.
[E528.5 2nd. R46   1991]
973.7'445—dc20
                                                    91-6519
                                                      CIP

To Landmark College's students and alumni
who are engaged in a battle
against dyslexia

FOREWORD

One March day in 1862, General George B. McClellan, never averse to a little favorable publicity, granted passes to a small party of influential civilians that included Nathaniel Hawthorne and a British correspondent, Edward Dicey of *The Spectator,* to travel out from Washington into Virginia and report firsthand on his elaborate preparations for the peninsula campaign. Hawthorne, Dicey, and their companions were suitably dazzled by the miles of supply wagons, the busy fleet of transports that clogged the Potomac, the wharves and river-steamers crowded with eager, cheering men in blue. It seemed to Dicey impossible that such an army would not sweep all before it.

Toward evening, the little party headed back toward town, only to be halted on the Virginia side of the long chain bridge across the Potomac. "For hours we found it impossible to cross," Dicey wrote, "as a division of 16,000 men were marching over....With colors flying and bands playing, regiment after regiment defiled past us. The men were singing, shouting, cheering;...they chanted 'John Brown's Hymn,'...and the heavy tramp of a thousand feet beat time to that strange weird melody. As the New England regiments passed our train, they shouted to us to tell the people at home that we had seen them in Dixie's Land and on the way to Richmond. Ah, me! How many, I wonder, of those who flitted before us in the twilight, came home themselves to tell their own story."

One of the New Englanders who marched across that chain bridge and did come home to tell his own story was Elisha Hunt Rhodes of the Second Rhode Island Volunteer Infantry, just a few days short of his twentieth birthday but already promoted to Sergeant Major. Over the course of the war, he would cross the Potomac at least twenty-five more times in pursuit of victory, and take part in every major campaign undertaken by the great northern army named for that river, from First Bull Run to Appomattox.

Rhodes had had to obtain his widowed mother's permission before he could join the army as a nineteen-year-old private in July of 1861. He would leave it, a little over four years later, as the colonel in command of his Regiment, a sea-soned soldier at twenty-three. His account of what he lived through, lovingly compiled by his great-grandson and published here for the first time for a wide audience, is, I believe, one of the finest of the war—fresh, vivid, understated, utterly free of the ornate and imitative style with which more learned veterans managed to put some distance between themselves and the ghastly sights they saw.

Rhodes had the genuine soldier's innate distrust of false heroics: at its first taste of gunfire, he faithfully reports, his Regiment "immediately laid down without waiting for orders." But his pages are filled nonetheless with instances of heroism, and it is hard for a modern reader to understand how any man, enduring what Rhodes and his friends endured at Fredericksburg, Gettysburg, the Wilderness, Cold Harbor, or any one of a score of other battles, could have held on to his sanity.

No single soldier can be said to be representative of all his comrades. Armies, perhaps especially American armies, are made up of idiosyncratic individuals. But surely Elisha Hunt Rhodes can safely be said to have been speaking for most of his fellow-soldiers when, a few days before he was mustered out of the army, he looked back on his military career with understandable pride. "I have been successful in my Army life," he wrote, "simply because I have always been ready and willing to do my duty. I thank God that I have had an opportunity of serving my country freeing the slaves and restoring the Union."

Geoffrey C. Ward

INTRODUCTION

Elisha Hunt Rhodes, eldest son of Captain Elisha Hunt and Eliza Ann (Chace) Rhodes, was a lineal descendant of Roger Williams and was born in Pawtuxet village, Cranston, Rhode Island on March 21, 1842.

He attended schools in Pawtuxet as well as the Fountain Street Grammar School and Potter & Hammond's Commercial College in Providence. When his father, a sea captain and master of the costal schooner *Worcester,* was shipwrecked and drowned on Linyard's Cay, Abaco, Bahama Islands on December 10, 1858, Elisha was only sixteen and sole supporter of his family. He left school and went to work as a clerk in the office of Frederick Miller, a mill supplier, where he remained until June 5, 1861 when he enlisted as a private in Co. D, 2nd R.I. Volunteers. He remained in this regiment until it was disbanded on July 28, 1865. He participated in every campaign of the Army of the Potomac from Bull Run to Appomattox with rapid promotions up to the rank of Colonel in 1865.

On June 12, 1866 he married Caroline Pearce Hunt, daughter of Joshua Hunt of Providence and had two children: Frederick Miller, who married Annie Pierce Webb, and Alice Caroline, who married Howard P. Chace.

He took over the firm of Frederick Miller and formed Dunham & Rhodes Co., traveling throughout the South and West establishing contacts with many veterans in the cotton and woolen mill business.

After the war he maintained his interest in military affairs, and on June 25, 1879 he was elected Brigadier General, Brigade of Rhode Island Militia and held that command until 1893.

Elisha Rhodes was President of the Second Rhode Island Volunteers and Battery A Veterans Association and helped to organize reunions at battlefields with other veterans of the Union and Confederacy, carried on voluminous correspondence with other veterans (trading information and souvenirs), and helped raise funds for monuments for the cemeteries and battlefield parks.

General Rhodes was one of the founders, a charter member, and the first Commander of Prescott Post, no. 1, Grand Army of the Republic, Department of Rhode Island on April 12, 1867. In 1871 he was Assistant Adjutant General,

Dept. of Rhode Island, G.A.R. During the years 1872-73 he was Commander of the Department. He was Senior Vice Commander-in-Chief, Grand Army of the Republic in 1877 and Vice-President of the Army of the Potomac Society in 1877. He was a founder and the first President of the Soldiers' and Sailors' Historical Society of Rhode Island for seven years. He was Master of Harmony Lodge, No. 9, Free and Accepted Masons in 1886, and was the head of Golden Rule Lodge, Knights of Honor, and of What Cheer Assembly, Royal Good Fellows, Providence and Grand Master of the Grand Lodge of Rhode Island 1892-93.

He was a member of the Pawtuxet Baptist Church until 1867 when he joined the Central Baptist Church in Providence where he served as a Deacon and Superintendent of the Sunday School.

He served as a member of the Providence School Board for many years. From 1875 to 1885 he was Collector of Internal Revenue (Customs), District of Rhode Island, appointed by President Grant. In 1885 he was elected Assessor of Taxes in Providence.

General Rhodes was a member of the State Board of Soldier's Relief in 1889 and 1890 and was President of the Officers' Rifle Association during those years. He was also Chariman of the Home for Aged Men and Couples in Providence. He was urged to run for the office of Governor, but he declined.

Elisha H. Rhodes died at the age of 75 on Sunday, January 14, 1917, having spent his life in the service of his church, country, state and fellow men.

The diary and letters consist of various slips of papers from small notebooks, letters, with the largest portion a journal re-copied by him in 1885 onto uniform-sized sheets of paper. It is written very simply in contrast to the texts of speeches he delivered as an officer and as a veteran, but it was written as a journal for him to refer to in later years and the rest were letters written whenever he could find the time. His words need no embellishment to capture the feeling of a young man's view of the war. I have tried to add only explanatory notes and to verify names of people and places when I could not read the handwriting and have added other documents as noted, otherwise the manuscript is as he set it down.

R.H.R.

[*All of the illustrations used in the preparation of this volume have been selected from originals contained in the personal collection of Colonel Elisha H. Rhodes.*]

Regiment formed — Recruiting — Mustering In — Camp at Dexter Parade Grounds — Colors presented — New York — Baltimore — Washington — Reviewed by President — Camp Clark — To Virginia — Bush Camp — Centreville — First Action — Bull Run — Fairfax, Va. — Camp Brightwood, Md.

1861

The first Rhode Island Detached Militia under command of Colonel Ambrose E. Burnside has left the state for the seat of war. Military spirit runs high and I, in common with the other young men, feel that it is my duty to serve in the field. I tried hard to go with the First Regiment, but my mother being a widow and having two younger brothers to support, I resisted the inclination to enlist. At this time I am nineteen years of age and for two years have been employed at the office of Frederick Miller Esq., Reed and Harness Manufacturers, no. 92 Canal Street, Providence as a clerk. My mother lives in the village of Pawtuxet, and with her, and my sister and two brothers I spend my Sundays.

Late in the month of April Governor Sprague issued an order stating that the 2nd Rhode Island Volunteers would be immediately enlisted for three years service and called upon the citizens to enlist. Saturday night I visited my home and laid the matter before my mother. She at once refused her consent, and giving as a reason that I was her only support, I was forced to promise that I would remain at home until such time as she might consent to my enlisting. The next Sunday was a sorrowful one at our home. My mother went about with tears in her eyes, while I felt dissappointment that I could not express and therefore nursed my sorrow in silence. Sunday night after I had retired, my mother came to my room and with a spirit worthy of a Spartan mother of old said: "My son, other mothers must make sacrifices and why should not I? If you feel that it is your duty to enlist, I will give my consent." She showed a patriotic spirit that much inspired my young heart. I did not sleep much that night and rose the next morning (which was early in May) and took the omnibus at six o'clock for Providence. On the omnibus I met my old school mate, Levi F. Carr, and finding that his father had consented we agreed to enlist together. On reaching Providence we immediately went to the Infantry Armory corner of Weybosset and Dorrance Streets, and we took seats upon the stairs, it being only seven o'clock A.M. About nine A.M. Mr. William A. Arnold appeared, and upon enquiring we found that he had been appointed as a recruiting officer and was about to open the armory and receive recruits. We followed him into the armory and after he had properly headed a book for signature, Carr signed his name (he being my senior) and I followed.

The boyhood home of Elisha H. Rhodes in Pawtuxet, Rhode Island. Looking south on Broad Street, the house was opposite the corner of Sheldon Street. It is no longer standing.

Recruits began to come in rapidly, and by the end of the week we had more than one hundred names upon the books. The next Monday evening the company organized and elected officers as follows: Captain William B. Sears, First Lieutenant Thomas H. Carr, and First Sergeant James S. Hudson. We drilled day and night and I was especailly instructed by Mr. John E. Bradford, an old member of the Light Infantry Company. Standing before a long mirror, I put in many hours of weary work and soon thought myself quite a soldier. A call for recruits for the first Rhode Island Regiment having come, John E. Bradford and First Sergeant James S. Hudson left our company to join the First Regiment in Washington. I was elected First Sergeant, much to my surprise. Just what a First Sergeant's duty might be I had no idea, for I had never done duty in the militia and was ignorant of the first principles. We spent all our time in the Armory and talked of nothing but soldiering.

May 30, 1861—An order has been issued by Governor Sprague that after examination a company will be formed from the best men now enlisted in the First Light Infantry Company, National Cadet Company and Providence City Guards. During the day Major John S. Slocum of the First Regiment (He is to be Colonel of the Second.) and Surgeon Wheaton (Francis L.) made their appearance at the Armory and stated that only twenty-fine men would be taken from the First Light Infantry. Major Slocum asked for some one to act as clerk, and I was detailed for this purpose. The Colonel asked me if I was acquainted with the men and their general character, and on my saying that I knew them all quite well, he said: "We want only good men. Now when a good man comes in to be examined you look up. If the man is not all right you just go on with your writing." The first man that came in was my friend Levi F. Carr. I looked up. Dr. Wheaton caused him to strip off his clothes, and as Levi was a large robust young fellow, he gave him a severe examination. But he passed and went into another room. I then arose and said that I wanted to go. The doctor looked at me and said: "Young man, you cannot go. You are not fit to be a soldier." I begged of him to let me go and told him of the days I had drilled and how much work I had done. The Colonel finally asked me my age, state of health, if my father was living, and if my mother was willing for me to go. I answered his questions, and he said: "Put your name down. You can go." The doctor inquired if he should examine me, but the Colonel said: "No!" very decidedly. The doctor then said: "Why Colonel, he will be in the hospital in a week, and we shall have to send him home." "Well," said the Colonel, "We will send him home then." I was happy. The examination went on until a man came in who had enlisted and played the bully with us youngsters. He was a large fine built fellow, but I did not look up. The doctor said to him: "You cannot go. You are not a well man." The fellow looked his surprise and said: "What is wrong with me?" The doctor evidently did not expect this question, but he answered promptly: "You have a heart disease." (I doubt if the fellow had a heart for he was a tough customer.) He denied this and insisted upon being examined, but the doctor declined, and he went out. I explained the matter and we went on. As soon as the twenty-five men were selected I was ordered to march them to the Cadet Armory and report to Captain William H. P. Steere. It was my first command, and I made the most of it. I marched the squad through Dorrance, down Westminster Street, through Exchange Street, Exchange Place, across the bridge, through Steeple Street to North Main Street and up to the Cadet Armory in Arnold's Block. Here I formed the men in line and saluting Captain Steere said: "Twenty-five men from the infantry for your company, sir." The Captain said: "I do not want them," and turned away. I did not know what to do and so stood still. It seems that Captain Steere had already formed his company and in order to make room for us he had been obliged to turn out twenty-five men. The Captain finally came up to me and said: "What were you in the Infantry Company?" I replied: "I was First Sergeant, Sir." "Well," said the Captain, "You are a private here. Take your place in line." As I did not know much about sergeants or privates and cared less, I was satisfied. Levi Carr was a sergeant in the Infantry and the Captain continued him in office. At night I wanted to go home, but the Captain said that I was a soldier and must sleep in the Armory. So I slept upon the floor with a lot of other fellows and howled most of the night, much to the disgust of the Captain. As we were still citizens we claimed the right to do about as we pleased. Here we drilled for several days. One evening the Captain came to me, and taking me by the arm, led me to the left of the company and putting me on the flank said: "Rhodes, you are now Eight Corporal." This made me feel all right towards the Captain, but just what an Eight Corporal had to do I did not know. And why I should be eight I did not at the time understand.

June 5, 1861—Today our company marched to a building on the east side of Eddy Street near Clifford Street and was mustered into the U. S. Service by Colonel Loomis, U.S.A. The scene was a solemn one and the

E.H. Rhodes as 8th Corporal of Company "D."

impression made upon our minds will last a long time. We marched back to the Armory, and during the evening I was fitted out with a uniform. It consisted of a blue flannel shirt worn with the flaps outside of the pants, grey pants, fatigue or forage cap and shoes. It was after dark, but I immediately donned my new rig and receiving permission I walked to Pawtuxet, five miles distant, reaching there about nine P.M. Now I was an object of curiosity to my school friends. My mother shed many tears but was still willing that I should go. This was my last visit home before leaving for the war.

2nd Lieut. William Ames

June 6, 1861—Went back to Providence and resumed drill in the Armory. No more could I control my own movements, and we were kept shut up in the Armory most of the day.

June 7, 1861—Our company was designated as Company "D" and the following company officers were appointed by the Governor:

Captain William H.P. Steere

First Lieutenant Edward H. Sears

Second Lieutenant William Ames

Today the Regiment formed for the first time and marched to Exchange Place where services in memory of Stephen A. Douglas were held.

June 8, 1861—The Regiment formed on Exchange Place and marched to the Dexter Parade Ground where a camp was laid out and named Camp Burnside in honor of the Colonel of the First Rhode Island Detached Militia. Sibley tents were issued and at night most of the companies were under canvas, but Company "D" for some reason failed to receive their tents. At noon the entire Regiment marched down street to Railroad Hall for dinner, but by supper time the sheds on Dexter Street opposite to the camp were ready and we took supper there. The sheds, four in number, were built of rough lumber and were 100 by 25 feet. This night our company had to look for quarters to sleep and our Captain marched us to a carpenter shop, corner of Cranston and Gilmore Streets, where we slept upon the benches and floors. We did not howl all night either, for we found that as we were now soldiers regularly mustered into the U.S. Service we couldn't do as we pleased.

Sunday June 9, 1861—This morning the Regiment marched to the First Baptist Church on North Main Street and listened to a sermon by Dr. Caldwell.

Wednesday June 12, 1861—After dress parade a set of colors was presented to the Regiment by the ladies of Providence. This presentation attracted a large party of ladies and gentlemen and was conducted with great ceremony. Speeches were made by prominent citizens and much enthusiasm shown by the men. Hon. Jabez C. Knight, Mayor of Providence, made the presentation.

While encamped on Dexter Parade Ground, I performed my first duty. Captain Steere ordered me to report to Colonel Slocum with two privates armed with side arms (bayonets). On arrival at the Colonel's unit he said to me: "Corporal, take this paper and obey the instructions given." I read the paper and found that it was an order to proceed to a house on Richmond Street and there arrest a deserter and bring him to camp dead or alive. The "dead or alive" part caused me some uneasiness, but I started with my guard, consisting of Thomas W. D. Markham and James M. Bronson, privates of Company "D". On arriving at the house a young lady told me that the man that I was looking for was her brother and that he was sick in bed upstairs. I insisted upon going up and entering a room found a young man groaning in bed. After some conversation during which he told me that he was very ill, my suspicions were excited, and by a sudden movement I stripped off the bed clothes and found that he had turned in boots and all. I made him get up and we went out into the street. Here he asked me to wait on the sidewalk while he went into a beer saloon, but I reminded him of my order which I had already read to him, laying stress upon the "dead or alive" section and we went on. We all sat down upon the steps of Grace Church and waited for an omnibus. He tried to persuade me to get into the omnibus first and let him sit next to the door in order that people might not think him a prisoner. I reversed this and let him get in first and I took a seat by the door. On arrival at camp I turned my prisoner over to the guard. This little adventure made some talk in the Regiment, some of the men claiming that they would not have obeyed the order to arrest the man. But most of the men took a more soldier-like view of it and thought it right to obey orders.

June 16, 1861—This morning the Regiment attended service at Grace Church and Bishop Thomas M. Clark preached. In the afternoon I tried to get a pass to go to Pawtuxet but did not succeed. The Captain did give me a pass to go out of camp but not to leave the city. He made me wear my belt and cartridge box, which rig I did not like, but not knowing enough of the world to disobey orders, I kept it on while I

The 2nd Rhode Island parades through Exchange Place (now Kennedy Plaza) in Providence on their way to join the Army of the Potomac.

made farewell calls upon my friends. At night we had dress parade and the camp was filled with the friends of the soldiers. Frederick Miller presented me with a Smith and Wesson seven shooting revolver and a holster to carry it in. All sorts of useful and ornamental articles were given to us by our friends. I had a silver spoon, knife and fork and a knapsack full of traps that were supposed to be of use to me.

Wednesday, June 19, 1861—Today we have orders to pack up and be ready to leave Rhode Island for Washington. This is new business for us and the work of taking down the tents is slowly performed. Toward night we slung our knapsacks and moved down High, Westminster, and South Main Streets to Fox Point where we went on board the side-wheel steamer *State of Maine*. The streets were crowded with people and we were observed continually. My knapsack was heavy; in fact it was so heavy that I could hardly stagger under the load. At the wharf an immense crowd had gathered and we went on board our steamer with mingled feelings of joy and sorrow. After leaving the wharf I with others fell in for rations. A man stood beside a cask or barrel, and as I passed he threw into my haversack that I held open a piece of boiled corned beef. It proved to be entirely of fat, and as I did not like fat, I threw it overboard and made a supper upon dry bread. The Colonel made us go to bed early and so spreading my blanket upon the floor of the saloon I went to sleep. We were not allowed to make any noise and soon all was quiet.

Thursday, June 20, 1861—We arrived this morning in New York, and as I had only visited New York once before I enjoyed the sail up to the city. We touched at a wharf and after remaining a few minutes steamed down the harbor and landed at Elizabeth Port, New Jersey. Here we found a long train of cars, and we were soon on board and off for Harrisburg, Pennsylvania. All day we dragged along or waited at stations for other trains. We moved so slow that at times the men got off and walked. We had to sleep on the train and being crowded the night was one of much discomfort, and when morning came it showed a party of very weary men. We descended upon the contents of our haversacks for food and the supply was limited.

June 21, 1861—Today we are still on the cars and on the road between Harrisburg and Baltimore. We move slow and are much interested in the scenes from the windows. The little towns and hamlets through which we pass turn out apparently all their inhabitants who stare at the Yankees as if we were wild beasts. Just before dark, ammunition was issued to Companies "C" and "D". We were given three rounds each which were placed in our cartridge boxes. It being the first warlike ammunition I had ever seen I examined mine with much interest. A few percussion caps were also handed to each of us. We were ordered not to load our muskets until orders were given and not to fire until we got the word from our Captain. Our muskets are old fashioned smooth bore flint lock guns altered over to percussion locks, and the cartridge contains one round ball and three buck shot. We arrived in Baltimore after dark and disembarked from the cars to march through the city to the Washington Depot. Immense crowds met us at the Depot and the streets were lined with people who shouted for Jeff Davis and abused us roundly. But we said not a word and plodded on. Governor Sprague was with us and many questions were asked concerning him, but remembering our orders not to speak to anyone we took no notice of the people or their talk. The march nearly killed me for my knapsack was so heavy that I could hardly move, but fear of the people kept me from falling out of line, and at last we reached the Washington Depot. Here we took the cars and the balance of the night was passed on the road to Washington only forty miles distant.

Saturday June 22, 1861—Hurrah we are in Washington and what a city! Mud, pigs, geese, Negroes, palaces, shanties everywhere. We marched out to a place called Gales Woods where we are to camp and stacked arms in Camp Sprague, the home of the First Rhode Island Detached Militia. Here we were cordially received by our Rhode Island comrades and breakfast given to us. I took breakfast at the "Tigers' Retreat" this being the name given to the barracks of Company "A", or National Cadets of the First Regiment. After breakfast we went down into the woods and pitched our tents. Our camp has been named Camp Clark in honor of Bishop Thomas M. Clark of Rhode Island. Well, this looks like soldiering and also work.

Sunday June 23, 1861—Our first Sunday from home, and it has been a queer one to me. At eleven A.M. our Regiment joined with the First Regiment in church service. The scene to me was a solemn and impressive one. Our Chaplain, Rev. Thorndike C. Jameson, preached a fine sermon. The camp has been full of visitors all day and things have been lively. Not much like a Sunday in Rhode Island, but yet we have tried to keep the day holy and recognize the fact that God is still our Lord.

Monday June 24, 1861—Today we brushed up and marched into Washington and were reviewed by the President. As we passed the

White House I had my first view of Abraham Lincoln. He looks like a good honest man, and I trust that with God's help he can bring our country safely out of its peril. I was not well pleased with the appearance of the city, but was struck with the magnitude of the public buildings. The Capitol, although unfinished, is a magnificent structure and every American should be proud of it. After the review we returned to our camp.

Thursday June 28, 1861—For the past few days we have been busy putting Camp Clark in order, and now we shall settle down to work and drill. Today we had a Union dress parade with the First Regiment on their parade ground. It was a fine sight to see two large Regiments drawn up in line. The parade concluded with prayer and singing the Doxology by the men.

Sunday June 31, 1861—We are having a rain today and so services have been omitted. We have employed our time in writing letters to our friends and in reading. Our Sibley tents are very comfortable and we feel quite at home. We march to our meals up to the camp of the First Rhode Island where the food is cooked. We have excellent food and not at all as I thought it would be. If we take the field I guess there will be a change of diet. Plum pudding, gingerbread and milk and other good things are served daily.

Camp Clark, July 4, 1861—Our first Independence Day in the army and we have had a grand celebration. Rev. Augustus Woodbury, Chaplain of the First Rhode Island Detached Militia read the Declaration of Independence to both the First and Second Rhode Island Regiments at nine A.M. Prayer was offered by Chaplain Jameson of the Second Rhode Island Volunteers and a fine oration delivered by Rev. Father Quinn, Assistant Chaplain to the First Rhode Island. Captain Cyrus G. Dyer, Company "A", Second Rhode Island Volunteers followed with an excellent poem. At twelve noon a national salute was fired by the Light Battery and we were invited to a fine dinner. Prof. Benoni Sweet, a member of Company H, Second Rhode Island gave an exhibition of tight rope walking. Our camp has been full of people all day. In fact we are in the habit of seeing many distinguished men at our parade. Night before last (July 2) there were present the Hon. Salmon P. Chase, Secretary of the Treasury, Colonel John C. Fremont the great path finder, James F. Smith, Esq. of Rhode Island and others.

July 9, 1861—We have had a sad accident today. While on drill a caisson belonging to our battery exploded and killed two men and wounded three others. This sad affair has cast a gloom over our camps and it gives us our first idea of the terrible effect of gun powder. Governor Sprague has taken up his quarters with our Regiment.

Camp Clark, July 11, 1861—President Lincoln and wife paid our camp a visit today and received a fine reception from the troops. In the afternoon both Regiments had a dress parade after which we passed before the President in review. We began to hear rumors of a movement by the army but we do not know much about it.

I have taken my turn at guard duty and cannot say that I like sitting up nights. As I am a corporal I do not have to stand guard or walk a beat, but as corporal I have charge of one of the reliefs which in our camp numbers sixteen men and have to post them as it is called or march them to their beats. Every few minutes some sentinel will call our Corporal of the Guard post no. 1,2, or 16 as the case may be, and I have to take my gun and run down to his post and find out what is wanted. As we follow the line of sentinels other corporals have to stop and give the countersign which makes delays. Of course there is no enemy near, but we are made to do duty the same as if the Rebels were in Washington. I do not complain of this for I want to know the whole duty of a soldier.

Governor William Sprague

July 16, 1861—We have orders to be ready to move, but where no one can tell. Rations are being cooked and we expect to march very soon. It begins to look warlike, and we shall probably have a chance to pay our southern brethren a visit upon the sacred soil of Virginia very soon. Well I hope we shall be successful and give the Rebels a good pounding.

Camp Clark, July 16, 1861—Hurrah! We are all packed and waiting to move. Our haversacks are filled with salt pork and hard bread and our canteens with water. This morning my Captain (Steere) sent for me and said: "Corporal 64," (This is my company number and the Captain uses it in speaking to the men.) "You are detailed to remain in camp with a guard to look after the tents and Company property while the Regiment is absent." I objected to this plan and finally told my Captain that if he left me in camp I would run away and join the Regiment on the road as soon as it became dark. He tried to convince me that I was too slight built to march, but I insisted that I would go, orders or no orders, and he finally told me to go to my tent and pack up my traps, and that he would detail another corporal to remain in camp. I packed up such things as I thought I should need and left my treasures that have accumulated in the Company chest. Our large felt hats with a blue cord and brass eagle were left in the First Sergeant's tents. Just before the Regiment moved Captain Steere sent me with two privates to report to Colonel Slocum in great haste. We went up to headquarters on the run and the Colonel pointed to a citizen just outside of the camp and told me to arrest him. The man ran and we ran chasing him for at least a mile down New York Avenue towards the city. He ran up a flight of stairs on the outside of a house and entered the second story. We followed him, but after searching the house thoroughly we were obliged to return to camp without a prisoner. It appears that this man assaulted a little girl who was selling pies in camp, and when spoken to by the Colonel he fled the camp. On returning I took my place in line and we moved out into the street. Here we met the Second New Hampshire Volunteers and the Seventy-first New York Militia, who with the First and Second Rhode Island Regiments are to form a Brigade under the command of Colonel Ambrose E. Burnside of the first Rhode Island. A regular officer has joined our Regiment. He is from Rhode Island and is the son of our Surgeon Francis L. Wheaton. His name is Frank Wheaton and we understand that he is to be our Lieutenant Colonel. He is a handsome fellow and looks as if he would fight.

We moved through Washington with crowds of people looking at us from the sidewalks and houses, and at last reached Long Bridge and crossed into Virginia. It is my first visit to the Old Dominion and every object is of interest. At the head of the bridge on the Virginia side is a large fort called Fort Runyon. We saw several forts on the hills and soldiers in all directions. It was nearly dark when we crossed the river, so our march has been short. We camp at a little place called Annandale and our Regiment stacked arms in a large meadow. Rail fences were plenty and we soon had fires burning and coffee cooking in our cups. The novelty of this scene interested me very much, and I enjoyed the evening sitting by the fire and speculating on what might happen on the morrow. As we have no tents with us, we lay upon our rubber blankets spread upon the ground and slept soundly.

July 17, 1861—I awoke this morning feeling a little stiff and with my clothes wet with dew. But the hot sun soon dried our blankets, and after taking breakfast on the contents of our haversacks, we moved out into the road and continued our march. Company "D" Captain Steere was detailed as flankers for the Brigade, and while the troops marched in the road, we took the fields on the right of the column. It was a grand sight, the long line of soldiers with their bright gun barrels, with now and then a battery moving between two regiments. Our Company marched in single ranks by the flank with intervals of several paces between the men. We tried to keep the road in sight but could not always do so, as we had to pass through several pieces of thick woods. On the way we found an old railroad embankment, and I never saw black berries more plenty. We stopped and ate what we wanted and then moved on. About noon I left the line with two other men and went to the top of a hill where we saw to our left and rear a church spire and several houses. Believing it to be Fairfax Court House I called Captain Steere who examined the country with his field glasses. The Captain ordered the Company to assemble and then formed a square. In this manner we marched down the hill in the direction of the town and entered by a side street. As we entered the main street we saw a number of knapsacks which the Rebels had thrown away, and our boys wanted to stop and examine them, but the Captain made the Company march on, and we were soon in the main street and in about the centre of the village. We halted some minutes before we saw the head of the main column coming up the street. A Rebel flag was flying from the Court House but none of our boys thought of taking it down until the Regiment arrived. The flag was taken down by Andrew McMahon, Company "A", Second Rhode Island Volunteers. Here we joined our Regiment again and Company "D" went into camp in the yard of the mansion formerly occupied by the Rebel General Beauregard. I found a subsistence return which gave the number of men and when rations were issued the day before. I gave this to Captain Nelson Viall, and he sent it to General Hunter. Some of the men tried to enter the houses, but the officers soon put a stop to this, but not before a piano was broken up and taken into the yard. Private Thomas Parker of our Company "D", an old English soldier who had served in the Crimea, came down the street with a large Bible under one arm and a picture of General Washington under the other. Captain Viall saw him and sent him back to the house and made him restore them. The only thing that I took was an old rooster and I had a lively time catching him. I chased him about the yard until he ran under a corn crib. Leander Shaw, a private in our Company went under the crib on his hands and knees and passed him out. We killed him and took off his feathers in great haste. At night I put him in a kettle and agreed to watch while he cooked. As I had no salt I could only add hard bread to the mess and some time late in the night I awoke my chum Fred. A. Arnold and a few others and we tried to eat him. But he was tough, and we had to give it up. And I lay down near a fence for a little sleep, satisfied that I knew very little about boiling roosters.

Private Thomas Parker, described by Rhodes as an "old English soldier". Parker served throughout the war in the 2nd R.I. without rising above the rank of Corporal which he attained in 1863. After the war he enlisted in the regular U.S. Army and is shown here in his post-war uniform wearing his medals, the Congressional Medal of Honor and a large silver medal, presented to him by Gen. Frank Wheaton, engraved on both sides with all his battles and their dates.

July 20, 1861—Today we left Fairfax Court House and encamped a few miles beyond, near Centreville. Here we built shelters with pine and cedar boughs and call the camp "Bush Camp." Here we have heard our first hostile shot, and we wonder what is to follow.

July 21, 1861—About two o'clock this morning we left "Bush Camp," and marching down the hill, through Centreville, found the woods obstructed by wagons and troops that had failed to start on time. Soon the Second left the main road and struck off to the right, through a wood path that had been much obstructed. As we led the Brigade the task of clearing the road fell to us, and hard work we found it. About nine o'clock in the forenoon we reached Sudley church, and a distant gun startled us, but we did not realize that our first battle was so near at hand. We now took a side road that skirted a piece of woods and marched for some distance, the men amusing themselves with laughter and jokes, with occasional stops for berries. On reaching a clearing, separated from our left flank by a rail fence, we were saluted with a volley of musketry, which, however, was fired so high that all the bullets went over our heads. I remember that my first sensation was one of astonishment at the peculiar whir of the bullets, and that the Regiment immediately laid down without waiting for orders. Colonel Slocum gave the command: "By the left flank—MARCH!" and we commenced crossing the field. One of our boys by the name of Webb fell off of the fence and broke his bayonet. This caused some amusement, for even at this time we did not realize that we were about to engage in battle.

As we crossed the fence, the Rebels, after firing a few scattering shots, fled down a slope to the woods. We followed to the brow of the hill and opened fire. Our Battery came into position on our right and replied to the Rebel artillery, which was sending their shell into our line. On what followed I have very confused ideas. I remember that my smooth bore gun became so foul that I was obliged to strike the ramrod against a fence to force the cartridge home, and soon exchanged it for another. There was a hay stack in front of our line, and some of the boys sheltered themselves behind it. A shell from the enemy striking covered the men with hay, from which they emerged and retook their places in line. About this time, Private Thomas Parker of Co. "D" captured a prisoner, a member of the Louisiana Tiger Regiment, and as he brought him back to the line was spoken to by Colonel Slocum.

Colonel Slocum had crossed a rail fence in our front and had advanced nearer to the brow of the hill than the line occupied by the

Colonel John S. Slocum

Regiment. As he returned and was in the act of climbing the fence, he fell on the side next to the Regiment. I, being the nearest man to him at the time, raised him up, but was unable to lift him from the ground. Calling for help, Private Parker dropped his gun and came to my assistance. Together we bore him to a small house of the left of the line and laying him upon the floor, sent for Colonel Burnside, Surgeon Francis L. Wheaton and Chaplain Thordike Jameson, who all arrived in a few moments, a lull in the fight having occurred.[1] Chaplain Augustus Woodbury and Assistant Surgeon James Harris, of the First Rhode Island Detached Militia were already in attendance.[2] With the sponge, from my cap, I washed the blood from his head and found that the bullet had ploughed a furrow from rear to front through the top of his head, but had not lodged. His ankle was also injured, having two wounds upon it. While unable to speak, he yet appeared conscious, and at my request would move his hand from his wounded head. When it was decided to place the Colonel in an ambulance, I took the door from its hinges with my gun screw driver, and assisted in carrying him on this door to the ambulance. The Second Regiment was engaged about thirty minutes without support, when the balance of the Brigade was brought on to the field and the battle became general. The Eighth Georgia Regiment was in our immediate front, and received the benefit of our fire. Shot and shell were continually striking in or near our line and the troops became much scattered. Losing my own Company I joined Company "F", under command of Lieutenant William B. Sears, and remained with them until the battle ceased and we withdrew to replenish our ammunition.

Frank Wheaton

About three o'clock in the afternoon the enemy disappeared in our front and the firing ceased. We considered that a victory had been won. The wounded were cared for and then orders came for us to retire to a piece of woods in our rear and fill our boxes with ammunition. We found the First Rhode Island in the woods with arms stacked and some of the men cooking. I met friends in the First Regiment and congratulated them on our victory, little expecting the finale of our day's fighting.

The firing, which had gradually receded, now seemed to be nearer, and soon a shell fired into the woods told us that the enemy had returned the combat. I cannot explain the causes of what followed. The woods and roads were soon filled with fleeing men and our Brigade was ordered to the front to cover the retreat, which it was now evident could not be stopped. Lieutenant-Colonel Frank Wheaton who on the fall of Colonel Slocum, had assumed command, posted the Regiment to the left of our first position and behind a fence. The field was soon clear of troops, excepting our Brigade, all of which except the Second Rhode Island, were posted farther back from the brow of the hill. The Rebels came on in a splendid order, pushing two light field guns to the front of them. We received their fire and held them in check until the Brigade

William B. Sears

had taken up their march, when we followed—the last to leave the field. The Rebels followed us for a short distance, shelling our rear, and then we pursued our march unmolested, until we reached the vicinity of the bridge that crosses Cub Run. Here a Rebel battery opened upon us from a corner of the woods, and the stampede commenced. The bridge was soon rendered impassible by the teams that obstructed it, and we here lost five of the guns belonging to our battery. Many men were killed and wounded at this point, and a panic seemed to seize upon every one. As our Regiment was now broken, I looked for a place to cross the stream, not daring to try the bridge. I jumped into the run and holding my gun above my head struggled across with the water up to my waist. After crossing, the Regiment gradually formed again, and we continued our march to Centreville where we found Blenker's troops posted across the road to protect the retreat. We passed through their ranks, and entered our old grounds, "Bush Camp," supposing the retreat to be at an end.

Tired, hungry and wet, we laid down, only to be awakened about eleven o'clock that night to resume the march towards Washington, in the midst of a rain storm. The Regiment filed out of camp and marched to Fairfax Court House in good order and rested in the streets. Crowds of soldiers were hurrying by and the streets were blocked with trains. After halting a few minutes we started again and soon, in the darkness, rain and crowd, became broken up to some extent. Of the horrors of that night, I can give you no adequate idea. I suffered untold horrors from thirst and fatigue but struggled on, clinging to my gun and cartridge box. Many times I sat down in the mud determined to go no further, and willing to die to end my misery. But soon a friend would pass and urge me to make another effort, and I would stagger on a mile further. At daylight we could see the spires of Washington, and a welcome sight it was. About eight o'clock I reached Fort Runyon, near Long Bridge, and giving my gun to an officer who was collecting them, I entered a tent and was soon asleep. Towards noon I awoke and, with my Company, endeavored to cross Long Bridge, but fell exhausted before reaching the Washington side. My officers kindly placed me in an army wagon and I was carried to camp, where with rest and proper care, I soon recovered and went on duty.

The loss of the Regiment in this disastrous affair was ninety-three killed, wounded and missing. Of this number, four officers were killed, namely, Colonel John S. Slocum, Major Sullivan Ballou, Captain Levi

Tower and Captain S. James Smith. Twenty-six enlisted men were killed or mortally wounded. My Company, "D," lost four killed, three wounded, one of whom died, and one missing.

On returning from the Battle of Bull Run, the Second Rhode Island Regiment entered the old camp at Gales Wood and was reorganized. Lieutenant-Colonel Frank Wheaton became Colonel, Captain William H.P. Steere Company "D" Lieutenant-Colonel and Captain Nelson Viall Company "C" Major.

Capt. Levi Tower

[At this point the editor takes the liberty of inserting a letter found in the papers of Elisha H. Rhodes written by Corporal Samuel J. English, Company "D," Second Rhode Island Volunteers.]

Camp Clark, July 24th/61
Dear Mother   *Washington, D.C.*

I rec'd your letter of the 21st shortly after our return to camp and take the earliest opportunity of writing. Yes, we have been & gone and done it. Last Thursday the 16th our brigade consisting of the two Rhode Island regiments, the New York 71st and the New Hampshire 2nd took up our line of march for Fairfax Court House. We crossed Long Bridge about 3 o'clock and continued on for six miles where we bivouacked for the night. Nothing occurred of importance to disturb our slumbers except the passing of troops bound on the same expedition. We commenced our march early in the morning, the 2nd R.I. regiment taking the lead and acting as skirmishers, Co. A taking the advance on the right; Co. D acting as flankers; Co. F acting as rear advance on the right of the column, Co. K[?] acting as advance on the left. Co. C as flankers and Co. G as rear guard. I cannot state exactly the strength of our forces at the time, but should judge there were seven or eight thousand, including 1500 cavalry and two Batteries of artillery with two howitzers belonging to the New York 71st Regt. When within half a mile of the village of Fairfax, word was sent that the rebels' battery was directly in our line of march. Our artillery was immediately ordered to the front and fired three shots into it, making the sand fly, and showing pretty conclusively that the birds had flown. All the time this was taking place your humble servant was skirting around in the woods as a skirmisher and arrived in the village ahead of the main column. As our company arrived the streets presented the scene of the wildest confusion: old negroes running around, some laughing, some crying and some swearing at a fearful rate. The streets were strewn with the knapsacks, haversacks, canteens, blankets, shirts and most every article pertaining to camp life. The houses were deserted and in some places the tables were set for dinner and coffee warm on the stove. After strolling around a short time we quartered ourselves in the park of Gen. Lee and made ourselves as comfortable as circumstances would permit. The cavalry in the meantime pursuing the retreating rebels and capturing 30 of their men. What particularly pleased me was that the company that lost the mess was the Palmetto Guards and Brooks Guards of South Carolina, having lost all of their camp equipage and barely escaped with their lives. But to continue, the next day our colors started for Manassas but halted and camped three miles this side of Centreville, waiting for our troops and reinforcements to come up; the second regiment being somewhat in advance of the main army; we stay here for three days and Sunday the 21st about 2 o'clock the drums beat the assembly and in ten minutes we were on our march for Bull Run having heard the enemy were waiting to receive us, our troops then numbering 25 or 30 thousand which were divided into three columns ours under Col Hunter taking the right through a thick woods. About eleven o'clock as our pickets were advancing through the woods a volley was poured in upon them from behind a fence thickly covered with brush; the pickets after returning the shots returned to our regiment and we advanced double quick time yelling like so many devils. On our arrival into the open field I saw I should judge three or four thousand rebels retreating for a dense woods, firing as they retreated, while from another part of the woods a perfect hail storm of bullets, round shot and shell was poured upon us, tearing through our ranks and scattering death and confusion everywhere; but with a yell and a roar we charged upon them driving them again into the woods with fearful loss. In the mean time our battery came up to our support and commenced hurling destruction among the rebels. Next orders were given for us to fall back and protect our battery as the enemy were charging upon it from another quarter, and then we saw with dismay that the second R.I. regiment were the only troops in the fight; the others having lagged so far behind that we had to stand the fight alone for 30 minutes; 1100 against 7 or 8 thousand. It was afterwards ascertained from a prisoner that the rebels thought we numbered 20 or 30 thousand from the noise made by us while making the charge. While preparing to make our final effort to keep our battery out of their hands, the 1st R.I. regiment then came filing over the fence and poured a volley out to them that drove them under cover again; they were followed by the New York 71st and the New Hampshire 2nd regiments; with 2,000 regulars bringing up the rear who pitched into the "Sechers" most beautifully.[3] Our regiments were then ordered off the field and formed a line for a support to rally on in case the rebels over powered our troops. When the line had formed again I started off for the scene of action to see how the fight was progressing. As I emerged from the woods I saw a bomb shell strike a man in the breast and literally tear him to pieces. I passed the farm house which had been appropriated for a hospital and the groans of the wounded and dying were horrible. I then descended the hill to the woods which had been occupied by the rebels at the place where the Elsworth zouaves made their charge; the bodies of the dead and dying were actually three and four deep, while in the woods where the desperate struggle had taken place between the U.S. Marines and the Louisiana zouaves, the trees were spattered with blood and the ground strewn with dead bodies. The shots flying pretty lively round me I thought best to join my regiment; as I gained the top of the hill I heard the shot and shell of our batteries had given out, not having but 130 [150?] shots for each gun during the whole engagement. As we had nothing but infantry to fight against their batteries, the command was given to retreat; our cavalry not being of much use, because the rebels would not come out of the woods. The R.I. regiments, the New York 71st and the New Hampshire 2nd were drawn into a line to cover the retreat, but an officer galloped wildly into the column crying the enemy is upon us, and off they started like a flock of sheep every man for himself and the devil take the hindermost; while the rebels' shot and shell fell like rain among our exhausted troops. As we gained the cover of the woods the stampede became even more frightful, for the baggage wagons and ambulances became entangled with the artillery and rendered the scene even more dreadful than the battle, while the plunging of the horses broke the lines of our infantry and prevented any successful formation out of the question. The rebels being so badly cut up supposed we had gone beyond the woods to form on for a fresh attack and shelled the woods for full two hours, supposing we were there, thus saving the greater part of our forces, for if they had begun an immediate attack, nothing in heaven's name could have saved us. As we neared the bridge the rebels opened a very destructive fire upon us, mowing down our men like grass, and caused even greater confusion than before. Our artillery and baggage wagons became fouled with each other, completely blocking the bridge, while the bomb shells bursting on the bridge made it "rather unhealthy" to be around. As I crossed on my hands and knees, Capt. Smith who was crossing by my side at the same time was struck by a round shot at the same time and completely cut in two.[4] *After I crossed I started up the hill as fast as my legs could carry and passed through Centreville and continued on to Fairfax where we arrived about 10 o'clock halting about 15 minutes, then kept on to Washington where we arrived about 2 o'clock Monday noon more dead than alive, having been on our feet 36 hours without a mouthful to eat, and traveled a distance of 60 miles without twenty minutes halt. The last five miles of that march was perfect misery, none of us having scarcely strength to put one foot before the other, but I tell you the cheers we rec'd going through the streets of Washington seemed to put new life into the men for they rallied and marched to our camps and every man dropped on the ground and in one moment the greater part of them were asleep. Our loss is estimated at 1,000, but I think it greater, the rebels loss from three to five thousand.*

[Ed. Note: The letter ends here on the very bottom of the paper, crowded together, but no signature. It appears to be complete. The following consists of ten handwritten pages, unsigned, labelled "Historical Notes on 1st Bull Run" with a note that it was "found in papers of Gov. Wm. Sprague, Sept. 9th, 1892."]

"On Saturday the 21 of July the Secretary of War visited the several camps at Centreville, and in company with Genl McDowall and staff and Gov. Wm. Sprague, reviewed the division under the command of Col. Kay. The Secretary intended to have remained in camp over night; but being informed by Gov. Sprague, who with others, had reconnoitered the enemy, that their number, as near as it could be ascertained amounted to at least 75,000 men, supported by batteries to such an extent that their position was almost impregnable, he deemed it necessary to return immediately to Washington and send foward at once the fifteen reserve regiments. This was necessary in order to support the main body, then about to move to Manassas. Genl McDowall heartily thanked the Governor for his information, saying at the time, he was very glad the Secretary of War had learned the facts on the ground from him, otherwise the Secretary would have told him (McDowall) 'You want everything.' In the evening the Commanders of Divisions and Brigades asembled at Genl McDowall's quarters to learn the orders for the ensuing day. They were read at ten o'clock, and the various com mands instructed to move foward the next morning and commence the attack without waiting for reinforcements. No comments were made when the orders were read, the commandants present merely inquiring as to the position which each was to assume. The several divisions were directed to move forward at half past two o'clock. While one division was to threaten the battery of the previous day's battle, another under Tyler was to engage the batteries on the Washington Turnpike, but with

positive orders not to cross. Hunter's division was to move in the rear of Tyler's, his march supposed to [be] masked by that column, then to the right across Cub Run, through the woods to a ford some 7 or 9 miles up Bulls Run. Crossing the Run they were to attack the enemy in the rear and get between them and Manassas Junction. This important and perilous duty devolved upon Col. Hunter's division. It consisted of two Brigades, viz. Col. Burnside's containing the 1st and 2nd Rhode Island Regiments with the second Battery of 6 pieces of rifles cannon; the 2nd New Hampshire and 71st New York, making some thirty-five hundred men; and Col. Porter's Brigade about the same number of men, consisting of Regulars, Marines, Cavalry, a Battery of Artillery [three inch space in MS] both brigades amounting to about 7,000 men. They marched promptly without waiting for breakfast at 2½ o'clock, but were afterwards delayed one or two hours by Tyler's Brigade. Two shots were heard in the direction of Tyler's column after we had marched some two miles. These were the only shots the divisions engaged in battle heard from him, although he was expected to engage the enemy. One company of skirmishers under Capt. Dyer of the 2nd R.I. regiment was thrown out, and during the march to Bulls Run, no halt was made excepting that required to keep the skirmishers in advance. At the Run the skirmishers were increased to five companies, all taken from the second Regiment. Several civilians were taken, but though in the immediate vicinity of the enemy, could give us no information concerning them. They were greatly alarmed for their safety. A negro being interrogated as [to] their number at this crossing replied that there were 35,000. Gov. Sprague and Capt. Woodbury then went forward to reconnoiter but could learn nothing. Two vollies of musketry were heard in the distance, and soon after Col. Porter of the 2nd Brigade, who was in advance, returned to Col. Hunter and reported the enemy in front. In the meantime the division had been advancing, and our skirmishers engaging those of the enemy drove them from the woods. Col. Slocum gallantly led into action the balance of the 2nd regiment—5 companies which had been posted on the left in an open space formed by the woods. No position being assigned the Battery, Gov. Sprague posted it on the right of the 2nd Regiment. The cavalry were posted on the road on a line with the Regiment and Battery but about ¼ or ½ a mile distant. Col. Hunter being wounded left the field in charge of Col. Porter—he being the senior officer then on the field. Genl. McDowell was in the column on the field. The Second Regiment and Battery were exposed to the whole fire of the enemy for nearly half an hour. Two regiments of the enemy were discovered in a cornfield within fifty paces of them seeking to gain their right and by so doing outflank our position and get between us and the river. Col. Burnside's Sharpshooters coming up, opened upon them a sharp fire. The shells of the Battery exploded among them in rapid succession, making terrible havoc in the ranks. They had advanced within twenty paces of our lines when the timely appearance of the 1st. R.I. and 71st New York changed the current of battle. By a well directed fire they checked their advance, and after a

Ambrose E. Burnside

while silenced their battery, and drove them from the cornfield into the woods half a mile distant. At this time the enemy displayed the stars and stripes, and by this cowardly trick led our men to slacken their fire and saved themselves from almost certain destruction. The fire of the enemy from the woods became so hot that Col. Burnside applied for aid. The third Infantry and a battery of Regulars came to our support, receiving vociferous cheers from the men. They drove back the enemy and established the line of battle at right angles from its first position. The destruction of the enemy in the cornfields, in front of the woods, and in the woods themselves was terrible. Men lay in whole lines piled one upon the other all over the field. The Rhode Island Regiments had also suffered badly—having lost 2 field officers, Col. Slocum and Major Ballou and 2 Captains. Their ammunition was exhausted and they fought 3 hours in imminent danger of destruction. They were now permitted to withdraw from the battle, as well as the 5 companies who had been acting as skirmishers, and ordered to stack their arms in the woods. Prior to this the Brigade of [space] came onto the field and advancing by the woods took a position in front of the new line of battle. Capt. Reynolds' Battery being on the right, supported their advance, and shot among the most distant of the enemy's batteries. It had previously succeeded in silencing the battery in front of the first position. Two guns were forwarded by Gov. Sprague almost to the enemy's lines, notwithstanding a raking fire of 2000 men and the charge of the enemy's cavalry. The hill upon which the Battery was posted was nearly a mile long. Along the sides of this hill fronting us were the enemy's batteries, stretching away in numberless tiers and protected by their long lines of Infantry. As we advanced upon them the whole line opened its fire upon us. The effect was terrible. Our troops could present but one Regiment at a time, and upon this one Regiment their whole force could deliver their fire. Our men being somewhat disheartened, in reply to efforts made to rally them, said: 'Give us officers and we will advance.' Three guns were so hot that it was almost impossible to use them. Here one was dismounted and slung under its limber, and another rendered useless by a cannon ball. Many of the horses had been killed. It was utterly impossible to carry on the battle successfully under such circumstances and against such odds, and when the enemy, reinforced by Johnson, charged upon our men, the Regulars, Cavalry, and all the troops retreated precipitately in the greatest confusion under a perfect avalanche of balls. The panic stricken crowd cut loose the horses, and mounting them fled from the field. Word had been passed by Gov. Sprague to prepare the R.I. Regiments to cover any retreat that might be made. They were already drawn up in line but were repeatedly broken by the frantic flight of the other troops. Their muskets which they had stacked in the woods were overturned, and everything was in the greatest disorder. The two Regiments were marched slowly from the field, covering as well as they could the panic stricken multitude. As Col. Burnside led them from the field he opened an effectual fire upon the enemy. One gun only was brought from the field. Gov. Sprague, being with the rear guard making every effort to rally the troops, was not aware of the condition of his guns until the retreat from Centredale [sic. Centreville]. The two Regiments might have saved them, but the horses being stolen or disabled, they could not have carried them to Washington. Gov. Sprague sent forward a guard to show the way to Centreville. The enemy did not follow our retreat. When within two miles of the road, in an open space, the enemy poured in upon us from an eminence to the right a raking fire. The troops sought shelter in the woods at the left and were finally led into the road which they had left in the morning. Here again the enemy opened fire upon us. This was very destructive. We had expected to meet here the reserve ready to protect us. Everything was in confusion. Baggage wagons were piled one upon another, the guns crowded together, and men lay all around, some dead, others wounded, and dying. The order to retreat from Centreville was very unexpected. When it came the R.I. Regiments were refreshing themselves and preparing to make a stand against the enemy. These Regiments were fresh, in good order, and able to have stopped the retreat. They could have saved the guns and other property had they received such orders. The enemy's forces were so placed that they could deliver their whole fire from 30 Regiments, without exposing but one front. Their batteries were planted on the side of a hill, in the shape of a cone, each supported by Infantry, and it was utterly impossible with the force at our disposal, probably not more than 4,000, engaged in the fight at any one time. Had the enemy been more active and brave, few of our men would have escaped to tell the sad tale of the fight."

July 25, 1861—The First Rhode Island Detached Militia left us this night for home, their time being expired.[5] It made us feel lonesome to see them march away to the depot in such good spirits while we are to remain and fight on. They exchanged their Springfield rifle muskets for our smooth bores before they left. I understand that we are to take possession of the barracks at Camp Sprague.

July 27, 1861—We are now in the barracks at Camp Sprague, but from the rumors I am led to believe that we are to move soon for a new camp.

Head Quarters Co. D 2nd Reg RIV
Camp Clark, Washington, D.C.
July 28, 1861

My Dear Sister,

I rec'd your letter last night. I will try to give you all the particulars of the Battle. We left our camp on Sunday, July 21st at 2 o'clock in the morning. We started without breakfast and only a little hardbread in our haversacks. We marched until about 10 o'clock A.M. when our pickets were fired upon. We were on a road with woods on one side. In a few minutes we received a volley and the orders were given for the 2nd R.I. Reg. to charge. We started and charged through the woods into an open field. We had about 700 men. We came out upon about 5,000 of the Rebels who started on the run for the woods on the other side of the valley. We marched to the brow of the hill and fired. Our battery came up and opened fire. The enemy opened fire from several masked forts and cut down our men in great numbers. We loaded and fired as fast as we could. This was the time that Wm. Aborn was shot. He was fighting bravely when he was shot through the neck. He fell into a dry ditch and then got out and crawled into the woods. He no doubt died immediately as the wound was a bad one. Some of us got separated from our Co. and joined Co. F. We were near a fence. Col. Slocum was with us. He took a prisoner and loaded his gun and fired it. The Co. was ordered to fall back, but I not belonging to it stayed near the Col. He tried to get over the fence and received 3 wounds. I was the only man very near him when he fell. I tried to get him alone, but I found I could not carry him a great while. I called for help and an Old Crimea soldier named Thos. Parker came and helped me. We carried him to a house and I was left with him after the firing ceased. When we left I brought his spurs and delivered them to the Lieu. Col. He thanked me very kindly for them. As I rec'd the credit here I did not think of Parker. We drove the Rebels away from the fields, but our powder gave out and they received new men, so we had to retreat. Our two Regiments protected the men as they marched off. The Rebels ran into the field with shots from their artillery and cut us off. They fired several shells at us and killed a good many men. We continued to retreat until we reached Washington. [Remainder of letter missing.]

July 30th—Nothing but drill and guard duty. Even the late battle has become an old story. Some of our men actually became crazy from the excitement. I have recovered my strength and feel that I could make another campaign without much trouble.

Aug. 6th, 1861—All of the sick of our Regiment were sent away today in charge of Surgeon Francis L. Wheaton. Today we picked up our traps and started for a little place called Brightwood about four miles distance. We marched out the 7th St. Road, and after passing the hotel at Brightwood turned down a country road and went into camp on the farm of a Mr. Ray. The day was fearfully hot and with our loaded knapsacks we suffered much. Here we are to make a permanent camp and to be brigaded with other Regiments.

Aug. 11th, 1861—Our camp named Camp Brightwood is in Maryland just outside of the District of Columbia lines and is on the road to Rockville in one direction and Bladensburg in another. Today we received quite a number of recruits for our Regiment. I was on picket out on the road when they arrived.

Aug. 30th, 1861—The month has been passed in hard work. We have built a large fort and named it Fort Slocum after our first colonel. The city of Washington is now surrounded by a chain of forts and is considered safe from attack. We have shoveled many weary hours but feel that our labor will do some good. General Darius N. Couch is in command of our Brigade which consists of the 2nd Rhode Island Volunteers, 7th and 10th Mass. Volunteers and 36th N.Y. Volunteers. Camp life is dull, but I suppose that it is part of a soldier's duty, and it will be lively enough before we reach home again. Well, it is all for the Union.

Sept. 1, 1861—Mustered for pay today.

Sept. 29, 1861 Sunday—Services were held this morning, and in the afternoon preparations were made for a move, but the orders did not arrive and so we remain in camp. A beautiful day clear and bright. Have received a box from home containing many good things which however did not last long.

Sept. 30, 1861—The Regiment packed up again ready to move. Arbors were torn down, bed sacks emptied and straw burned, and at night line was formed ready for the march. After remaining in line for an hour orders came to dismiss the men.

Oct. 1, 1861—Still waiting to move. It is rumored that the Rebels made an advance upon the forts near Chain Bridge, but retreated without attacking. Company "D" went on picket duty last night. I being one of the corporals on the color guard did not go with them, but on the afternoon of the 1st took out the mail to the men.

Oct. 7, 1861—A severe rain storm with thunder and lightning. Co. "D" doing duty as camp guards. The Regiment was inspected by one of Gen. McClellan's staff officers. Work goes on at Fort Slocum. In digging, a bed of iron ore has been found. Some of the forts are practicing with heavy guns. Tents leaked and we got wet.

Oct. 10, 1861—We have just heard of the arrival of the 4th R.I. Volunteers in Washington. Chestnuts began to be ripe, and we have

Entered according to act of Congress in the year 1861 by J.B. Rassenthal in the Cle

CAMP BRIGHTWOOD

some everyday in camp. Persimmons are also beginning to be eatable and are gathered whenever found.

Oct. 11, 1861—This morning I procured a pass and visited the camp of the 4th R.I. Volunteers. I stopped at Camp Sprague where I found Battery "E" R.I. Light Artillery and called upon Frank Butts who is serving as a corporal. I then went on to the camp of the 4th. R.I. and showing my pass to the sentinel was sent to the sergeant of the guard, then to the officer of the guard, and then to the officer of the day who finally admitted me. This Regiment wears fine clothes, and the officers sport gold epauletts and the sergeants woolen ones. It was a curiosity to me as our Regiment has never tried to dress up very fine. Governor Sprague was present in camp, and the band played on the parade. I saw

oe of the Eastern Distr of Penna.   I.N. Rosenthal Lith 50 Chesnut Phila

2ᴅ RHODE ISLAND,
Col. Frank Wheaton, Comdg

several of my Pawtuxet friends.

Oct. 12, 1861 Sunday—Names of men in no. 5 mess:
Corporal Elisha H. Rhodes
Corporal William C. Webb
Private George F. Phillips
Private Thomas W.D. Markham
Private Noah A. Peck
Private Cyrus W. Johnson
Private Sidney M. Turner
Private Hollis H. Martin
Private John C. Tiffany
Private William A. Turner
Private William E. Reynolds

Yesterday we had another alarm and were ordered to march immediately, but the orders were countermanded. I am getting weary of marching orders and wish that we could move, for we have been in Camp Brightwood for two months, and I know every tree within two miles of camp. I have charge of the mails for Co. "D." I go to the Captain's tent every evening, assort the letters and take them to camp. The men crowd around me while I read off the names upon the envelopes. Some look pleased, take their letters and enter their tents, while others ask in a disappointed tone if I am sure that I have none for them. Chaplain Jameson's wife and daughter are in camp with him. We expect to receive our California colors next Tuesday. Dress parade closes this quiet Sunday evening. Chaplain Jameson preached this forenoon, and Gen Don Carlos Buell and staff were interested attendants. Governor Sprague arrived last Tuesday evening. The Regiment formed with the band and received him with proper honors. He made a speech which called out loud cheers. He is a favorite with our boys. Army life is not so disagreeable as I imagined it would be, and I trust that I am prepared to do my whole duty unto death if it is required. I trust that I shall be able to live, or die if need be, like a Christian soldier.

Oct. 16, 1861—We have just finished our so-called California oven to warm our tent. It is a large hole in the centre of the tent covered over with stone with one canal, or passage, to carry off the smoke and another to let in a draft of air. The passage ways are under ground, and we left off the top stone of the oven to put in wood. It works well and keeps us very warm. Bishop Clark of Rhode Island arrived today just as we marched out for dress parade. He addressed the Regiment and told us that Captain Steere, who is absent, is improving and will soon join us. We are having Battalion drill every day and the movements are usually made at the double pace.

Oct. 17, 1861 Thursday—Today at one P.M. the Regiments marched about three miles to the vicinity of Columbia College where we joined the other Regiments of the Brigade. (7th & 36th New York) and were drilled by Gen. Darius N. Couch, our Brigade Commander. General Buell was present and both officers complimented Colonel Wheaton and their 2nd Regiment upon their proficiency. We returned about dark, and as the line was dismissed I accidentally stepped into a hole and

Members of Company "D." Left to right: Pvt. George L. Smith, Pvt. Fred A. Arnold and Pvt. George H. Smith.

turned my ankle. I was told that since the Mexican War there had not been held a Brigade drill in the U.S. It was a fine sight to see so many troops moving upon the open plain.

Oct. 18, 1861 Friday—Being lame I was excused from duty with the color guard today and so had a good opportunity to witness the presentation of the stand of colors presented by Rhode Island citizens living in California. At one P.M. our Regiment was formed in line, the men wearing their best uniforms and white gloves. The 4th Rhode Island and a Pennsylvania Battery on our left. Generals Buell and Couch with many other officers were present. The troops were reviewed by Governor Sprague and about 3 P.M. President Lincoln and party arrived, and another review by the President took place. The colors were presented by Governor Sprague. The drums sounding and the Batteries firing a national salute. The Regiment then closed en masse, and Bishop Clark delivered an address and a chaplain present offered prayer. It was dark before we were dismissed and wended our way to our tents for supper while the officers and guests accompanied Colonel Wheaton to his quarters and partook of a turkey dinner. We *soldiers* had *rice* for supper. We have had a regular holiday or 4th of July and I have enjoyed the occasion. Colonel Wheaton had a bower of green built and ornamented with flags which added to the picturesque scene. The Regiment looked fine wearing their new cross belts with brass plates. The Colonel presented the members of the color guard with new white gloves.

Oct. 20, 1861 Sunday—Regular services held today. Sergeant Andrew Bates and Corporal William Baker of the 4th Rhode Island have been with me today and we have visited Fort Slocum which looks very warlike with its large iron guns frowning from its embrasures. Captain Edward H. Sears has resigned the command of "D" and is to take a position as First Lieutenant in one of the Rhode Island Batteries. We cannot tell who will be our new Captain. We would like to see Lieutenant William Ames promoted but fear that we shall be disappointed.

Oct. 21, 1861 Monday—Company "D" is on picket today. I rode out to the lines in a baggage wagon that carried their rations and distributed the mail.

Oct. 23, 1861 Wednesday—Cold and rainy. Not much going on and the boys hover over their fires in the tents.

Oct. 25, 1861—Still very cold. Lieutenant Ames received a box of blankets from Rhode Island and distributed them to our company. Several boxes have arrived and one of them is for me. They all searched for *liquors* before they were delivered to the men. I approve of this plan as it saves much trouble, as some men are inclined to get drunk when the opportunity offers. I visited Fort Slocum today. Some of the 4th Rhode Island Regiment visited our camp today.

Oct. 27, 1861 Sunday—Rev. Mr. Osgood of Lynn, Mass. preached to the Regiment this morning. At dress parade an order was read announcing the death of Colonel Baker of the California Regiment killed at Ball's Bluff.

The men have employed their time today in making visits upon their comrades in other camp areas. New dress coats were issued today, but as all the companies did not receive them we did not wear them at dress parade. I still like the Rhode Island blouse the best, as it is loose and more comfortable. We make the best of everything and are becoming quite ingenious in inventing all sorts of conveniences for use in our tents.

Oct. 30th 1861—Today we had a fine drill. The following Regiments took part and the drill was held near Kalorama Heights. 2nd Rhode Island, 7th Mass, 36th New York, 1st U.S. Chasseurs (65th New York), 23rd Penn, 61st New York and 1st Long Island Volunteers. The 6th Penn. Cavalry "Rush's Lancers" were drilling at the same time. A Cavalry charge astonished us somewhat, but I prefer to be on foot with a good musket in my hands. Our Regiment has drilled the formation of square to resist Cavalry and we think we are in fine condition for service. We are disgusted with the newspaper talk about the Army. If the stay-at-home heroes would come out here they would change their minds about Army life and movements.

Nov. 5, 1861 Tuesday—Much to my surprise Colonel Wheaton sent for me today and asked if I would like to be detached as clerk at the Headquarters of our Division commanded by Genl. Don Carlos Buell. Of course I said yes, and so the order was made out and read at dress parade. George Clendennin, whose place I take, has been made Sergeant Major of the 2nd Regiment. I regard this appointment as a promotion and certainly as a great favor, for it will relieve me from all night duty as well as drills. General Buell's Headquarters are in tents in a field near our camp and one is assigned to me as an office. The General is undoubtedly a good soldier, but I am inclined to believe a martinet, for he requires the clerks to stand while he remains in the office tent. But he is kind to me and I rather like his style. So goodbye to the 2nd R.I.

Vols. for the present, and I shall do my duty in my new position, for aside from the satisfaction of doing right, I know that if I conduct myself aright that I shall receive further favors and perhaps promotion. Near our Headquarters is Mr. Ray's house and I find it pleasant to visit him there at times.

Nov. 9th 1861—General Buell was relieved from the command of the Division today and has been ordered out west.

Nov. 10, 1861—General Erasmus D. Keyes arrived this morning and assumed command of the Division. As he entered the tent we arose, saluted, and remained standing as we did with General Buell. The General said: "Sit down boys and attend your work. I don't want you to stand up for me. When I come in you say: 'Good morning, General,' and I will say: 'Good morning, boys,' and that is all that I require." We were somewhat surprised, for both Generals are regulars and we thought all regulars were alike. However we are pleased with our new chief and expect to have pleasant times with him. We have not seen all of his staff as yet, but Captain Charles C. Suydam and Lieutenant Bradbury C. Chetwood have reported. Captain Suydam is to be Assistant Adjutant General and Chetwood A.D.C. The Captain is a tall slight built young man and a lawyer by profession. He is very pleasant to us, and as I am to serve under him, I have watched him very carefully. A guard is detailed daily from the troops for service at Headquarters. There are 3 Brigades in the Division commanded respectively by Gen. Darius N. Couch, John J. Peck and L.P. Graham. The 6th Penn. Cavalry and four Penn. Batteries are attached to the Division. Quite a little army in itself.

Headquarters Keyes Division, Washington, D.C. Nov. 24/61 Sunday—During the past week General Keyes moved his headquarters to Washington, and we are now located on the corner of Penn Avenue and 19th Street in the 4th story of a building formerly occupied by General McClellan. We came in baggage wagons and brought only our desks and table. Furniture will come after a while if we can find any. Today I have taken a walk in the President's grounds and then visited the camp of the Michigan Cavalry Regiment. Although I see soldiers every day, yet there is a fascination about them to me, and I never neglect an opportunity to visit a camp. I came back by way of the Washington Monument and admired this splendid structure although it is in an unfinished state. If it is ever completed it will be a worthy monument to the "Father of his country." I have not attended church today, as the work in the office kept me busy until after church hour.

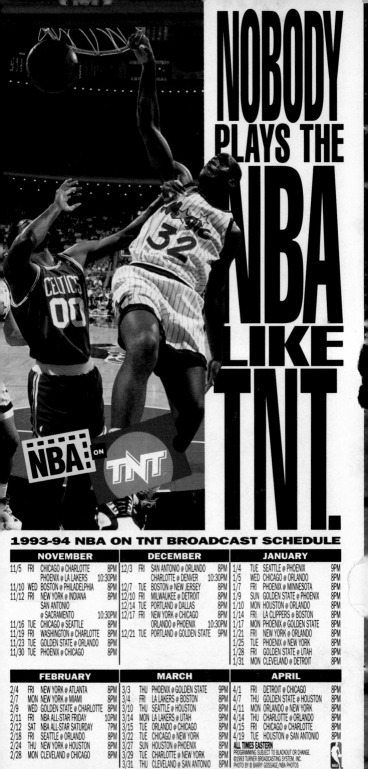

NOBODY PLAYS THE NBA LIKE TNT.

1993-94 NBA ON TNT BROADCAST SCHEDULE

		NOVEMBER	
11/5	FRI	CHICAGO @ CHARLOTTE	8PM
		PHOENIX @ LA LAKERS	10:30PM
11/10	WED	BOSTON @ PHILADELPHIA	8PM
11/12	FRI	NEW YORK @ INDIANA	8PM
		SAN ANTONIO	
		@ SACRAMENTO	10:30PM
11/16	TUE	CHICAGO @ SEATTLE	8PM
11/19	FRI	WASHINGTON @ CHARLOTTE	8PM
11/23	TUE	GOLDEN STATE @ ORLANDO	8PM
11/30	TUE	PHOENIX @ CHICAGO	8PM

		DECEMBER	
12/3	FRI	SAN ANTONIO @ ORLANDO	8PM
		CHARLOTTE @ DENVER	10:30PM
12/7	TUE	BOSTON @ NEW JERSEY	8PM
12/10	FRI	MILWAUKEE @ DETROIT	8PM
12/14	TUE	PORTLAND @ DALLAS	8PM
12/17	FRI	NEW YORK @ CHICAGO	8PM
		ORLANDO @ PHOENIX	10:30PM
12/21	TUE	PORTLAND @ GOLDEN STATE	9PM

		JANUARY	
1/4	TUE	SEATTLE @ PHOENIX	9PM
1/5	WED	CHICAGO @ ORLANDO	8PM
1/7	FRI	PHOENIX @ MINNESOTA	8PM
1/9	SUN	GOLDEN STATE @ PHOENIX	8PM
1/10	MON	HOUSTON @ ORLANDO	8PM
1/14	FRI	LA CLIPPERS @ BOSTON	8PM
1/17	MON	PHOENIX @ GOLDEN STATE	8PM
1/21	FRI	NEW YORK @ ORLANDO	8PM
1/25	TUE	PHOENIX @ NEW YORK	8PM
1/28	FRI	GOLDEN STATE @ UTAH	8PM
1/31	MON	CLEVELAND @ DETROIT	8PM

		FEBRUARY	
2/4	FRI	NEW YORK @ ATLANTA	8PM
2/7	MON	NEW YORK @ MIAMI	8PM
2/9	WED	GOLDEN STATE @ CHARLOTTE	8PM
2/11	FRI	NBA ALL-STAR FRIDAY	10PM
2/12	SAT	NBA ALL-STAR SATURDAY	7PM
2/18	FRI	SEATTLE @ ORLANDO	8PM
2/24	THU	NEW YORK @ HOUSTON	8PM
2/28	MON	CLEVELAND @ CHICAGO	8PM

		MARCH	
3/3	THU	PHOENIX @ GOLDEN STATE	9PM
3/4	FRI	LA LAKERS @ BOSTON	8PM
3/10	THU	SEATTLE @ HOUSTON	8PM
3/14	MON	LA LAKERS @ UTAH	9PM
3/15	TUE	ORLANDO @ CHICAGO	8PM
3/22	TUE	CHICAGO @ NEW YORK	8PM
3/27	SUN	HOUSTON @ PHOENIX	8PM
3/29	TUE	CHARLOTTE @ NEW YORK	8PM
3/31	THU	CLEVELAND @ SAN ANTONIO	8PM

		APRIL	
4/1	FRI	DETROIT @ CHICAGO	8PM
4/7	THU	GOLDEN STATE @ HOUSTON	8PM
4/11	MON	ORLANDO @ NEW YORK	8PM
4/14	THU	CHARLOTTE @ ORLANDO	8PM
4/15	FRI	CHICAGO @ CHARLOTTE	8PM
4/19	TUE	HOUSTON @ SAN ANTONIO	8PM

ALL TIMES EASTERN
PROGRAMMING SUBJECT TO BLACKOUT OR CHANGE.
©1993 TURNER BROADCASTING SYSTEM, INC.
PHOTO © BY BARRY GOSSAGE/NBA PHOTOS

13 NOV

NBA INSIDE STUFF 12:00 noon •	
Milwaukee @ New York	7:30
Philadelphia @ New Jersey	7:30
Boston @ Chicago	7:30
Utah @ Dallas	7:30
Phoenix @ Houston	7:30
Golden State @ Denver	7:00
San Antonio @ L.A. Clippers	7:30
Atlanta @ Seattle	7:00

UN 14 NOV

Sacramento @ New Jersey	
Cleveland @ L.A. Lakers	
Detroit @ Portland	

15 NOV

Houston @ Philadelphia	7:30

16 NOV

...ston @ New Jersey	7:30
...tah @ Orlando	7:30
...nto @ Atlanta	7:30
...te @ Indiana	7:30
...a @ Milwaukee	7:30
... @ Dallas	7:30
... @ Denver	7:00
... @ L.A. Lakers	7:30
... @ Golden State	7:30
... Portland	7:30
...Seattle	5:00

NOV

...elphia	7:30
...shington	7:30

SAT 2...

NBA INSIDE	
NBA RISING	
Utah @ N...	
Orlando @ Ne...	
Miami @ Wa...	
Charlotte @ Atla...	
Boston @ India...	
San Antonio @ Milw...	
Denver @ Minnes...	
L.A. Clippers @ Housto...	
Cl...nix...	
...enix ...n St...	

SUN 21...

L.A. Lakers @ New Jersey	
...n @ Detroit	
...cramento	
...land	

MON 22 NOV

Indiana @ Boston	
Miami @ New York	
L.A. Clippers @ San Antonio	

TUE 23 NOV

Charlotte @ Washington	7:...
Golden State @ Orlando	8:0...
L.A. Lakers @ Atlanta	7:3...
L.A. Clippers @ Dallas	7:30
Chicago @ Houston	7:30
Denver @ Portland	7:30
	7:30

WED 24 NOV

Golden State @ Min...	

But I expect to begin to attend church regularly next Sunday, and I know I shall enjoy it for I have not attended service in a house for five months.

Dec. 6/61—Keyes' Division was reviewed by General McClellen. I improvised the opportunity to visit Camp Sprague and call upon friends in Battery "G."

Dec. 8/61 Sunday—Warm and pleasant. General Keyes has rented a house in the same block with headquarters and is keeping house with some of his staff. Miss Nellie Keyes, his daughter, is at home with him.

Dec. 22/61 Sunday—Warm and pleasant. I rode out to Camp Brightwood today and visited the 2nd R.I. Vol. On my way back stopped at Camp Sprague and called upon the R.I. boys in the Battery stationed there.

One day is much like another at headquarters. We have a room where four of us "Clerks" sleep. Corporal Elisha H. Rhodes, Private George Reading 1st Long Island Volunteers, Private Isaac Cooper 62nd New York Volunteers, and Private_____ _____ Volunteers. In the room we have four iron bedsteads with good bedding all borrowed from a neighboring attic where they were stored by the former occupants of this building who kept a young ladies school. The desk that I use is marked:

> "Nellie Gwin is my name,
> America is my nation
> California is my native state.
> The Lord bless all creation."

We get up at seven o'clock and go over to a restaurant opposite for breakfast. After breakfast, a smoke. At 9 A.M. office hours begin and the General comes in promptly. During the day the General sometimes goes out to camp and many officers call at the office. General Couch is particularly neighborly and is very kind to us clerks. The morning reports from Brigade Headquarters begin to arrive at about 10 A.M. There are 13 Infantry Regiments, 1 Cavalry Regiment and 3 Batteries in the Division. It is my work to consolidate the morning reports and at 3 P.M. they are sent to General McClellan's Headquarters. After three P.M. the office hours are over and we go out for our dinner. During the evening one clerk must remain in the office, and the others are at liberty to go where they please. For this duty I get my Corporal's pay, $13.00 per month, 30 cents per day for rations and 35 cents per day for extra services. On this we manage to live very comfortably. We have time to visit the interesting points in the city, and I have a horse that I can use at pleasure. I often take rides out to the camps and begin to feel quite at home upon an Army horse. Letter writing usually occupies my evenings, although I occasionally spend an evening with young ladies whose acquaintance I have made.

Dec. 30/61—This afternoon, seeing the General alone in the office, I stepped up to him and said: "General, I want to go home." "Want to go home, and for what?" he replied. As I could not think of an excuse, I blurted out: "I want to see my mother." "Is she sick?" he asked. "No," I replied, "I hope not." He then asked me how long since I left home and if I was ever away for so long a time before. I told him I had been in the service seven months and never been away from home alone before. "Well," said the General, "You have been a good boy, and you shall have a furlough for ten days." So I have made out my papers and shall start as soon as they are signed.

Dec. 31/61—Today after office hours I rode out to Camp Brightwood, and my Captain Stephen H. Brown signed my furlough. Colonel Wheaton was inspecting the 36th New York Volunteers, and I rode over to their camp. The Colonel very kindly affixed his approval to the paper, and I then took it to Brigade Headquarters at the old Brightwood Hotel. General Couch first endorsed the papers as not being in proper form, but upon my explaining that I copied the form from the U.S. Army Regulations, he wrote another endorsement of approval.

Capt. Stephen H. Brown

Washington — Camp Brightwood, Md. — Prospect Hill, Va. — Camp near Chain Bridge — US Transport John Brooks — Newport News, Va. — Warwick Court House, Va. — Camp near Young's Farm — Williamsburg — Camp near Pamunkey River — White House Landing — Macon's Plantation — Cold Harbor, Va. — Gaines Mills, Va. — Hanover Court House, Va. — Mechanicsville, Va. — Fair Oaks, Va. — Charles City Crossroads, Va. — Malvern Hill, Va. — Harrison's Landing, Va. — Camp near Yorktown, Va. — Downsville, Md. — Cherry Run, Md. — Union, Va. — White Plains, Va. — Baltimore, Va. — Stafford Court House, Va. — Fredericksburg, Va.

1862

Washington Jany 1st 1862 Headquarters Keyes' Division—At 12 o'clock noon General Keyes, accompanied by Generals Couch, Peck, and Graham with their respective staffs, called upon President Lincoln. General Keyes was dressed in his ordinary uniform with shoulder straps, trousers tucked into his boot tops and with cover on his forage cap. The other generals wore full dress uniforms, chapeaux, and presented a marked contrast to General Keyes. This amused General Keyes very much, and he commented on it upon his return, and ended with his usual threat to send us back to our Regiments if we ever repeated anything that he had said.

Washington has been very gay today and the streets full of people out for a holiday. Officers in showy uniforms and ladies elegantly dressed are making New Year calls.

General Keyes has approved my application for a furlough and the papers have been sent to General McClellan.

Jany 2nd 1862—My application for a furlough did not come back this morning with the mail from Army Headquarters. I called General Keyes' attention to the fact, and he told me to go to Army Headquarters, give his compliments to Captain Mason and ask that the papers be approved and sent back to me. Captain Mason undertook to scold me for coming to General McClellan's office upon such an errand, and for some time I could get no satisfaction. But I happened to see my papers in a file of documents and calling his attention to the one, he very ungraciously signed his name and dismissed me after expressing his views of what he called my "impudence." I reported the affair to General Keyes who called for "the spurs he wore in Florida" and the sword he "wore when he fought the Indians" and strode down the stairs in great anger. On his return he only said: "I will teach these young officers not to insult my clerks." I was satisfied with the result of the affair and started for Providence on the night train."

Washington Hotel Baltimore, Md. Jany 12/62—I arrived here at 10 A.M. on my return from my furlough, and as it is Sunday there are no trains for Washington today. I have had a delightful visit to my home and feel cured of homesickness, but fear that I may have another attack some day. On my way I met two Rebel prisoners on their way to Fortress Monroe to be exchanged. One of them told me that he belonged to a North Carolina Regiment and was captured at Hatteras. He said the fight was a one-sided affair, that the Yankees got them in a corner and then shelled them out. They were paroled.

In the afternoon I visited the Fort upon Federal Hill, and one of the soldiers on duty showed me about and explained the situation. It is one of the most extensive earth works that I have seen.

Monday Jany 13/62—I took a very early train for Washington where I arrived before my fellow clerks were out of their beds. In the afternoon I rode out to Brightwood and visited my comrades in the 2nd R.I. and delivered messages to them from friends at home.

Tuesday Jany 14/62—Snow and mud is the rule today. I am back in the traces and doing my work as of old.

Washington Jany 17th 1862—A beautiful day and warm as spring. But the streets are in a terrible condition from mud, being much cut up by heavy teams. Isaac Cooper, one of the clerks, has started for home on an eight days furlough. The 2nd U.S. (Regular) Cavalry, who have been doing mounted Provost guard duty, have been relieved by the 6th Penn. Cavalry or Rush's Lancers. These soldiers look well as they sit upon their horses at street corners and are armed with long lances with red flags.

Sunday Jany 19th 1862—A pleasant day and the usual routine work in the office to perform. Attended church in the evening at the 20th Street Methodist.

Jany 20th 1862—Today all the Army officers in Washington are to be presented to Hon. Edwin M. Stanton, the new Secretary of War. (Not being an officer I am out.) An order has been issued forbidding any more furloughs, so I was just in time.

Jany 22nd 1862—A new Regiment of Penn. troops was added to our Division today. They waded past the office in the mud and slush and looked a little disconsolated. Their colonel was formerly a chaplain in a three months regiment. We have drawn from the Quartermaster's Department tents for General Keyes and staff and also for the clerks, orderlies, etc. I saw Gov. William Sprague downstairs in General Barry's Office. The driver of the hack did not know who his passenger was until I told him. He told me a funny story true or false. It was that the Governor applied at the Provost Marshal's office for a pass to cross the river to Virginia. The sentinel (a regular soldier) not knowing him, refused him admittance to the office because it was after office hours. The Governor, without making himself known, went out to George-town and trying to cross the Canal fell in. The hackman was very much amused and somewhat astonished when he found out the name of his queer passenger. The weather is bad and the roads almost impassable, so I stay in the office instead of taking my usual rides.

Jany 24/62—Walking down street today a soldier in a Zouave uniform spoke to me, and it proved to be William W. Aborn of Pawtuxet, R.I., a private in my Company "D" 2nd R.I. Vols. Aborn was severely wounded at the Battle of Bull Run July 21st 1861 and left for dead upon the field. He was carried to Richmond as a prisoner and has just been released. I took him to the office with me and shall send him home in a few days.

Jany 25/62—I rode out to Brightwood today and came back in a rain and hail storm. Lt. Col Wm. H.P. Steere has gone to Phila.

Jany 26th 1862—A fine day at last and I enjoyed a ride after office hours out to Georgetown. William Aborn is still with me and will go home as soon as his papers are properly made out.

Jany 29/62—General Keyes is in New York on "Leave of Absence" and General D.N. Couch is in command of the Division. It is rumored that Lieutenant Chetwood ADC is engaged to Miss Nellie Keyes, daughter of the General. They go to ride nearly every day in the mud and appear to be having a good time. We soldiers however are not supposed to know about such affairs. Quite a difference between being an enlisted man and an officer, but it is all right, and I am treated well.

William Aborn started for Rhode Island today.

Jany 31/62—Mud, mud. I am thinking of starting a steamboat line to run on Penn. Avenue between our office and the Capitol. If I was owner of this town I would sell it very cheap. Will the mud never dry up so that the Army can move? I hope so, for I am tired and weary of mud and routine work. I want to see service and have the war over so that I can go home. But I suppose the powers that be know what they are about and perhaps after a while I may be sighing for my comfortable quarters in Washington. We are to have another clerk to assist us in our work, and rumor says more staff officers.

Sunday Feby 2nd 1862—After office hours I rode out to Camp Brightwood but found the roads almost impassable by reason of mud. General Keyes has returned from his leave of absence.

Thursday Feby 6/62—Mud and rain and no prospects of a move. It is reported that the Senate expelled Senator Bright of Indiana for the crime of treason.[6] All Copperheads should be punished, for they are too cowardly to fight us in front, so they stop us in the rear.[7] Orders have been issued that all passes must be approved by the Division Commander. This makes extra work for the clerks.

Feby 14/62—We have just received news from the Burnside Expedition and are rejoicing over the victory for the Union which has been won. Also that the Rebel General Price has been defeated in the west. The 4th Battery "C" 1st Rhode Island Light Artillery came over from Virginia this morning and exchanged their brass guns for steel rifle cannon. The Battery made a fine appearance in the streets.

Sunday Feby 16/62—A pleasant day which has caused the snow in the streets to disappear. The 5th U.S. Cavalry made a parade a few days since.

Monday Feby 17th 1862—I turned out at Reveille as usual. When the drums sound from the camp of the regulars on a square near our Headquarters I always get out of bed although not obliged to do so. I like to keep my soldierly habits. This is a cold icy day. Orders have been issued to allow the soldiers in camp to visit Washington often. This order will be popular.

Feby 22, 1862 Washington's Birthday—It rained in the morning but at noon it cleared, and I rode out to the camp of my Regiment and helped the boys to celebrate. Isaac Cooper, clerk, and John Simmons (2nd R.I.), orderly, went with me. Professor Benoni Sweet, a private in the Regiment had finished his rope walking, but we we were in time for

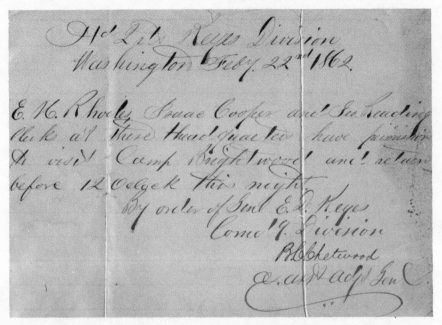

Pass used by E.H. Rhodes on his visit to Camp Brightwood, February 22, 1862.

the celebration. A double row of pine trees was planted around the entire camp and hung with paper lanterns. Company "D" (my company) had the name of "Buell" in letters of evergreen extending the length of the Company street or the distance of six tents. The Regiment was inspected by a Colonel of Regulars, and he was very complimentary, and said that the muskets were the first that he had ever seen. Companies "C & D" carried off the honors and the question has not been decided between them. A Penn. Battery fired a salute from the heavy guns at Fort Slocum, and a large flag was raised at Colonel Frank Wheaton's quarters. In the officers' foot race Captain Henry H. Young won the prize which was advertised as a trumpet. It proved to be a *tin horn*. A sack race for the men made much sport, and a clam chowder in Rhode Island style closed the exercises of the day. In the evening a huge barn fire was started and all the paper lanterns lighted. The effect was grand. Lt. Col Wm. H.P. Steere had the finest display at his quarters. The walls of his hut were covered with white paper adorned with gilt stars. The wood work was painted with scenes by Sergt. Richard Kruger

Co. "D" and flags inscribed with the names of Slocum and Ballou were suspended from the ceilings. Crowds of citizens and soldiers thronged the camp and all were delighted. We returned to Washington late in the evening and found that many residences were illuminated in honor of the "Father of his Country." Another Regiment has been added to our Division. We shall have an Army under General Keyes if we keep on.

Monday Feby 24/62—Today we have had a severe gale which smashed the windows in our office, much to the delight of General Keyes, who remarked: "Now we shall have some fresh air." A church on 13th Street was blown down and several dwellings damaged. The Potomac River rose several feet, and the water dashed over Long Bridge.

Feby 26/62—This afternoon I went down to the Capitol and heard Senator Henry Wilson speak upon the question of expelling disloyal members.[8] If I had my way I would hang every Copperhead. I saw Vice-President Hamlin in the Chair as Presiding Officer. Rumors of movements are plenty, and we keep our traps packed ready for a start. Some of the troops (not our Division) have moved into Virginia. In the evening I attended a fair on 20th Street held by a Methodist church and had a pleasant time. Cooper and I went home with some young ladies.

Sunday March 2/62—Still packed up and ready to move, but the orders are countermanded almost as soon as received. I want to go, I want to get out of Washington, and I want the war to end.

President Lincoln's son died Feby 21st, and the Departments were not illuminated on Washington's Birth Day. I attended the 20th Street Methodist church this evening. I go there because it is the nearest church. The Pastor preached his farewell sermon.

It has snowed all day. This may delay our move, but we shall start soon.

March 6/62—General Lander's funeral took place today and was a very solemn affair. Gen. McClellan was one of the pall bearers, and General Keyes and staff attended. Bishop Clark of Rhode Island preached the sermon. I hope I shall be ordered back to my Regiment soon. Not that I am dissatisfied with my position here, and the General is very kind to me, but I want to be with the boys in the next campaign and do my part as a soldier. I have no fear of the future. If I die upon the battlefield I hope to receive the reward of the righteous and feel resigned to God's will.

March 7/62—A fine day and troops have been moving in the streets.

Sergeant-Major E.H. Rhodes with his friend Levi Carr.

It is said that they are crossing into Virginia. Our turn will come soon.

March 9/62 Camp Brightwood, 2nd R.I.V.—Well, I have had my wish and here I am back to my Regiment again as a soldier. Saturday while visiting the camp, Colonel Wheaton sent for me and informed me that I had been promoted to be "Sergeant Major" of the Regiment. Well, well, who would have supposed that this would ever have happened? To say that I was delighted would be very tame. Corporal William G. Bradford Co. "G" is to take my place as clerk at Division

Headquarters. This morning my traps were brought out to camp, and I was mustered as Sergeant Major. I have received many congratulations from officers and men, and I am very happy. Tomorrow I shall receive my sash and sword. I shall mess with the officers by special arrangements. General Keyes expressed himself as much pleased with my promotion and said that I had served him faithfully and that he was glad to see me prosper. He said something about young men being ambitious for promotion, but his remarks would apply equally as well to himself. He was very kind to me, however, and I shall always remember him with gratitude. The former Sergeant Major George C. Clendennin has been made a Second Lieutenant. Levi Carr (Pawtuxet) has returned from his furlough. Direct your letters to:

Sergt Major E.H. Rhodes
2nd Regt R.I. Vols.
Camp Brightwood
Washington, D.C.

Corporal is played out.

Lieut. George C. Clendennin

Monday March 10/62 3 A.M.—At midnight orders came to march, and the men are busy cooking their three days' rations. I got my promotion just in time to go with them. Let us trust in God that he will guide and protect us. Levi Carr is on guard tonight as Sergeant of the Guard.

8 o'clock A.M.—The Regiment left camp at 8 o'clock and marched to Tennally Town, Maryland joining the Division on the road. We then crossed the Potomac River at Chain Bridge. The bridge is protected on the Maryland side by a large earthwork mounting many heavy guns. The roads were bad until we crossed the river and then became hard and firm. After marching about eight miles on the Leesburg Pike we went into camp near Prospect Hill. Col. Wheaton took possession of a brush hut and invited me to share his quarters with him. I started out this morning very brave and determined to carry my knapsack on my back, but soon weakened and placed it in a wagon. It will be carried for me hereafter, or I shall leave it behind me.

Camp on Prospect Hill, Va. March 11/62—Still in camp with orders to stay here. I called on General Keyes today. The old man is happy, for the Army is on the move. He passed our Regiment yesterday and was loudly cheered by the men. Today we have Guard Mount and Dress Parade, and I made my first appearance as Sergeant Major. Tonight the country is lighted up for miles with the campfires. We do not know our destination and do not care if it only means an advance and the close of the war.

Today one of our men found a shell upon the Lewinsville Battlefield and foolishly put some fire into the vent, when it exploded and killed a soldier.[9] This event has cast a gloom over our Regiment.

Camp near Chain Bridge, Va. March 15/62—Yesterday we were ordered back to this place, and we are now in the Fourth Corps D'Armee. General Keyes commands the corps and General Couch our Division. I am glad for General Keyes, for he deserves his promotion. As we took no tents with us, we are having a hard time sleeping out of doors. Last night it rained, and we suffered much from cold and wet. At dark we were ordered to march back to Brightwood where we arrived about midnight tired out and wet. We expect to leave here again soon, some say to join General Burnside. I hope this is true, for I should like to serve under so gallant a soldier.

Camp Brightwood, Md. March 17/62—Back in our old quarters and pretty well used up. Saturday night it rained so hard that the men could not sleep, so we crossed the bridge and following the river down to Georgetown reached our old quarters. Many of the men are sick, and we left them all along the road. But they will probably all come in today, and a little rest will set them all right. We are cooking six days' rations for another move which will be by water without much doubt. The baggage has been sent off and we are waiting for orders.

March 19/62—Still at Camp Brightwood waiting, waiting. Gov. Sprague was in Camp today.

March 21/62—I am twenty years of age today. The past year has been an eventful one to me, and I thank God for all his mercies to me. I trust my life in the future may be spent in his service. When I look back to March 21/61 I am amazed at what has transpired. Then I was a peaceful clerk in Frederick Miller's office. Today I am a soldier anxious to move. I feel to thank God that he has kept me within his fold while so many have gone astray, and trust that he will give me Grace to continue to serve Him and my country faithfully. I have now been in service ten months and feel like a veteran. Sleeping on the ground is fun, and a bed of pine boughs better than one of feathers. We are still waiting for orders which must come very soon. Many of the men are broken down by the late march, but I am stronger than ever.

Camp Brightwood, D.C. Sunday March 23/62—This morning we had divine service on the parade and the chaplain preached a sermon. This afternoon we received the bodies of Colonel John S. Slocum, Major Sullivan Ballou and Captain Levi Tower, officers of the 2nd R.I. killed at the Battle of Bull Run, Va. July 21/61. The remains were escorted by Gov. Sprague. The Regiment presented arms as the procession passed, and the remains were placed in the surgeon's quarters. I have before me a statement signed by Gov. Sprague and read upon Dress Parade as follows: *"The Rebels supposing the remains of Maj. Ballou to be Col. Slocum disinterred the body, removed the clothing, and burned the body to ashes."* The Governor collected all the remains he could and brought them to Camp. The other bodies were buried lying upon their faces. This to us is horrible, and the 2nd Rhode Island will remember it when they meet the foe again.[10]

Camp Brightwood, Tuesday morning, March 25/62, One o'clock— We are to leave Camp at 7 A.M. to take steamer, destination unknown. So Goodbye old Camp Brightwood where we have had lots of fun and learned a soldier's duty. May God bless and prosper us.

Camp Brightwood, March 25/62—We left camp this morning and marched about three miles, where we waited until dark and then again returned to camp. We never get away from Washington.

March 26/62—This morning we left Camp Brightwood again and marching through Washington to the Sixth Street wharf embarked on the side wheel steamer *John Brooks.* The 36th New York Volunteers are on the same boat. Our steamer sailed down the Potomac and joined the fleet at Alexandria. I should think that there were one hundred vessels in sight, among them the *Canonicus* and *Golden Gate* from R.I. The Stonington steamers are also in the fleet. Here we anchored for the night, and I slept in the ladies' cabin. The boat is crowded and the men not very comfortable. The night was passed in singing.

U.S. Transport John Brooks, Potomac River, March 27/62—This morning we started down the river towing two schooners loaded with horses. The weather is warm and the scene is delightful. The ships are gaily decorated with flags, and it looks more like a pleasure excursion than an army looking for the enemy. We passed Fort Washington on our left and a band played the "Red, White, and Blue." Our band responded with "Hail, Columbia." On our right we passed Mount Vernon, and our band played "Washington's March." The river here is very wide. General Keyes is just ahead of us on the steamer *Daniel Webster,* which is the flag ship of the fleet. The Rebel batteries appeared to be deserted, and a large fire was seen at Acquia Creek.

Friday morning March 28/62—This morning when I turned out we were nearing Fortress Monroe, and a large fleet of war vessels, including the little *Monitor,* and transports were anchored in Hampton Roads. We landed at the wharf and marched about three miles to the town, or what remains of the town, of Hampton. This town was burned last August by the Rebels, and only six or eight buildings are standing. Battery "E" 1st Rhode Island Light Artillery is encamped quite near to us.

Newport News, Va., March 29/62—We are now at Newport News where the Union Army can be found. The next place is Yorktown where the Rebels will be found.

March 31/62—Our tents have come, and we are in comfort again. Plenty of beef, pork, ham, bacon, etc. Yesterday I had a beefsteak and sweet potatoes. Very good living for a soldier. I called at General Keyes' Headquarters yesterday. I am well and contented as usual. Camp life agrees with me.

Warwick Court House, Va., April 6/62—As I write the booming of cannon show that our boys are at work. This is a queer place of only a few houses. We arrived here last night—the Rebels retreating from Youngs Mills as we approached. We were immediately sent out on picket duty taking with us two pieces of artillery. We advanced to the river and posted our guns. This morning we discovered a Rebel fort, and our guns have been throwing shells across the river into it. They replied quite briskly, but as our Regiment is in the woods we have so far escaped any losses. The main body of the Rebels is at Yorktown, and we shall be there soon. I am cheerful and in good spirits, trusting that God will bring us in safety to victory.

April 12/62—Still at Warwick Court House. Great was our joy last night when the mail arrived, for it was the first one for several days. We are still in front of the Rebel forts, a distance of two miles separating us. I have been sleeping in the attic of a log house, but now have a tent. We have taken several prisoners in our skirmishes, and they all seem to be glad to get out of the Rebel Army. Both sides are building forts, and a great battle cannot be long delayed. May God help us to win the victory.

Camp Winfield Scott, Va., April 15/62—We are still at Warwick Court House. The affair that we had with the Rebels when we first arrived on the night of April 5th was the first time that we have fired upon the enemy since Bull Run. Our boys behaved well and kept up a rattle of musketry as long as the enemy remained in sight. As the river separated us (Warwick River), we did not come to close quarters. The Rebel pickets showed us some haversacks and canteens marked 2nd R.I.V. which they captured at Bull Run. They inquired for Governor Sprague.[11] We are living in the fields without tents, and every man cooks his own rations.

April 15/62—Yesterday I made a long tramp to see the sights. I went as far as Young's Mills where we first found the Rebels as we approached on the night of April 5th. I examined their deserted forts and was surprised to find that they had such comfortable quarters. Their old camps looked like villages with well built huts of pine slabs. The forts are on the brow on a hill beneath which is a swamp. A pond was made by a dam and a gate was all in readiness to open and let the water upon us had we attempted to pass the swamp. For some reason the Rebels did not wait for us to attack but fled at our approach. We still hear the Guns at Yorktown. General George B. McClellan paid our Regiment a visit today and was well received by Rhode Island cheers and music by the band. He rode in front of our line, took off his hat and said: "Good night my lads; we will find out what is in front of us and then go at them." The General is very popular with the troops, and we expect great things from him. Cooking coffee and soup in the same tin cup is not my forte, but I have to do it or starve.

April 18/62—Levi Carr and myself went out this morning to take a look at the Rebel forts and watch our men shell them. We could not see a single Rebel as Berdan's Sharpshooters keep them from showing themselves.[12] We saw a poor fellow, belonging to the 2nd Vermont Regiment laying dead upon a pile of boards. Last night the firing was terrific, and we could not sleep for the noise. As we are but a short distance from the Rebel lines, I wonder that they do not shell our camp. We have built breastworks of sand to protect our guns.

April 23/62—We have just returned from a march towards York- town where we had a small fight. The Rebels drove in the pickets of the 2nd R.I. and 7th Maine Vols. and fired into our camp. We formed and drove them back. General Davidson, who was in command, praised us highly. I never saw a cooler man than Col. Wheaton. When under fire he is always smiling, and the men catch his spirits. Last night we returned to Warwick Court House. Adjutant Samuel G. Smith is now on General Keyes staff, and First Lieut. William Ames is acting as Adjutant. We never get lonesome now, for something exciting is going on all the time.

April 25/62—Today I borrowed the Adjutant's horse, and with Chaplain Jameson, took a ride. We visited a place called Deep Creek where a steam mill was located before we arrived, but the engine had been taken away. We crossed the creek and kept on until we reached Young's farm at the mouth of the Warwick River. Young is said to be a quartermaster in the Rebel Army. His plantation contains some five thousand acres, and he did own one hundred slaves. A large three story house stands upon a hill and the chimneys are on the outside. About a dozen cabins are clustered in the yard while a path leads down to the spring house. The house faces the river and a beautiful flower garden is in front. I picked a fine bouquet and took it back to our camp. The beach in front of the house is covered with fine black and white sand. The Rebels have some forts on the other side of the river, but although we walked on the beach they did not fire at us. The Rebel gun boat *Teazer* came up last Tuesday and fired a 65 lbs shot through one of Young's barns. The seige of Yorktown goes bravely on, and some day it will be ours.

Camp near Young's Farm, April 30/62—Monday the Rebel gun boat *Teazer* shelled our Batteries near Young's Farm, and as it was supposed that they would land troops, our Regiment was sent down. We reached this place at one o'clock Tuesday morning and were put into Young's house and the windows darkened. This morning we moved to a piece of woods and have a fine camp. Our Batteries are shelling the Rebels across the river, and it sounds like a 4th of July celebration. We can hear the Rebels beat their drums in their camps, but ours are quiet as we do not want to show our position. We can hear our shell go over to the Rebel lines, and if they enjoy it as much as we do they are having a fine time. Levi Carr was out on picket duty last night. There is a fine peach orchard near us, but alas the peaches are not ripe. The news of the capture of New Orleans has been received, and it gives us great joy.[13] Well, the war will end in God's own time and we shall have peace. But the Rebels must lay down their arms before the United States will make peace with them.

Battlefield of Williamsburg, Va., May 7th 1862—Sunday last we received news of the evacuation of Yorktown, and we were ordered to leave our camp at Young's Farm and join the main Army. We crossed the river at Lee's Mills and then followed the line of forts and rifle pits until midnight when we encamped in a deserted Rebel camp. Everything denoted the haste in which the Rebels left their works. It rained hard all night, and we lay in the mud and water but felt happy, for now it was our turn to chase and the Rebels to run. Early Monday morning we moved towards Williamsburg, and about noon we began to hear the roar of cannon and rattle of musketry. We pushed on through mud that caused teams to be mired and batteries to halt, but by taking advantage of the woods and fields where the ground was not so soft or cut up, our Division arrived under fire at 4 P.M. Here we were placed in the reserves and remained until nearly dark when our Brigade was pushed to the front and took position in the edge of a piece of woods about six hundred yards in front of Fort Magruder. Until dark we could see the Rebel gunners load and fire the cannon from the fort, and we had to stand it, for we were ordered for some reason not to fire. All night the shells continued to burst over our heads, and in the mud and discomfort we prayed for daylight. Sometime after midnight we could hear the rumble of teams in the direction of Williamsburg, and just as day began to break Major Nelson Viall and myself crawled towards the fort. After approaching quite near and not seeing anyone we arose and walked up the glacis and looked into an embrasure. Behold, the fort was deserted. We hurried around to the rear and entered the gate. The ground was covered with dead men and horses. I found in one of the tents left standing some documents that gave the number of the garrison. While we were in the fort the 10th Mass. charged across the open space and entered the fort. They were surprised to find two Rhode Island soldiers already in possession. Both General Couch and Gen. Charles Devens who commands our Brigade made speeches to our Regiment and thanked the men for their coolness under fire. The field presented a horrible appearance, and in one small spot I counted sixty dead bodies. The Rebels threw away much of their baggage, and the road is filled with broken teams and gun carriages. Our Cavalry are now in pursuit, and many prisoners are being sent to the rear. Thank God for this victory and may we have many more and so end the war.

May 8th 1862—Monday night orders were received for a Light Brigade under command of General George Stoneman to be formed and follow the retreating Rebels. The 2nd R.I. Vols, Col. Frank Wheaton; the 98th Penn. Vols, Col. John F. Ballier; the 6th U.S. Cavalry; the 8th Illinois Cavalry, Col. Farnsworth Robertson's and Tidball's regular Batteries were detailed for this duty. Colonel Wheaton commands the two Infantry Regiments and Lt. Colonel Steere the 2nd R.I. We are now fifteen miles from Williamsburg on the road to Richmond, and we pick up prisoners every mile. The bugle has just sounded the advance and we must move.

Camp near Pamunkey River, Va., May 11/62—Friday our Cavalry came up with the Rebels and charged through the lines, and falling into an ambush, turned and came back. The Cavalry lost three killed and several wounded but brought back a number of prisoners. The Rebels opened with skill and we were ordered to move up. Our Artillery replied and the Rebel rear guard moved on. We followed to this place and are now waiting orders. Food is scarce, and all that we have to eat is the cattle killed by the way. No bread or salt in the Regiment and I am most starved. But it is all for the Union and we do not complain.

May 12th 1862—Left camp in the evening and marched to White House Landing on the Pamunkey River. Here we found three gun boats, and we feel more comfortable. In the evening we attended an outdoor jubilee meeting held by the Negroes. One of them preached a sermon. He tried to prove from the Bible that truth that every man must seek his own salvation. He said: "Bretheren, the Scripture says,'Every man for himself. Every tub on its own bottom.'" Not exactly Scripture, but it came near the truth. Our chaplain addressed the slaves, and the scene was a wild one.

White House Landing, Va., May 13/62—This is historic ground for in yonder house George Washington was married.[14] From this house Colonel Wheaton has procured a fine black saddle mule. We are now within twenty-four miles of Richmond, and heavy firing can be heard in the distance. Franklin's Division is arriving by way of the river and West Point.

Macon's Plantation, Va., May 16/62—Wednesday we left the White House and came to this place, a distance of three miles, and on the Richmond and West Point Railroad. Last night one of the Rebel General Stewart's orderlies came into our Cavalry lines by mistake and was captured. Two of our companies had a brush with the Rebels yesterday. We are on a high hill and our Batteries command the country round about. This farm is owned by a Dr. Macon. One of our gun boats fired an eleven inch shell that landed in his yard. Property is respected as much as it was in Washington. Even the generals sleep out of doors, and the rights of the people are respected. The men living here are surprised at this, as they were told the Yankees would destroy everything. The female portion of the population are very bitter and insult every soldier they meet, or rather think that they do. One of them said as the U.S. flag was borne by her house: "I never expected to live to see this day." If the Rebels were not in our front we could ride to Richmond by rail in a short time as the distance is only about twenty miles. General McClellan visited our camp.

Cold Harbor, Va., May 20/62—Saturday night we left Macon farm and marched about two miles and encamped, and remained until Sunday noon when we marched a short distance and went into camp again. Yesterday we marched to this place which is about twelve miles from Richmond and four miles to the Chickahominy where the Rebels say they have prepared the last ditch. We have had a tedious march. Every night wood was placed under our wagons ready to light and destroy them if the enemy should surprise us. The men have been obliged to wear their equipment day and night, and we have resorted to all sorts of tricks to deceive the Rebels. Sometimes at night we would build fires in all directions to lead them to believe that a large force was following them. Had they known that we were only about four thousand strong, they could have turned and destroyed us, but not without a fight. Yesterday our Cavalry captured a Rebel train with one hundred barrels of flour and fifty mules. The plantations as a rule are deserted but show that this was before the war a delightful country.

Gaines Mills May 20/62, 6 P.M.—We moved to this place this afternoon, and Richmond is only nine miles off. At the mill I found some meal and shall have jonnycake for supper.[15] I would give a good price for a good meal, for most of the time we have been short of food. Our Batteries are planted to command the Chickahominy River nearly two miles distant. The Rebels have a Battery in position on the other side of the river. Our advance has been slow. After marching a few miles we wait for the main Army to come up. The Negroes are delighted to see us, but the whites look as if they would like to kill us. One man was surprised when I told him that at the North the schools were open and the mills running. They seem to think that the North must be suffering the same as the South. I have enjoyed the march up the Peninsular very much, and thanks to Colonel Wheaton and Major Viall I have a chance to ride some.

Near New Bridge, Chickahominy River, May 24/62—We left our camp last night for a place called "Ellisons Mills." Just as we reached a bridge over a creek bang goes a gun, and a shot struck within ten feet of me. I thought my time had come and stood stupidly waiting for it to explode. But it proved to be a solid shot. Soon the shells were flying all around us and one of our Batteries went into position and replied. Our second shot dismounted a Rebel gun and they changed position and opened again. They fired about one hundred shots and then limbered up and left.

This morning we crossed the creek and our Cavalry went on and destroyed a portion of the Richmond and Fredericksburg Rail Road. A Regiment of Infantry from General Davidson's Brigade accompanied by a Regiment of Cavalry crossed New Bridge and brought back thirty-two prisoners besides killing and wounding several. Our side lost seven men. From a hill nearby we can see the spires of the churches in Richmond. Col. Lowe makes an ascension in his balloon every day.[16] It has rained nearly all day, and we are wet and uncomfortable. The Negroes are queer people and seem to understand the war. They leave for Fortress Monroe as soon as they can get to our rear. I pity them in their degradation, but the whites are to blame. Strawberries and peas are ripe, and we get a few occasionally. After the above described skirmish we found that we were near a place called Mechanicsville, and

I went into the town. The houses were riddled with shot fired from both sides during the fight.

Near Hanover Court House, May 28/62—Yesterday we returned to our old camp, and the men were ordered to pile their knapsacks in heaps and leave them and marched three miles to the place where the Cavalry tore up the rail road on Saturday. We found that the Rebels had repaired the track, and the Cavalry scouts reported that a train was coming from the direction of Hanover. We put some Artillery in position, and as the cars came around a curve we sent a polite message to stop in the shape of a few shells. The train stopped and about seventy-five soldiers jumped off and took to the woods. Captain Edward Stanley went down to the train and ran it up to our lines. There were four cars loaded with ammunition, and other stores. We destroyed the track by tearing up the rails. Huge piles of ties were made and the rails laid across. When the fire reached the rails they bent of their own weight and so they became useless. We opened a culvert and ran the engine into it, after which we bent all the rails we could and built a huge fire over it all. The cars were blown up after taking out such things as we needed. I procured a fine pair of new grey pantaloons. During all this a terrible battle was going on only four miles from us at Hanover Court House where General Fitz-John Porter gained a victory over the Rebels and took many prisoners. I saw about 400 of them as the Cavalry were taking them to the rear. We captured nearly all the soldiers that were on the train. This morning the Rebels came upon us in force, and as our work of destruction was finished, we returned to our camp where we left our knapsacks.

Near Mechanicsville, May 31/62—The place where we destroyed the railroad is called Atlee's Station. It is rumored that the advance guard is to be broken up and that we are to return to General Devens' Brigade in the 4th Corps. Fighting has been going on all day, and we still hear the roar of the guns in the distance. We are at a place called the Four Corners.

Near Mechanicsville, Va., June 4th 1862—We are still in this position and appear to be on the right of the Army. Great battles are being fought, but we are not being called upon. Our time will come soon enough. Saturday was a day of carnage. Our Division suffered terribly. General Charles Devens, Jr., our Brigade Commander, and General Peck (John J.) were wounded. Col. Riker of the 62nd New York, or Anderson Zouaves, was killed. General McClellan has issued an order in which he states that he shall share the dangers of the battlefield with us (Why not?) and talks about relying upon the bayonet. We can see the Rebel guns, and the shells fly over our camp. They sound like a steam whistle. We have not tents, and our blankets are wet most of the time. But it is all for the Union. May God help us. Several of the men are sick and some have died, but my health is good, and I keep up my spirits. We expect to have blouses issued soon to take the place of the coats the men have been wearing. Tomorrow will complete my first year in the Army. It has been one of hardships, but I am glad that I enlisted and want to see the end of the war with the Union restored and peace again in our land. I cannot say when we shall move. We are kept here for some wise purpose without doubt and are ready to do our duty when called upon.

Near Mechanicsville, Va., June 8/62—Sunday has come again, and it is unusually quiet. The cannonading which has been continuous for the past week is hushed today as if in reverence. For a week we have had queer weather. The mornings have been pleasant, but towards night we have had terrific thunder storms with heavy rains, and the men sleep in wet clothing. I wonder that we are not all sick. Every night we have our traps packed ready for a move, but so far we have not been disturbed. The Artillery fire up to today has been constant, and our chief amusement is speculating on where the shells will strike. The balloon goes up every day, and prisoners say that the people of Richmond stand upon the street corners and watch its movement. The Rebels occasionally fire a shell at it but have not succeeded in reaching it as yet. Yesterday a heavy Battery opened on the Rebel works. In a house or shanty near our camp lives a woman with her daughter and two small sons. Her oldest is in the Rebel Army. She asked for a guard, and I went over with a corporal and a guard to investigate. They were very much alarmed and said they were afraid of our men. I left the guard. This is a sample of what we are doing in Virginia. The men are fighting against their country, and we are guarding their families and even feeding them. But humanity demands this much. We have only used houses for hospitals for very sick men. When the weather will permit we have dress parade, but without music, as we do not care to inform the enemy of our location. After parade we usually have religious service, and as a rule the men give good attention. Mr. Jameson, our Chaplain, preached to the Regiment today in the woods. This morning a careful inspection of the Regiment was made.

Near Mechanicsville, June 11/62—Hurrah! The Paymaster is in camp and is paying off the officers and men.

Near Mechanicsville, Sunday June 15/62—For two days we have been constantly under arms, and as our baggage has been sent to the rear with all the trains, we are not very comfortable. The men sleep part of the time and take turns standing to arms. The Cavalry hold their horses by their bridles, and it looks like work coming. One day last week a carriage containing Mrs. General Robert E. Lee of the Rebel Army with her daughter and two other ladies passed our camp escorted by Union Cavalry. She was sent South under a flag of truce. How she came to be left in the North I do not know.[17] I rode over to Battery "C" 1st R.I. Artillery a few days since. They are near the Chickahominy River and facing the Rebels. The pickets on that line are good natured and exchange papers. There are several houses near our camp, and I took supper at one of them a few nights since. The first meal eaten by me in a house for a long time. We have to detail a good many men to protect the gardens, or the people would starve. I do not see what they can do for food next winter, but they are reaping the fruits of their folly.

Near Fair Oaks, Va., June 20/62—Stoneman's Light Brigade is at last disbanded, and we are back to our old Brigade. Last Wednesday we started at 4P.M. and crossed the Chickahominy at the so-called Tammany Bridge. It is built of pine logs and crosses both swamp and stream. It is nearly one mile in length and was built I believe by a New York Regiment. After crossing we encamped for the night and the next morning joined our Brigade. The Mass. boys (7th & 10th Regt.) and the 36th New York were very glad to see us back. We camped in a heavy oak wood in the rear of some earthworks built by our Brigade. The railroad runs very near our camp and cars are passing continually. I was boy enough to run down and see a train pass, and it was the first sight of civilization that I have seen for a long time. General Keyes' quarters are near our camp, and I made him a call. Adjutant Sam J. Smith of the 2nd who is on Keyes' staff is said to have behaved very bravely in the last fight. New uniforms were issued to our Regiment today. It consists of a dark flannel blouse and light blue pants. Our officers have taken to soft black hats. William B. Westcott called to see me last night. He is now Quarter Master Sergeant of Battery "G" 1st R.I. Artillery. Lieutenant-Colonel Steere has been promoted Colonel of the 4th R.I. Vols and will leave us soon. Major Nelson Viall has been promoted Lieutenant-Colonel of our Regiment. He is a splendid officer and man and has been very kind to me.

Near Fair Oaks, Va., Sunday June 22/62—Mr. Jameson, our Chaplain, preached this morning from the word "Gospel." The sermon was excellent and I trust will do some good. We have Christian men in the Regiment, but there are many who take no interest in religious matters. I trust that God's spirit will move upon their hearts and turn them to repentance. Just before dark last night the Rebels undertook to drive in our pickets but did not succeed. They kept up constant firing all night and sleep was out of the question.

This morning at three o'clock the whole Army was under arms, but so far all is quiet. My friend, Benjamin Hubbard started for the White house with several hundred dollars belonging to Company "D" to send home. He was captured by Rebel Cavalry. Our sutler also was captured with several thousand dollars. Col. Steere left us today for the 4th Regiment. He was cheered as he left camp. The 4th will have a good Colonel.

Near Fair Oaks, Va., June 26/62—The old Second has again been in battle, and although many have been killed and wounded I, by the goodness of God, escaped unhurt.

Yesterday morning the 25th, our advanced pickets had a severe skirmish with the Rebels, and our Brigade under General Ives N. Palmer was moved forward to their support. We crossed the old battlefield of Seven Pines which is a graveyard, and many of the bodies are only half buried. Some only have a little earth thrown over them and are partly exposed. Here we halted until noon when we again advanced and pressed the enemy back for a mile or more while our Artillery threw shells over our heads into the woods in our front. On reaching a piece of woods with an open space in front two guns from a regular battery were brought up and fire was opened upon the Rebel camps. After some time a Rebel battery replied. Their first shots went high, but came nearer and nearer, and as the range of our guns was ascertained the Regulars retired down the road to our rear. The Rebels continued their fire, and soon a shell came crashing through the swamp and exploded in the ranks of Company "A" killing two men and wounding another. Now the shell and canister came thick and fast, and several were killed and others wounded including Captain Stanley of Company "E." The firing ceased at dark, and we commenced to build a rifle pit in the swamp, but as fast as we dug out the mud the water would run in. We struck across a trench where the dead of Fair Oaks were buried, and the result was simply horrible. General Philip Kearney was engaged on our left and drove the enemy from his front. Some time in the evening our pickets were attacked by Rebel Infantry, but we dropped our spades and drove the enemy back. Three times during the night did they try to drive us from the swamp but failed each time. It was very dark, and the flames from the muskets and cannon of the Rebels lighted up the scene while the bullets buzzed like bees. I was busy taking orders from Colonel Wheaton (who took command of the Brigade during the night) to the other Regiments. I did not like the work, but it was duty, and I try to do my duty always. The firing would at times almost cease and then be renewed with new force and fury. Our men behaved splendidly and Colonel was as cool as if on drill. At daylight we were relieved by other troops and retired to a fort in the rear where after waiting to see if we were to be attacked, and the Rebels not appearing we returned to our old camp. As far as known we had five men killed and about twenty-five wounded. My friend Fred A. Arnold Co. "D" was wounded, but I hope will recover. He was hit in the leg.

Charles City Crossroads, Sunday morning June 29/62— Well, the Grand Army is on the retreat. After the battle of the 25th General McClellan determined to raise the siege of Richmond and fall back to the James River. The 2nd R.I. and the 6th Maine Volunteers were sent on in advance, and since we left the front we have heard constant firing in our rear. The immense depot of supplies at Savage Station was burned to prevent its falling into the hands of the enemy. I did not expect this would be the result of our campaign, but I suppose it is all right. We have marched night and day, and no one will know how much the Army has suffered. No sleep, scant food, and tired almost to death. We arrived at this place this morning and were attacked by a Regiment of North Carolina Cavalry. With the help of two guns with us we about ruined this Cavalry Regiment and took many prisoners. As we were concealed in the woods the enemy rode right up to us and did not hit even one of our men. I caught a Rebel and brought him to Colonel Wheaton. He had a Colt revolving rifle which I took from him, and the Colonel tells me that he will send it home for me. We were ordered to move on, and so took our prisoners into line and marched again towards the James River.

Monday June 30/62— At early hour this morning we arrived at a place on the James River called Hacksville Landing. After resting a short time we turned back on the road and at night reached Malvern Hill.

Malvern Hill July 1/62—O the horrors of this day's work, but at last we have stopped the Rebel advance, and instead of following us they are fleeing to Richmond. The battle of today is beyond description. The enemy advanced through fields of grain and attacked our lines posted upon a long range of hills. Our gun boat threw shell over our heads and into the Rebel lines. All attempts to drive us from our position failed and at night the Rebels retired. Our Regiment supported the Batteries of our camps and did not suffer much, but saw the whole of the grand fight.

Harrison's Landing, James River,[18] July 3/62—We left Malvern Hill last night and in the midst of a pouring rain marched to this place where we arrived early this morning. O how tired and sleepy I am. We have had no rest since June 24th, and we are nearly dead. The first thing I noticed in the river was the steamer *Canonicus* of Providence. It made me think of home. We stacked arms and the men laid down in the rain and went to sleep. Lieutenant-Colonel Viall threw a piece of canvas over a bush and putting some straw upon the ground invited me to share it with him. We had just gone to sleep when a Rebel Battery opened and sent their shells over our heads. We turned out in a hurry and just in time, too, for a shot or shell struck in the straw that we had just left. This shot covered Colonel Viall's horse with mud. We were ordered to leave our knapsacks and go after this Rebel Battery. But our men could hardly move, and after going a short distance we halted and other troops went on in pursuit. Battery "E" 1st R.I. Artillery sent out some guns and I hear that one of the Rebel guns was captured. We returned to our knapsacks and the men are trying to sleep.

July 4th 1862—This morning all the troops were put to work upon the line of forts that have been laid out. As I was going to the spring I met General McClellan who said good morning pleasantly and told our party that as soon as the forts were finished we shoud have rest. He took a drink of water from a canteen and lighted a cigar from one of the men's pipes. At Malvern Hill he rode in front of our Regiment and was loudly cheered. I have been down to the river. I rode the Adjutant's horse and enjoyed the sight of the vessels. Gun boats and transports are anchored in the stream. Rest is what we want now, and I hope we shall get it. I could sleep for a week. The weather is very hot, but we have moved our camp to a wood where we get the shade. This is a queer 4th of July, but we have not forgotten that it is our national birthday, and a salute has been fired. We expect to have something to eat before long.

Soldiering is not fun, but duty keeps us in the ranks. Well, the war must end some time, and the Union will be restored. I wonder what our next move will be. I hope it will be more successful than our last.

Harrison's Landing, Va., July 9/62—The weather is extremely hot, and as the men are at work on the forts they suffer much. The Army is full of sick men, but so far our Regiment seems to have escaped. The swamp in which we lived while in front of Richmond caused chills and fever. I have been very well, in fact not sick at all. Lt. Col. Nelson Viall of our Regiment is now in command of the 10th Mass. Vols., their field officers being all sick or wounded. Fred Arnold is in the hospital in Washington. Last night President Lincoln made a visit to the Army. As he passed along the lines salutes were fired, and the men turned out and cheered. We see General McClellan nearly every day, and he often speaks to the men. How I should like to see my home. In God's own time we shall meet on earth or in Heaven. I have been busy all day preparing muster and pay rolls. We hope to get some money some day.

Sunday July 20/62—Routine work goes on in camp with drills and picket duty. During the last week we have had much rain and our camp has been flooded. This morning the sun made its appearance and the mud is drying up. Dr. Carr left for home last night. Capt. Edwin K. Sherman, who left us two weeks ago on a sick leave, died in New York before he could reach his home. Lieut. Lewis E. Bowen has resigned on account of sickness. Chaplain Jameson preached to us this morning amid the cannonading of our gun boats up the river. This is the first time the Rebels have molested us since the day we arrived here. Colonel Wheaton is in command of the Brigade, as General Palmer is sick. The Colonel started for Fortress Monroe this morning. General Devens, our Brigade Commander, who was wounded at Fair Oaks is expected back soon. Lt. William Wheaton, brother to the Colonel, is now an aide to General Palmer. Yesterday Major Davis USA inspected our Regiment, and we are soon to be supplied with clothing which we much need.

Harrison's Landing Sunday July 27/62—We are having a fine day and commenced regular camp duties the same as at Camp Brightwood. After "Guard Mount" the Regiment was paraded in front of Colonel Wheaton's quarters and we had church service. The men were seated in the form of a hollow square, and the Chaplain preached from the centre. Some of the men are very much interested, while others are totally indifferent to what is going on. The band is now playing in front of the Colonel's tent, and crowds of soldiers are listening to the music. The

Surgeon George W. Carr

Colonel has returned from his visit to Mrs. Wheaton at Fortress Monroe. The Sloop of War *Dacotah* has arrived. Lieut. Wm. Ames' brother is an officer on board of her. Some of the Rhode Island Artillery boys paid me a visit today.

July 31/62—I have been quite sick for a few days but am all right again now. Col Wheaton has recommended me for promotion to Second Lieutenant, for as the letter reads: "Good conduct in the different engagements on the Peninsular." I suppose my commission will come soon. Hurrah. Yesterday the Army was under arms as it was reported that the Rebel iron clad *Merrimac* was coming. Well let her come, and bring the Rebel Army with her. We can take care of them now. I have received a box. The cake was spoiled, but the other things were all right.

Harrison's Landing, Va. Aug. 2nd 1862—Today we moved our camp back into a pine grove. Shelter tents have been issued to the men. Each man has one piece about six feet long and four feet wide. Two men button these pieces together, and by throwing it over a ridge pole, supported at each end, a shelter is formed. It is open at each end and serves to shield from the sun, but makes a regular shower bath when it rains. The men carry each a piece of tent in their knapsacks. We have a fine camp with regular company streets. Tonight we had a fine dress parade followed by Divine Service. We have a large open field near our camp which we use for parades and drills. It is rumored that we are to move. I hope it will be towards Richmond.

Aug. 3/62—Thursday morning about 1 o'clock a gun was heard followed by the bursting of a shell near our camp. This was repeated, and soon the gunboats joined in with the heavy shots and we had music. We found that a Rebel Light Battery had taken position on the south side of the James and opened upon our fleet of transports, some of the shells coming over to the camps. The gunboats drove the enemy away, and the next morning troops crossed the river and burned the houses that gave the enemy shelter. We are looking for recruits, but so far in vain. If men are not patriotic enough to volunteer to save the country I hope a draft will be ordered.

Aug. 7/62 Friday—Thursday night Gen. Sedgwick's Division had a sharp night at Malvern Hill and our Division was ordered to support them. At 7 A.M. we started with two days rations. We first went down to the James River and then followed a road near the bank in the direction of Richmond. Three miles from camp we reached the plantation of Hill Carter. Although a Rebel Mr. Carter is glad to have his property protected. He has a fine farm and a small village of story and half houses painted white for his slaves. They look fine in the moonlight. Two miles on we reached the village of Shirley. This is one of the finest little towns I ever saw. The houses are of brick and have neat lawns in front. A neat brick church stands on the main street. It is said that Mr. Carter owns this village, and that he had one thousand slaves. About three o'clock A.M. we halted and formed in line with guns loaded. At daylight our pickets reported the enemy in sight, but they did not attack us. At noon we moved to a hill near by, and a waggon train passed us bound for Malvern Hill. About 10 P.M. we moved on to Turkey Bridge and were soon ordered back to camp, reaching it about daylight this (Friday) morning very tired and sleepy. The movement is said to have been a feint to draw troops from Richmond and give our General Pope a chance to operate north of Richmond. We brought back several prisoners. Tonight I rode down to the James River for a bath and enjoyed it much.

Aug. 10/62—I took a ride today and visited Battery "G" 1st R.I. Artillery and saw William Westcott. I stopped at the camp of the 64th New York Vols. and called on my own cousin, Arnold Rhodes Chase. As I never met him before I rather enjoyed the novelty of meeting an unknown relative. He is soon to be made a Captain.

O, how hot the weather is, and many of our men are sick. We had church service today and an interesting sermon. I do not know what the next move will be but think we shall leave this place altogether. If we are to advance on Richmond again, why did we leave Malvern Hill? Since writing the above, orders have been received to move tomorrow with six days' rations. I do not know what it may mean.

Aug. 14th 1862—All of our baggage has been sent off, and we are waiting for orders to march. Where, we do not know as yet.

Camp between Williamsburg and Yorktown, Aug. 19/62—For some time we have been suspicious that General McClellan intended to leave Harrison's Landing, as all of the baggage had been sent off. Our Division left camp about daylight on Saturday last and marched about eight miles, when we halted, as the roads were blocked with teams. Sunday morning we started again and reached the Chickahominy River near its mouth about dark. We made twenty miles and crossed the river on a pontoon bridge which was about half a mile in length. Gunboats were lying at anchor near each bridge to protect it. After crossing we camped for the night. Yesterday we continued on and passing through Williamsburg reached this camp which is about five miles from Yorktown. So far we have seen no enemy. No one knows where we are bound, but some think we are to join Pope's Army.

Aug. 20/62—This morning we left camp and marched through Yorktown, and we are now in camp near the village. The old forts are still standing and shot and shell can be picked up most anywheres. It is said that we are to go to Fortress Monroe, but what for no one can find out. I am well but do not like the appearance of things. We are moving in the wrong direction it seems to me. Well, I hope it will turn out all right.

Camp near Yorktown, Va., Aug. 24/62—Sunday night again and I fear we are no nearer the end of the war than we were when we first landed at Fortress Monroe five months ago. But then we have learned some things, and now I hope we shall go ahead and capture Richmond.

We have moved our camp from near the river to a hill where we get plenty of pure water from a spring. This is a great luxury, for in most of our camps we have been obliged to go long distances for water. This hill was occupied by General Fitz-John Porter's Corps during the late siege, and we occasionally find shot and shell lying about. Each company has a wide street, and we have a parade ground in front of the camp. It looks now as if our Corps (Keyes 4th) would remain on the Peninsular, as most of the other troops have been sent away. I was much surprised at the appearance of Yorktown. We entered town through a gate in a fort built upon a bluff. There are not more than twenty houses in the village and some of these must have been built before the Revolutionary War for they are of the gamble roof style and all tumbling down.[19] Passing through the main street we saw the old forts built by the British Army when it was beseiged by Washington in 1781. Some of these forts were used by the Rebels. Still further on we saw the Rebel works built of bags of sand covered with earth. Some of them were on high bluffs with deep ravines in front. Some of the Rebel guns are still mounted, while others lay upon the ground dismounted by our fire. Passing through another gate we came to the open plain which separated Yorktown from our batteries. Here we halted for a short time, and I visited a large lot enclosed by a rail fence over the entrance to which were the words: "Union Cemetery." Here our brave boys were buried after the capture of the town. One member of my old company "D" is buried here. In the open field were other graves marked 12th Mississippi Regiment. The plain was covered with holes with dirt piled in front and were used by Berdan's Sharpshooters who kept the Rebel gunners down. We marched on to our old lines where we saw the Batteries for heavy guns and mortars. A darkey said that the shell from our guns "played a tune like a fiddle." We passed through the old camps and encamped near the river. I visited with Levi Carr in one of our bayonet earthworks. It is in the yard of a plantation. The owner told me that he moved away when the fight began, but he might have remained in safety for not one Rebel shot struck his house. He said that he owned hundreds of acres of land, but could only raise two and a half dollars in money, and that he got from our people. The people are very poor indeed. They are reaping their reward. General Keyes and General Devens are standing beside the tent talking to Colonel Wheaton.

Near Yorktown, Va., Aug. 27/62—We are under orders to take transports, but no one knows where we are to go.

Friday Aug. 29/62—We left our camp today and marching to the wharf at Yorktown embarked on the side wheel steamship *S. R. Spaulding* and started up Chesapeake Bay.

Sunday Aug. 31/62—We arrived at Alexandria this morning after a pleasant sail from Yorktown. Here we learned that a battle had been fought at, or near, Manassas. We landed and marched in the direction of the old Bull Run ground where we understand our forces have met the enemy.

Sept. 1st 1862—Today we passed through Fairfax Court House and formed line of battle at Germantown with a battle going on two miles in our front. It rained in torrents, and I never in all my life ever heard such thunder or saw such lightning. It seemed as if Nature was trying to outdo man in the way of noise, for all the time the cannon roared and muskets rattled while the air was filled with flying missiles. But Nature won, and the battle ceased. We camped on the field for the night amid the dead and dying.

Sept. 2nd 1862—This morning we found the entire Army retreating and our Division was left to protect and cover the rear. As soon as our lines were formed our troops that had been fighting the day before passed through to the rear. As the Rebels came in sight we too moved off with the gallant 1st Rhode Island Cavalry with us. The Rebels shelled us lively, but we did not stop and reached Alexandria all right about midnight.

Sept. 3/62—Today we took a steamer at Alexandria and went up the Potomac past Washington, through the draw at Long Bridge and landed at Georgetown. From here we marched up the river and crossed Chain Bridge into Virginia again. It is hard to have reached the point we started from last March, and Richmond is still the Rebel Capital.

Camp near Chain Bridge, Va., Sept. 5/62—Last Wednesday after landing at Alexandria, Levi Carr and myself procured a quart of milk, and as we had only one cup and one spoon sat down to take turns in enjoying our feast. As we were eating Colonel Wheaton called: "Lieutenant Rhodes!" I went across the railroad track to where he was standing where he took me by the hand and congratulated me on my promotion. Well, I am proud, and I think I have a right to be, for thirteen months ago I enlisted as a private and I am now an officer.[20] I am grateful to God for all his mercies to me.

Near Orcutts Cross Roads, Va., Sept. 7/62—Yesterday we marched to this place which is near a ford of the Potomac River some fifteen

2nd Lieut. E. H. Rhodes

miles above Washington. I have been assigned to my old Company that I came out in. "D." Captain Stephen H. Brown, Captain Dyer of Company "A" and Captain W.B. Sears of Company "F" wanted me, but as Company "D" held a meeting and passed resolutions asking the Colonel to assign me to their Company I decided to join them. I am very happy over my promotion, for I am one of the youngest officers, being only 20 years old and seven months. Direct letters to Lieut. E.H. Rhodes, Co. "D" 2nd R.I.V., Devens Brigade, Couch's Division.

Near Poolesville, Md., Sept. 11/62—We arrived here last night and are waiting orders. It is said that we are to guard Edwards ferry, but I do not know. The Rebels are in Maryland and are now about nine miles from us. Most people seem to be glad to see the Union Army. Corporal William L. Bradford has been made Sergeant Major in my place. He belonged to Company "G."

Pleasant Valley, Md., Sept. 16/62—We are almost nine miles from Harper's Ferry. Yesterday we passed a battlefield and saw many dead lying unburied. We expect a fight any moment now. I send this by a sutler who is going to the rear.

Near Williamsport, Md., Sept. 21/62—Yesterday we had a skirmish here with the enemy's rear guard. And this morning they have recrossed into Virginia. Thank God Maryland is clear and free from the Rebel Army. The old Army of the Republic can fight after all, and I think that the Rebels found it out by this time. In my next I will give you an account of our late movements.

Near Williamsport, Md., Sept. 23/62—After leaving Poolesville we marched through the mountains towards Harper's Ferry. The scenery was delightful and reminded me of stories of fairy land as we looked off into the valleys. Little villages with white church spires were seen in all directions. The finest town that we have seen is Jefferson. Near Burketsville General Franklin's Corps (the 6th) had a fight, and we passed over the field the next day. The fight was on the rocky side of a mountain, and we saw the dead lying where they fell. We passed through the town and formed in line just beyond. Here I was placed in charge of a plantation with a guard. One of the ladies became insane from fear and excitement. We remained here two days and then went on to Brownsville where our Regiment was sent into the mountains after some Rebel Cavalry, but did not find them. The mountain side was steep and we found climbing hard work.[21] The next morning, the 17th, we saw the Battle of Antietam fought almost at our feet.[22] We could see the long lines of battle, both Union and Rebel and hear the roar as it came from the field. The Rebel trains of waggons were moving all day towards the river. At dark we marched down the mountain and started for the battlefield where we arrived and went into camp. The next morning we were put in the front lines. I have never in my soldier life seen such a sight. The dead and wounded covered the ground. In one spot a Rebel officer and twenty men lay near a wreck of a Battery. It is said Battery "A" 1st R.I. Artillery did this work. The Rebel sharpshooters and skirmishers were still at work and the bullets whizzed merrily. At noon the Rebels asked and received permission to bury their dead, and the firing ceased for awhile but commenced again in the afternoon. The 2nd R.I. was ordered forward and we charged up a hill and driving the enemy away took possession. Here we lay all night with the bullets flying over us most of the time.

The next morning the enemy shelled our Regiment, but it was their last shots, for as we moved forward they retired, and we entered Sharpsburg. The town is all battered to pieces and is not worth much. Here we remained until midnight of the 19th when we moved to Williamsport. It was reported that the Rebels were here in force. After forming our lines the entire Division moved on the town with flags flying. It was a grand sight to see our long lines extending through fields and woods, hills and dales, make this advance. Picket or skirmish firing was going on in front, but after marching some distance we halted. Several were killed in the Division and many wounded. Sunday morning we found that the enemy had recrossed the river. O, why did we not attack them and drive them into the river? I do not understand these things. But then I am only a boy.

Near Downsville, Md., Sept. 26/62—We have been in camp here now for three days and may remain for some time. We are enjoying a season of rest, and I think that we need it, for what with marching and fighting we are weary and used up. Clothing is scarce, and what is pleasant we are soon to have some soft bread. Hard bread is good, but soft bread is better.

Near Downsville, Md., Tuesday Sept. 30th 1862—Still in Maryland with all sorts of rumors about our next move. The days are hot and the nights cold, and just now we are having beautiful weather with moonlight nights, which makes guard duty very pleasant. I suppose that we shall be looking for winter quarters soon.

We have a mess composed of the following officers: Capt. Samuel B.M. Read and Lieut. Benjamin B. Manchester of Co. "I," Lieut. Edward A. Russell commanding Co. "C" and Captain Stephen H. Brown and Lieut. Elisha H. Rhodes of Co. "D." We have attached to our mess three servants to carry our blankets, shelter tents and a few simple cooking utensils. When we halt the servants put up our shelter tents and find us straw if possible. They do our cooking and look after things generally. Near our present camp there lives an old lady who supplies our mess with soft bread. On the march salt pork toasted on a

Lieut. Edward A. Russell

stick with hard bread and coffee is our principal diet. Today we found a bee tree in a grove near camp. The tree was promptly cut down and found to be well stored with honey. What a treat it was to us. The bees charged on the Regiment and accomplished what the Rebels have never done, put us to flight. We manage to buy some extras now such as chickens and bacon, and our men are quite expert in discovering places the people will sell food. Being in a loyal state of course foraging is not allowed and everything is paid for. Today we commenced our regular drills, and as Captain Brown was sick and we have no First Lieutenant, I took the command. I had not been on a Company drill for about a year, but found that it all came back to me, and I had no trouble. We are now attached to the Sixth Army Corps commanded by Major-General William B. Franklin. The Divisions are commanded by Generals Henry W. Slocum, William F. Smith and Darius N. Couch. We are still in Couch's Division. The Sixth Corps has a fine reputation, and we shall probably see much service with them. Sunday last a soldier of Co. "A" died and was buried with military honors.[23] It was not an unusual scene for us, yet it is always solemn. First came the muffled drums playing the

"Dead March" then the usual escort for a private. Eight privates, commanded by a corporal, with arms reversed. Then an ambulance with the body in a common board coffin covered with the Stars and Stripes. Co. "A" with side arms only followed while the Company officers brought up the rear. On arriving at the grave the Chaplain offered prayer and made some remarks. The coffin was then lowered into the grave, and three volleys were fired by the guard, and then the grave was filled up. The procession returned to camp with the drums playing a "Quick March." Everything went on as usual in camp as if nothing had happened, for death is so common that little sentiment is wasted. It is not like death at home. May God prepare us all for this event which must sooner or later come to all of us.

Near Downsville, Md., Sunday Oct. 5th 1862—On Friday last our Corps (6th) was received by President Lincoln accompanied by General McClellan. In spite of our old, torn and ragged clothes the troops looked well as the lines stretched over the hills and plains. Chaplain Jameson has gone to Rhode Island, so we have had no service today. We expect the Paymaster in a few days.

Oct. 8/62—Our camp is in a fine oak grove near Downsville. This town boasts of a church, school house, a small store and about twenty houses. It is really a very pretty little town. We have found most of the villages in Maryland to be neat, and the tall church spire looks better than the jail we found in every Virginia town even if there were not more than six or eight houses. The people in Maryland appear as a rule to be loyal to our government and have suffered much during the past few weeks. The nights are cold, and, as our shelter tents furnish poor protection, the men spend a good deal of the night about huge camp fires. But we do not complain, as it is all for the Union. The war will not end until the North wakes up. As it is now conducted it seems to me to be a grand farce. When certain politicians, Army contractors and traitors North are put out of the way, we shall succeed. General McClellan is popular with the Army, and we feel that he has not had a fair chance.

[NOTE. 1885. Since I wrote the above as a boy, I have changed my mind in regard to Gen. McClellan. I now honestly believe that while he was a good organizer of Armies, yet he lacked the skill to plan campaigns or handle large bodies of troops.]

General D.N. Couch who has commanded our Division for such a long time is to leave us and take command of the Second Corps. We are sorry to part with him, for he is a gallant soldier and has looked after the comfort of his men. The 2nd Corps are to be congratulated upon having so good a soldier to lead them.

Near Downsville, Oct. 10th 1862—Mrs. Wheaton, the wife of our Colonel, is in camp. She is very kind to the officers and men and is a great favorite with all. Gen. Charles Devens is now in command of our Division and Colonel Wheaton commands the Brigade. Lt. William Ames is sick in Washington. It is reported that he is to be made Major of the 12th R.I. Vols. Well, he will make a good one. The weather is very fine and we have had no rain for a long time. Orders have come for us to move and we are all ready, but know nothing of our destination. Virginia probably.

Camp near Downsville, Md., Oct. 15th 1862—For the past four days it has been cloudy and very cold and as the men have no overcoats they suffer some. We are, however, expecting new clothing very soon. We are very much ashamed that the Rebels were allowed to make their late raid into Pennsylvania. If this Army cannot protect the loyal states we had better *sell out* and go home. I ought not to complain, but I am mortified to think that we did not catch some of the Rebel raiders. We are all ready for a move. Let me describe the camp after marching orders are received. We see an orderly or staff officer dash into camp with his horse covered with foam, and he says: "Colonel Wheaton, your Regiment will move in fifteen minutes." The orders are sent around to the Captains, and down comes the shelter tents, blankets are packed up and haver-sacks filled with rations. Perhaps, and it usually happens, all the straw is burned, when another orderly rides leisurely into camp and says: "The order to move is countermanded." Then we go to work, set up our shelters and get ready to live again. Some of the men will be quite glad while the growlers who always find fault say: "It is always so, and we never shall leave this camp." The same men will want to get back after marching a few miles. I am acting Adjutant for a few days.

Camp near Cherry Run, Md., Oct. 22, 1862—Last Saturday night about dark we were ordered to march in great haste. Our Division passed through Downsville and arrived at Williamsport about 9 P.M. and halted for an hour. Williamsport is quite a town and has three hotels and several good stores. The Rebels crossed the Potomac at this place after the Battle of Antietam. We left here and marched seven miles farther to Clear Spring, or as the Negroes say: "Clar Spring." The night was dark and the roads stony and we were very tired when we went into camp in a wet field from which the corn had just been cut. We used corn stalks to sleep upon and they felt under me like young trees. Clear Spring is a charming little town and is quite a business place.

Sunday morning we followed a road up the river and beside the canal, up, up and over a mountain. Five miles from Clear Spring we found a house with a large porch and a tall pole in front, from which swung a sign "Fair View Inn." After resting for a short time we descended the other side of the mountain and at the base found a shanty marked "Indian Spring Hotel by J. McAllister." Here we struck the National Road and followed it beside the river and canal until we reached Hancock, thirteen miles from Clear Spring and two miles from the Pennsylvania line. Here we encamped near the canal. The river was low and well worth seeing. We remained at Hancock until midnight Monday when we marched to this place which we reached at daylight yesterday. We are now at a ford on the Potomac River and may cross into Virginia. Assistant Surgeon George W. Carr has been promoted Surgeon with the rank of Major. He well deserves it. The weather is getting cold and the men suffer. Some nights it is impossible to sleep and this is filling the hospitals very fast. Our Regiment has escaped but we are better off than some.[24] I still keep in good health and spirits.

Cherry Run, Md., Oct. 26th 1862—Last Thursday afternoon the 2nd R.I. passed under the canal and forded the Potomac into Virginia again. The river is here about three hundred yards wide and about two feet deep. The water was cold as ice, but we took off our shoes, rolled up our pants and crossed over. My Company "D" was sent out on picket. I found a house where there were two pretty girls who claimed to be Unionist. They prepared a good supper for Captain Brown and myself. Our Cavalry went on to a place called Hedgeville and brought back as prisoners a Rebel Captain, a Lieutenant and eighteen men. The next morning we recrossed the river and returned to our camp.

Last Friday Levi Carr and myself rode to Clear Spring about five miles from camp. We enjoyed the trip very much. It is reported now that Capt. Cyrus G. Dyer Co. "A" is to be a Major of the 12th R.I. Vols and that Lieut. William Ames will be Major of the 11th R.I. Vols.

Near Downsville, Md., Oct. 30th 1862—Well here we are back again to our camp. Monday we left Cherry Run and marched to Williamsport and camped a short distance from the river. On the opposite bank the Rebel pickets could be seen. Also Rebel soldiers gathering corn and loading their teams. Last night we returned to this place. Well, what next?

Near Berlin, Md., Nov. 2nd 1862—Friday morning at daylight we left our camp near Downsville and marched twelve miles to Rohrsville where we camped for the night. Saturday we started again before light and reached this place which is on the banks of the Potomac. An Army pontoon bridge has been placed across the river and we expect to cross into old Virginia again very soon. Gen. Burnside's force has already crossed at this point, and we can hear cannon in the distance. I hope we shall join his forces, and it looks now as if we were at last to attack the enemy. Berlin is about six miles below Harper's Ferry. The cars run on one side of our camp and the canal boats on the other. The first boat that passed attracted much attention from our men to whom it was a great novelty.

General McClellan's Headquarters are near our camp. Surgeon Carr extracted a double tooth for me today. I thought the top of my head was coming off. I sat upon a log and held on, and so did the Doctor, but iron was too much for me and the tooth came out. I am happy. At a place called Smoketown we passed the Army hospitals where our wounded men are treated. It was a sad sight, and I thanked God that I have been spared.

Near Union, Virginia, Nov. 5th 1862—We crossed the Potomac Monday night and reached this place last evening. Fighting has been going on in our front, but the Rebels retire as we advance.

The enemy are at Ashby's Gap about nine miles from here. Levi F. Carr has been made Hospital Steward of the 2nd R.I. Vols. Oh, how cold it is. Last night when we reached camp we were nearly starved, but we picked up on the road two turkeys and had them boiled for supper.

White Plains, Va., Saturday Nov. 8th 1862—After leaving Union we marched to within a short distance of Ashby's Gap in the Blue Ridge and halted for the night. Thursday morning we marched down the Winchester and Alexandria Pike towards Washington and after making a cold day of it reached this place which is on the Manassas Gap Rail Road. We are now only fifteen miles from the old Bull Run field. The next place is Warrenton where we expect to go soon. How I would like to have some of those "On to Richmond" fellows out here with us in the snow. The ground is white with snow, and it is too cold to write. This morning we found ourselves covered with snow that had fallen during the night.

New Baltimore, Va., Sunday Nov. 9/62—Left camp at White Plains and reached this place at night.

New Baltimore, Va., Nov. 10th 1862—We camped on the side of a mountain and have hard work to keep from sliding off. This has been a sad day for the Army of the Potomac. Gen. McClellan has been relieved from command and has left us. He rode along the lines and was heartily cheered by the men. Gen. Ambrose E. Burnside of R.I. is our new Commander.[25] He also rode along our lines and was well received, being cheered as he passed. This change produces much bitter feeling and some indignation. McClellan's enemies will now rejoice, but the Army loves and respects him. Like loyal soldiers we submit.

New Baltimore, Va., Nov. 13/62—New Baltimore is a lonesome little village at the foot of the hill on which we are camped. From the hill we can see the deserted Rebel forts in the distance. Gen. John Newton has been assigned to the command of our Division and Gen. Charles Devens, Jr. has returned to the command of our Brigade. Col. Wheaton has been ordered to command of another Brigade for a few weeks.

Nov. 19th 1862—We are now five miles from Stafford Court House, twelve miles from Acquia Creek and fifteen miles from the city of Fredericksburg. We are encamped with our division in a large field. We left New Baltimore Sunday morning and marched to Weaversville on the Manassas Rail Road, not far from Cartletts Station. Here we camped for the night in the rain. Tuesday morning we marched to this camp. It is still raining and we are very uncomfortable and cannot tell where we are to go next.

Near Stafford Court House, Va., Nov. 23/62—I am cold, in fact half frozen. As I write some of the officers who are hovering over a huge fire are singing "Home Sweet Home." Well I should like to see my home. Our blankets are wet and we have had no sun to dry them in some time. Yesterday our Regiment was on picket. We struck a new section of country where rail fences were plenty and had good fires. The roads are in bad condition from mud. Supplies begin to come from Acquia Creek and we are happy. I get a little home sick sometimes.

Near Stafford Court House, Va., Nov. 26/62—Still muddy and more rain. The Adjutant is sick, and I have been acting as Adjutant again. We have had inspection of the Regiment.

Nov. 27/62—Thanksgiving Day in R.I. Well, I too have much to thank my Heavenly Father for. He has preserved my life and given me health and strength to do my duty. For all which I am devoutly grateful.

Near Stafford Court House, Va., Dec. 3/62—Yesterday we enclosed a piece of ground with a hedge of cedar and the officers of our mess pitched three *three* new A tents inside. We made a gateway and arched it with boughs and built a green screen in front of our tents. We built beds of boughs and as darkness came on we sat down to enjoy our new homes. An orderly came in and said: "The Colonel directs you that you have three day's rations cooked and be ready to move tomorrow morning." Well, we shall sleep one night in our new quarters, and that is worth something to us.

Colonel Wheaton has been promoted to Brigadier General. We are very glad for him but sorry to have him leave our Regiment. He is a fine soldier and gentleman. We hope Lt. Col. Viall will be promoted to Colonel. The paymaster finished paying our Regiment tonight, and many thousands of dollars will be sent to Rhode Island.

Dec. 4/62—I do not know exactly where we are. We left our camp near Stafford Court House this morning and marched to this place which is twelve miles below Fredericksburg and half way between the Potomac and Rappahannock Rivers. I know one thing—it is very cold on the hill where we are in camp.

Dec. 7th 1862—We are still in camp at the unknown place. Plenty of snow, ice, and cold. Col. Wheaton has gone to Washington for a few days.

Near Belle Plain, Va., Dec. 9/62—We have found a name for this section: "Belle Plain." We are all ready to move and probably will have to cross the Rappahannock River and attempt to drive the Rebels from Fredericksburg.[26]

Battle Field near Fredericksburg, Va., Dec. 14/62—We crossed the river Thursday night and have been under fire ever since. The Rebels are strongly entrenched, and we have not made much headway.[27] I write this on the battlefield.

Near Falmouth, Va., Dec. 16th 1862—Thursday Dec. 11th we left our camp about two o'clock in the morning and just at daylight reached the banks of the Rappahannock River below Fredericksburg. The river is narrow and for about five hundred yards back the ground is nearly of a level with the river. Back of this plain are high bluffs and here we had nearly two hundred cannon in position. These cannon were constantly firing and the roar was tremendous. The air was filled with shot and shell flying over our heads and into Fredericksburg. The Rebels did not often reply but would at times land a shot over onto our side. Just at sunset the 2nd R.I. was ordered to cross the bridge at a place now called Franklin's crossing. It is opposite a plantation owned by A.N. Bernard and is about three miles below the city. Companies "B," "I" & "K" first charged across the pontoon bridge with arms at a trail while the balance of the Regiment followed with loaded guns. As we reached the other side of the river the three companies rushed up the bank and deployed as skirmishers. The Regiment followed and as we reached the high ground received a volley that wounded two of our men. The Rebels retreated and we followed for a short distance. Night now came and as the remainder of our Brigade crossed the bridge they gave "Three cheers for the Regiment first over." Our entire Regiment was deployed across the plain in a semicircle from river to river and remained through the night. General Devens said to us: "Boys, you have had a hard time, but Rhode Island did well." The Army was looking on to see our crossing and we felt that we must do well.

Friday, Dec. 12th we were relieved from picket duty and joined our Brigade which was formed in line of battle near the river bank. By this time the entire left grand Division had crossed and the plain was covered with soldiers and Batteries of Artillery. About noon Artillery on both sides opened and one shell exploded in our Regiment. In fact one Rebel Battery on a hill seemed to have the range of our Regiment and a few men were hit.

Saturday Dec. 13/62—We slept upon our arms last night and daylight this morning found us in line. The battle began at an early hour and the shot and shell screeched and screamed over our heads. To our right we could see the fight going on for the heights beyond and back of Fredericksburg. General Sumner tried to take the hills but failed. The city was on fire in several places, and the noise was deafening. We could see the long lines of Union troops move up the hill and melt away before the Rebel fire. But we were not idle, although at times there would be a lull in our front and we could watch the fight on the right. At 3 P.M. our Regiment was sent down to the left of the line and ordered to support a Battery. This was no fun for us, for we had to stand the Rebel shells fired at the Battery. Just at dark the firing ceased, but what a scene was before us. The dead and wounded covered the ground in all directions. Ambulances were sent out to pick up the wounded, but the enemy opened fire upon them, and wounded were left to suffer. During the evening if a match was lighted it would bring a shell from the Rebel forts on the hills. At 8 P.M. we were ordered to the rear and our Division rested for the night.

Sunday Dec. 14/62—Today it has been very quiet with an occasional

Capt. Samuel B.M. Read

shell from the Rebels. We tried to keep the Sabbath the best we could. We lay all day in our rifle pits awaiting events.

Monday Dec. 15/62—Just before light our Regiment was sent to the front and pushed behind the bank of a road. Here we lay all day watching the enemy's forts. About three P.M. our Batteries opened firing over our heads, and as the Rebels replied the shots would cross in the air. It was not pleasant for us and somewhat dangerous.

Thursday Dec. 16/62—This morning at one o'clock our Brigade was formed in line to protect the rear of the Left Grand Division as it recrossed the Rappahannock River. We waited until all the troops had reached the Falmouth side and then our Brigade silently moved over the bridge. As soon as we reached the north side the bridge was broken up and the pontoons taken back from the river banks. We were the first to cross the river and the last ones to recross. The 10th Mass. Vols. was the last Regimental organization to cross the river, but a Bridge Guards detailed from the 2nd R.I. Vols. and under command of Capt. Samuel B.M. Read was the last troop to recross. The Rebels were on the south bank as soon as we left it. The Army has met with a severe loss, and I fear little has been gained. The 4th, 7th and 12th R.I. Regiments were in the main battle in rear of the city and their losses we hear are heavy. May God help the poor afflicted friends at home. I am tired, O so tired, and can hardly keep awake. We have had very little sleep since we first crossed the river. My heart is filled with sorrow for our dead, but I am grateful that my life has been spared. Mr. A.N. Bernard owns a place near where we crossed. He calls it Mansfield. His brother owns the place below which is called Smithfield. Bernard's house was shattered by shot and shell, one shot passing through a plate glass mirror. Bernard left in great haste and left his pistols and a purse laying on a table. His books were all scattered about the yard and fine china was used by the men to hold their pork. He has already dug a cellar and intended to build a new house soon. The bricks were piled up in his yard and served as a cover for Rebel skirmishers who fired upon us as we crossed the bridge. We captured one officer and several Rebel soldiers from behind his bricks.

Near Falmouth, Va., Dec. 21/62—We are now in camp and trying to repair our damage. Notwithstanding our late defeat, we all have confidence in General Burnside. If his plans had been carried out we should have won a victory. We hope to do better next time we try to cross the river.

Dec. 24th 1862—We are in trouble about our new Major and former Chaplain, Rev. Thorndike C. Jameson. Governor Sprague promoted him Major over all of the Captains. He is incompetent, and we do not want him with us. I hear that he is to be ordered before a board of officers for examination, and as he probably could not pass, I hope he will resign and leave us in peace. Jameson is not fitted for a soldier in some respects and ought to know it. He is brave, and that is all. Capt. Benoni S. Brown, Senior Captain, has resigned because Jameson was promoted over him.[28] General Wheaton has invited me to dine with him. We have commenced regular drills and camp duties once more, but a new movement will probably be ordered soon.

Christmas Dec. 25th 1862—We have passed a very quiet day and except that we have been excused from drill, the day has been like others. My brother-in-law, Colville D. Brown came today from Washington and made me a call. In the evening Lt. Col. Goff (Nathan, Jr.) of our Regiment and other officers came to my tent and we had a sing. I should like to be at home on this Christmas night.

Dec. 28th 1862—Today we received a visit from Rev. Augustus Woodbury of Rhode Island, formerly Chaplain of the 1st R.I. Detached Militia. Lieut. Robert H.I. Goddard (of R.I.) of General Burnside's staff came with him. We have had no service today as our former Chaplain is now a Major and Col. Viall would not allow him to preach. I think he was right, for Jameson is so unpopular that he could do no good by preaching to the men. He appeared on inspection this morning with a sabre on but did not meet with a very good reception.

Dec. 31/62—Well, the year 1862 is drawing to a close. As I look back I am bewildered when I think of the hundreds of miles I have tramped, the thousands of dead and wounded that I have seen, and the many strange sights that I have witnessed. I can truly thank God for his preserving care over me and the many blessings I have received. One year ago tonight I was an enlisted man and stood cap in hand asking for a furlough. Tonight I am an officer and men ask the same favor of me. It seems to me right that officers should rise from the ranks, for only such can sympathize with the private soldiers. The year has not amounted to much as far as the War is concerned, but we hope for the best and feel sure that in the end the Union will be restored. Good bye, 1862.

Lt. Col. Nathan Goff, Jr.

List of towns visited by the 2nd R.I. Vols since June 5th, 1861:

1.	New York	38.	Williamsport, Md.
2.	Elizabeth Port, N.J.	39.	Downsville, Md.
3.	Newark, N.J.	40.	Kudiesville, Md.
4.	York, Penn.	41.	Smoketown, Md.
5.	Easton, Penn.	42.	Rohrersville, Md.
6.	Harrisburg, Penn.	43.	Burkettsville, Md.
7.	Baltimore, Md.	44.	Berlin, Md.
8.	Fairfax Court House, Md.	45.	Jefferson, Md.
9.	Germantown, Va.	46.	Adamstown, Md.
10.	Centreville, Va.	47.	Brownsville, Md.
11.	Fortress Monroe, Va.	48.	Poolesville, Md.
12.	Hampton, Va.	49.	Tennallytown, Md.
13.	Young's Mills. Va.	50.	Lockville, Md.
14.	Warwick Court House, Va.	51.	Rushville, Md.
15.	Williamsburg, Va.	52.	Barnesville, Md.
16.	Barkamsville, Va.	53.	Sennaca Falls, Md.
17.	Burnt Ordinary, Va.	54.	Fair Play, Md.
18.	Slatersville, Va.	55.	Sharpsburg, Md.
19.	Cumberland, Va.	56.	Bakersville, Md.
20.	White House, Va.	57.	Fair View, Md.
21.	Gaines Mills, Va.	58.	Germantown, Md.
22.	Ellison Mills. Va.	59.	Lovettsville, Va.
23.	Mechanicsville, Va.	60.	Bolington, Va.
24.	Atlee's Station, Va.	61.	Phillemont, Va.
25.	Fair Oaks, Va.	62.	Wheatland, Va.
26.	Charles City Cross Roads, Va.	63.	Union, Va.
27.	Shirley, Va.	64.	Upperville, Va.
28.	Harrison's Landing, Va.	65.	Aldie, Va.
29.	Charles City Court House, Va.	66.	White Plains, Va.
30.	Savage Station, Va.	67.	New Baltimore, Va.
31.	Yorktown, Va.	68.	Cattlett's Station, Va.
32.	Alexandria, Va.	69.	Weaversville, Va.
33.	Georgetown, D.C.	70.	Spottswood Tavern, Va.
34.	Haxall's Landing, Va.	71.	Gunisonville, Va.
35.	New Kent Court House, Va.	72.	Stafford Court House, Va.
36.	Hancock, Md.	73.	Falmouth, Va.
37.	Clear Spring, Md.	74.	*

*And many other towns whose names I have forgotten.

Camp near Falmouth, Va. — "Pig Point" — Rappahannock River, Va. — Rumford Plantation — Fairfax Station, Va. — Manchester, Md. — Middletown, Md. — Funkstown, Md. — Hagerstown, Md. — Boonsboro, Md. — Berlin, Md. — Warrenton, Va. — Camp Sedgwick — Camp at Bristow Station, Va. — Chantilly Cross Roads, Va. — Warrenton, Va. — Kelly's Ford, Va. — Hazel Run, Va. — Camp Sedgwick, Va.

1863

Jany 1st 1863, Camp near Falmouth, Virginia—The new year opens, and we are still in camp with nothing new to report. Camp life goes on and it comes our turn to do picket duty on the river banks occasionally.

Pratt's Landing "Pig Point" Potomac River, Jany 6—Yesterday Levi Carr and myself rode over to the camp of the 4th R.I. Vols. and were joined by Lieut. Charles H. Hunt. We then visited the camps of Battery "D" and Battery "E" R.I. Artillery and finally called upon George H. Rhodes at the camp of the 1st R.I. Cavalry. On our return at night I was ordered to take command of Company "B" and go to Belle Plain. We made a start and after marching about two miles I was ordered back to camp. Monday morning our Regiment left camp and reached this place about noon. It is on the Potomac River at the mouth of Potomac Creek. Our camp is near the river bank, and we have a fine view of the shipping. Steamers and sailing vessels are constantly arriving and are discharged at the wharf. This morning we were marched to a ravine between two hills and set to work making a road. So the gallant Second is again shoveling Virginia. But it is not our first experience in this kind of work. If I live to get home I shall be fitted for any kind of work, for I have tried most everything since I have been in the Army. The road is hard to make, as we meet many brooks and frequent holes filled with mud and water. The brooks we bridge with logs and fill up the holes with brush. We are making what is known as a corduroy road. That is, we lay down logs length-wise of the road and then lay other logs across. In fact it is a continuous bridge. We are to stay three days and then be relieved by other troops.

Jany 9/63—We have finished our tour of duty and are now back to our camp near Falmouth.

Near Falmouth Jany 11/63—Major Jameson has resigned and left our Regiment. We are very glad to get rid of him, for we have had a constant quarrel ever since he was appointed. Adjutant Samuel J. Smith has resigned and will leave tomorrow. I do not know who will be appointed Adjutant, but I am now acting as Adjutant. I have this work to do quite often. There ought to be some promotions and I am entitled to a First Lieutenancy rank, but Governor Sprague is so angry with us all that I do not believe he will promote any of us. Well, we can stand it, and we have got rid of Major Jameson in spite of the Governor.

Near Falmouth, Va., Jany 15th 1863—No news, and all is quiet. But for our drills we should be unhappy in our laziness. We pay big prices here for things to eat. Butter is 60¢ per lb. Cheese the same. Bread 25¢ per loaf. Soft crackers 30¢ per lb. Cookies (which children and soldiers love) 3 cents apiece. Today I found a small cod fish at 16¢ per lb. It tasted good. Lieut. Benjamin B. Manchester has resigned and left. Capt. Brown and myself are all alone now in our mess. Capt. Samuel B.M. Read is acting as Assistant Inspector General on General Devens' staff. I spent last evening at General Wheaton's Headquarters and enjoyed myself very much.

> *Pawtuxet, R.I.*
> *Jan. 19, 1863*
> *Lieut. E.H. Rhodes*

Dear Brother,

I rejoice to hear from time to time good reports from our R.I. boys, and especially from the members of our church. So far as I have learned they have been kept by grace in the Ways of Righteousness. I pray they may ever be so kept. Near to my heart are they all.

My chief object of writing at this time however is with reference to the Chaplaincy of your regiment.

My heart is in the cause of our country. I want to be engaged both heart & hand. I learn that Jameson has resigned. If I can secure the election on the part of the officers I shall cheerfully enter the service— not for gain, not for earthly glory, but for the Cause of Truth as embodied in the great principle at issue; and for the cause of the soldiers whose welfare, present & eternal I would hope to be instrumental in promoting.

I am pleasantly located here, just married to a dear little wife; and have prospect of increased salary if I stay. But, I repeat it, my heart is in the cause of my country. Will you do for me what you can? I have written to Surgeon Carr & Col. Wheaton. The latter I am not acquainted with.

God's will be done & his name honored in the matter is all my prayer.

Very Truly Your Pastor,
J.D. Beugless

P.S. I send herewith to be shown to Col. W. & others, a recommendation I had at early opening of war for the position. I was then residing in Philadelphia.

B.

Camp near Falmouth Jany 24/63—Tuesday morning the Army broke camp and started for another attack upon the Rebels. Our Regiment marched up the river for about five miles to a place called "Beech Church." The roads were in good order and the troops in fine spirits. At dark it commenced to rain and we lay in the wet until four o'clock Wednesday morning. We found on leaving the woods that the roads were impassable by reason of mud. Daylight showed a strange scene. Men, Horses, Artillery, pontoons, and waggons were stuck in the mud. After making about two miles the waggons began to turn over and mules actually drowned in the mud and water. About noon we reached the river about eight miles above Falmouth. Here we waited for the pontoon trains, but they never came. The mud was too deep for them, and the teams lay back some distance. Here we lay until Friday when our Division was detailed to assist a regular Battery back to camp. The mud was so deep that sixteen horses could not pull one gun. The companies of men would take hold of a rope called a prolong and pull the gun out of the mire. It was hard on men and horses, but our boys did their duty as usual. Rations gave out and we became hungry, but found after awhile some hard bread on the road. Many horses and mules were lost. The Battery boys posted on the river bank say the Rebels put up a sign marked "Burnside stuck in the mud." Of course Gen. Burnside is not to blame for this failure. He could not control natural forces notwithstanding the views of certain newspapers who seem to think he could. If the weather had continued good I think the move would have been a successful one. We can fight Rebels but not mud. Capt. Stephen H. Brown is acting as Major of the Regiment, and I am in command of Company "D." I am still well and in good spirits, ready for anything that may turn up. I suppose another attempt will be made as soon as the weather becomes good and the mud dries up.

Near Falmouth Jany 27/63—We have a sad day. Colonel Nelson Viall has resigned and gone to R.I. He would not stand the indignities heaped upon us by Gov. Sprague and so gave up his position. Monday we visited him at his quarters with a band and gave him a farewell serenade. The Colonel cried like a child at parting with his old comrades, and we all felt very sad. The boys gave him nine hearty cheers, and then three groans for Gov. Sprague. Well, we shall see the end of this row sometime and Gov. Sprague will be sorry for his actions. Yesterday we had an inspection. Out of eighty men belonging to Co. "D" only forty are present for duty. Fred. A. Arnold has been discharged on account of wounds.

Near Falmouth, Va. Feby 1/63—An order was received today stating that two officers at a time from each Regiment would be allowed leave of absence. At this rate my turn will come in about one month. I have already sent up my applications and hope to see my home before long. The men of Co. "D" have built me a house. On the first floor we have a fireplace and table. Upstairs on a shelf we have a bed and a ladder to reach it. The floor of the second story only covers a part of the room and in fact is the bed. The walls are of hewn timber with spaces filled with mud. The roof is pieces of shelter tent. We moved in this evening and feel very happy in our new home.

Last Friday all of our officers called upon Gen'l Frank Wheaton and we were mustered into the U.S. Service. It seems that there was some informality about the previous muster. The General entertained the officers very finely. We hear nothing further about the Sprague trouble. I hope the Governor has thought better of his hasty words and perhaps will treat us better in the future. It is hard to have to fight the Rebels in front and our Governor in the rear.

General Burnside has been relieved from the command of the Army of the Potomac and Gen'l Hooker has taken command. A few more changes and I suppose the people north will think the war ended.

Feby 7th 1863—Our Regiment has been detailed for three days' picket duty beginning tomorrow morning.

Camp near Falmouth, Va., Feby 10/63—We have returned from our three days of picket duty, and I am glad to get back. We were posted on the banks of the Rappahannock near the place we crossed last December. I went in command of Co. "D" and with three companies occupied a plantation house near the river. We kept fires burning in the fireplaces and it was not so bad after all. The men occupied the Negro quarters. As firing at pickets is forbidden by each side the men were allowed to go down to the river banks. We did not allow our men to talk to the Rebels, but they kept up a stream of questions. They were anxious to know where the 9th Corps had gone. It seemed queer to see them only a few yards away in their gray clothes. One of their bands played every day, and we enjoyed the music with them. They were very anxious to procure New York papers and coffee, but we obeyed orders and did not give them any. On returning to camp we found a new Colonel had arrived. Col. Horatio Rogers, Jr., formerly Colonel of the 11th R.I. Vols. He seemed to be much surprised when he learned of our late troubles and that we were opposed to having him come to us as Colonel.

Colonel Horatio Rogers, Jr.

He sent for the officers this morning, and after a talk said he would send Lt. Col. Nathan Goff, Jr. home with a request that Governor Sprague would appoint him Colonel, and he (Rogers) would return to the 11th Regiment. Every man in our Regiment signed Lt. Colonel Goff's recommendations, and in fact it was signed by all the officers of our Division. Colonel Rogers is a splendid fellow, and we like him already. If Goff cannot be our Colonel I had rather have Rogers than any other outside man I know. His generous conduct towards Lt. Col. Goff has made him many friends among the officers already. Instead of making a great show of authority, he was very mild in his manner and it has had a good effect. I have just come from Surgeon Carr's quarters where I have had a talk with the Colonel. Captain Edward Stanley has resigned and started for home this morning. So they go, and we have only seven of the original officers left in the Regiment. Capt. Brown is still acting as major, and I command Co. "D."

Near Falmouth, Va., Feby 15/63—Yesterday Capt. Geo. C. Clendenin of Gen. Wheaton's staff, Capt. Samuel J. English, Capt. Edward A. Russell and myself took a ride. We went down to the river and saw the place where we crossed in December and then rode along the bank to Falmouth. We passed Fredericksburg on the opposite bank and could see the streets filled with Rebel soldiers. Some of them were busy making rifle pits across the streets where they come down to the river. Carriages as well as mounted officers were passing in the streets while many soldiers were on the bank watching the Yankees. After visiting the village of Falmouth we called at the camp of one of our R.I. Batteries and then returned to our own camp. Today it is raining and our usual Sunday inspection has been omitted. Friday night we had our first dress parade under the command of Col. Rogers. He pleased us very much.

Thursday Feby 18/63—The storm still continues and we sit over our fires and wonder what will happen next. Furloughs are still given to the men, and it is hard for me to tell who ought to go first.

Near Falmouth, Va., Feby 24/63—I have been laid up for a few days but am all right now. In handling some green bushes I got poisoned with sumac or ivy. This is the second time that this has happened to me since I entered the Army.

Near Falmouth, Va., March 12/63—Since the first of the month we have led a very quiet life. Drills take place when the weather will permit, but mud and rain is generally the rule. I shall start for R.I. before many days now I hope. It is a good time to leave, as we have nothing to do.

Capt.
Samuel J. English

Capt. Brown is on Court Martial duty, and I am in command of Co. "D" again.

Near Falmouth, Va., March 21/63—I am a man today, for it is my birthday and I am twenty one years old. Well, I begin to feel that I am an old man if hard work makes one old. I have had a birthday present—a leave of absence for ten days, and I appreciate it very much. I shall start for R.I. as soon as I can arrange my affairs and have pleasant anticipations of a happy time.

Near Falmouth, April 7th 1863—Back to my Army duties after a delightful visit to my home in R.I. Homesickness cured for the present but another attack expected. While at home Col. Rogers who was in R.I. on "Leave" had me promoted from a Second Lieutenant to Captain.[29] While I felt complimented by his kind appreciation of my services I declined the commission, because I did not care to step over the heads of ten First Lieutenants who are my seniors. I shall be satisfied to take my regular promotion and be made a First Lieutenant. Having a high regard for my fellow officers, I do not care to hurt their feelings.

On my arrival at camp I found that the news of my promotion had reached the Regiment, but the fact that I had declined the Captaincy had not been made public. I rather enjoyed the comments made by some of the officers who I am satisfied would *not* have declined. When it became known that I had declined and that First Lieut. John G. Beveridge was to have the commission of Captain, the tune of the growlers changed, and I was warmly thanked for my generosity. Well, this is a queer world, and one gets litle credit for good intentions. My conscience tells me that I did right in the matter, although the temptation was strong to accept the rank.

Last Thursday Gen. John Sedgwick reviewed our Division and on Friday last Gen. Hooker reviewed the Sixth Corps. Today our Brigade commander General Charles Devens, Jr. inspected and reviewed our Regiment. The General visited all the company streets and complimented us very highly. President Lincoln is to Review the Army of the Potomac tomorrow.

While at home I was surprised to find so little interest manifested in the war. The people seemed to take it as a matter of course, and hardly asked after the Army. The ladies however seem to be alive to the situation, and I hope their example will spur up the men to do all in their power to aid the Armies in crushing the Rebellion.

Rappahannock River, Va., Near Franklin's Crossing April 14/63— We are on picket again, and I am occupying a house owned by a Mr. Pollock. A young man, a nephew of Mr. Pollock, is here on a visit. He has but one leg, having lost the other while serving in the Rebel Cavalry. He is on his parole and so has the liberty of the plantation. Across the river and only a few yards distant I can see fifty Rebels gazing at the Yankees. Just beyond them is a large fort with long lines of rifle pits on each side. The Rebels are very anxious to get northern papers. A few minutes ago I saw one of their little boats made of a board with a paper

Lieut.
John G. Beveridge

sail and a tin can nailed upon the board come sailing across the river. I received the boat and took out of the can a late Richmond paper. The Rebel called out: "Send me a New York paper," but I declined as it is against orders. In accordance with orders I broke the boat in pieces, although a Rebel shouted that he would shoot me if I did not stop. But I broke the board, notwithstanding, and he did not shoot.

Gen. Thomas J. Jackson (Stonewall) came down to the river bank today with a party of ladies and officers. We raised our hats to the party, and strange to say the ladies waved their handkerchiefs in reply. Several

Rebel sentinels told us that it was Gen. Jackson. He took his field glasses and cooly surveyed our party. We could have shot him with a revolver, but we have an agreement that neither side will fire, as it does no good, and in fact is simply murder. We shall go back to camp tomorrow, as other troops will take our place on outpost duty. I am very well and try to enjoy myself.

Camp near Falmouth, Va., April 19th 1863—I have received my commission as First Lieutenant, have been mustered in and assigned to duty in the same Co. "D" and know the men well. Chas. Tinkham has been made Second Lieutenant of Co. "D" so for the first time since I have been an officer we have a full complement, or three officers to our company. The weather today is fine, and I have taken a long ride over to the Second Corps camps. The roads are in good condition, and we shall probably be on the move again soon. I hope so at any rate.

Lieut. Charles J. Tinkham

Rumford Place, Rappahannock River, April 29th 1863—At last a move. Last evening we left our camp and marched down to this place which is near the river. Gen. Brooks' Division of our Corps (the 6th) sent some men across the river in pontoon boats, drove the Rebels out of their rifle pits and then held the south bank. This morning several pontoon bridges were laid. Brooks' Division has crossed, but our Division (Newton's) is still on the north side. We expect to cross tomorrow morning. We have had no fighting yet except by the Batteries. They have exchanged shots several times across the river. Our Corps reports a loss today of two killed and seventeen wounded. The balance of the Army under Gen. Hooker has crossed the river above Falmouth, and a great battle will undoubtedly be fought. May God help us and give us victory. The Rebel lines are in plain sight, and the hills are covered with forts and rifle pits, but with God's help we can and will take them. We are to cross at the same place we crossed at in December last. I am now in command of Co. "B" and shall be probably for a long time as the Captain, Henry H. Young has been detailed upon the Brigade staff. I am well and confident of successful tomorrow. We shall try to take the same hills in rear of Fredericksburg that the Army failed to take in December last.

Saturday night, May 2nd 1863—The 2nd R.I. Vols. crossed the Rappahannock at 8 o'clock and camped with the 6th Corps near A.A. Bernard's house.

South side Rappahannock River, Sunday May 3d 1863—At one o'clock this morning the Sixth Corps following the River Road entered the city of Fredericksburg. The Rebels in the city fled to the forts on the hills in the rear, while the Corps formed for the attack in the streets. The 2nd R.I. formed in Princess Anne Street. At daylight the Rebels opened their guns from the forts on the hills and the shot and shell came crashing through the houses sounding like volleys of musketry. At 8 A.M. the 2nd R.I. advanced through the city and took position in rear of and as support to Battery "B" who were posted on a knoll with a mill pond in our rear. The Rebel shot and shell would come over our heads and explode over or fall into the pond. Battery "G" passed down to our right to go into position in a field. As they were crossing a small bridge over a stream, a shot hit one of the caissons and knocked it off the bridge. They soon got into position and opened, but the Rebels had a plunging fire from the hills and drove them away. They lost several men and many horses. Lieut. Benjamin E. Kelly of Battery "G" was mortally wounded. The Battery then moved to the hill where we were situated. Long lines of Infantry were deployed across the fields with Batteries stationed between the Brigades, and the advance was made. With loud cheers the lines moved up the hills and finally made a rush and Marye's Heights were in the hands of the Sixth Corps. Battery "B" fired over the heads of our men until the crest of the hill was reached and then ceased. We could see the Rebels from our position limber up their guns and leave with horses on the run. Captain T. Fred Brown of Battery "B" sighted a cannon at a Rebel gun just leaving a redoubt and hit the ammunition chest on the limber taking the men off as if with a stroke of lightning. As soon as we saw the Union flags planted on the hills our boys sprang to their feet for the brave storming party. The 2nd R.I. now joined the Brigade and advanced to the first line of hills and prepared to storm the second line. The 122nd New York Vols. were deployed as skirmishers and the 2nd R.I. Vols. followed as support. The Brigade commander ordered Col. Rogers to take a redoubt mounting three guns. We advanced at a double quick and the Rebels left their works, taking their cannon with them, but leaving one caisson in our hands. A Case shot burst in front of my company throwing a shower of iron about us. One iron bullet struck me upon my foot causing me to jump into the air, but only lamed me a little. I picked up the iron bullet and put it into my pocket and will send it home. The entire Heights were now in our hands, and here we rested until three o'clock P.M. when the Corps advanced some three miles and met the enemy again at Salem Church. The 2nd R.I. Vols. and 10th Mass. Vols. were placed in reserve and formed across the roads. After the attack was made by the front line, we could see the troops waver, and soon men began to retreat down the road. The next we knew the Rebels came in sight, and Col. Rogers was ordered to the front with the 2nd R.I. We advanced across a field to the brow of a hill and opened fire. Here our men began to fall, and the Rebels still advanced. Forward is the word again, and with a yell we rushed on to the Rebel lines which broke and fled for the woods. Men were falling here and there, but "Close up and forward" was the command and we kept on, cheered by the thought that we were doing good service while our Corps could reform in our rear. We entered the woods, but were stopped by the severe fire. Here we fought for an hour. As I commanded the color Company I had the centre of the Regiment and a good chance to observe our Colonel. If the line wavered Col. Rogers would seize the colors and lead us on. The Rebels had as

Prisoners a Regiment of New Jersey troops with their colors. We succeeded in releasing the troops and recapturing the colors. After the firing ceased we returned to the hill in our rear and reformed our lines. My Company "B" took into the battle 33 men, and we lost 11 killed and wounded. The Regiment lost 7 killed and 68 wounded beside 9 missing. Company "B" lost three of the killed. The Regiment received many compliments from Gen. Newton and Gen. Wheaton, and it seemed to be agreed that our last charge broke the Rebel advance and perhaps saved the Corps from disaster. Capt. William G. Turner and Lieut. Clark E. Bates were among the wounded.

Monday May 4/63—Artillery firing all day. The Rebels have taken possession of Fredericksburg in our rear and we are cut off from the river, but we have confidence in Gen. Sedgwick and shall get out of the scrape somehow. Heavy fighting is going on up the river where Hooker is trying to break through, but we do not know the result. It looks bad and we feel blue.

Tuesday May 5/63—Firing still going on and it seems to be all around us. Our wounded have been captured in Fredericksburg and nothing but good generalship can save the dear old 6th Corps.

At dark we left our lines, and marching in mud up hill and down we reached the Rappahannock River sometime in the night. Pontoon bridges were laid and the troops passed over. Straw and earth was packed upon the bridges to deaden the sound of the wagons and artillery. Our Regiment was left to guard the rear and finally we crossed with the Rebels dropping shell onto the bridge in our rear. The connections on the other side of the bridge were cut, and the boats floated over to the north side. As soon as we reached the opposite bank the men threw themselves upon the ground and slept.

Wednesday May 6/63—Cold with rain. I was ordered to take what remained of my Company and with Co. "I" Lieut. Charles A. Waldron go down and save the pontoons. As we reached the river bank I found the opposite shore lined with Rebels. An officer hailed me, and after a talk we mutually ageed not to fire without previous notice. As I could not save the boats without great loss of life, I agreed with the Rebel to let them alone. In fact his men had complete command of our side, and we were powerless to do anything. We built fires and the Rebels did the same, and we spent the day chaffing each other across the stream. Rations were all gone, and I was almost starved, but one of my men found a piece of pork in a deserted camp and generously gave me a slice.

Lieut. Charles A. Waldron

I ate it raw and it was good. After dark we got some long ropes and going down a ravine to the river we would make it fast to a boat. The men stationed around a bend in the ravine would then pull, and as the boat would grate upon the gravel and rocks the Rebels would fire a volley. But we kept on, and daylight showed all the boats safe up on the hills and the 2nd R.I.V. on the way to Falmouth.

Bank's Ford, Rappahannock River, May 6th 1863—Thank God I am alive and well. I shall be glad when the war is over and I can be civilized again. I do not like so much death and destruction.

Extract from a letter I wrote May 9/63 and published in the *Providence Journal; May 14th 1863.*

"Many of the Regiment unable to withstand the heavy fire broke and fled in confusion to the rear. Then came our turn to advance. Every eye was upon the Colonel for he never had been under fire with us and we knew him only by reputation. "Forward, Second Rhode Island!" was the word, and away we went in line of battle to the brow of a hill to stop the advance of the enemy who were everywhere driving our brave boys. Gaining the crest of the hill we gave them a volley and received their fire in return. "Forward" again shouts our gallant Colonel, and we charge down the hill with loud cheers for our starry banner and the anchor we bear upon our state flag and which we have sworn never to desert or dishonor.

The Rebels unable to stand our fierce assault turned and fled to the cover of the woods. We were soon in the woods and hotly engaged with them. When we wavered, Col. Rogers seized our flag and waving it over his head called for "three cheers" which were given with a will. Three times he carried the colors to the front and aided by the officers rallied the men to renew the battle. After firing ceased we retired to the hill and waited for the Rebels to appear and renew the fight, but they declined.

Col. Rogers is a brave man and the 2nd R.I. is more than satisfied with him. If all the officers of the 3rd R.I. Vols. are like the one they sent to us, it must indeed be a fighting Regiment. Lt. Col. S.B.M. Read and Major Henry C. Jencks behaved with great gallantry, and we feel that

Major Henry C. Jencks

we have three field officers that we can follow confidently in battle. Too much praise cannot be given to Corporals Kelley and Flier for the gallant manner in which they carried our colors through the entire battle.[30] All of the officers and men behaved bravely, and we have the credit of saving the Army from a stampede. This was the first engagement in which we have fired as a Regiment since the first battle of Bull Run, although we have been present and under fire at all the battles fought by the Army of the Potomac. We have to mourn the loss of many brave comrades, but we feel that they died in a glorious cause, striving to restore the Union founded by our fathers. Our Regiment is reduced to a small Battalion and we need more men. Will not our friends in Rhode Island rally and come to our assistance? We are in good health and spirits and if we meet the enemy again we hope to show them that R.I. is able to do her share in putting down the Rebellion through the Second Rhode Island Volunteers."

Near Falmouth Va., May 11/63—Back in camp again near where we passed the winter. The weather is very fine and warm. The 2nd. R.I. is spoken of in the highest terms of praise for the conduct of the late battle.

May 21/63—We have been fixing up our camp, and we look very fine. I do not imagine that we shall stay here very long for the weather is just right for a campaign. It is said that we have the finest camp in the Army. Each Company has a street one hundred and fifty feet long and fifty feet wide. The tents are all on the right hand side and shade trees have been planted. My Company "B" have an arbor of green the whole length of their street. In front we have a hedge and a gate-way. Over the gate in an arch of evergreen we have the name "Young Avenue" in honor of the Captain who is serving on the Brigade staff.

Last Monday our Division in command of Gen. Frank Wheaton was reviewed by the Corps commander, General John Sedgwick. The General was greeted with loud cheers by the troops. Gen. Wheaton wore the sash and belt presented him by our officers. When the reviewing party passed the 2nd R.I. General Wheaton called General Sedgwick's attention to us by saying: "This is the 2nd Rhode Island." They stopped and looked at us. After the review the officers rode through the camps.

Near Falmouth, Va., June 5th 1863—We have spent nearly a month in ordering our camp and now have orders to leave. In fact we are all packed up, and some of the troops are moving towards the river. This looks like another attack upon Fredericksburg. If we do not march

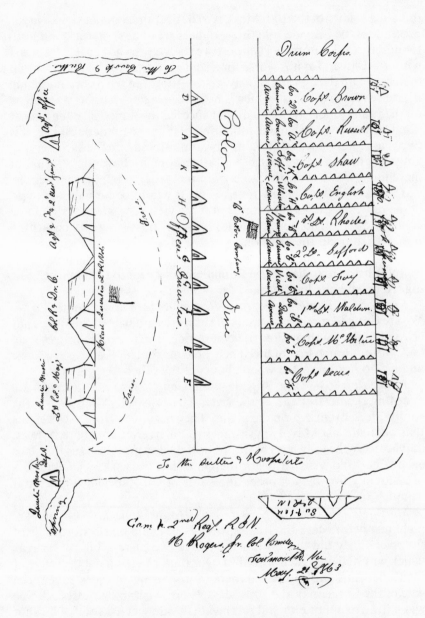

E.H. Rhodes drawing of the regimental camp, May 21, 1863.

tonight a soldier of the 10th Mass. is to be drummed out of service in the presence of the Brigade, and three soldiers are to be shot near Falmouth for desertion. Tomorrow I suppose we shall try to shoot a few Rebels. I wish it was over, for it is worse for a soldier to wait for a battle to begin than it is to do the fighting. Today it is very hot, and the troops marching by are covered with dust, which is not encouraging to us, as we shall be on the road tomorrow. If we do not succeed this time I shall be almost discouraged, for it will make four attempts to take Fredericksburg. It is two years today since our Regiment was mustered into the U.S. Service. Only one more and we expect, or rather hope, to have the pleasure of marching up Westminster Street with our tattered banners. When the war is over will be a happy time for us. It would be no pleasure to go home now, for I could not stay, but if the victory was won I should be content to remain at home in R.I. I hope my next letter will be written nearer Richmond than this one.

June 6, 1863—At 10 o'clock A.M. the 2nd R.I. left their camp at Falmouth and marched to the Rappahannock near to Franklin's Crossing. Here we halted and waited for orders to cross the river.

Rumford Plantation, Va., near Rappahannock River, June 7/63— We are camped on the north side of the river, and part of the Corps has crossed to the south or Fredericksburg side. The pontoon bridges were laid without much loss of life. The whole movement is a mystery to us, and we do not know the whereabouts of the other Army Corps.

June 9th 1863—Our Brigade with Gen. Wheaton's Brigade are guarding the north bank of the river. The other Divisions are on the south side, entrenched on the plains. They occupy in front the rifle pits that we made last May. I am sitting on a hill overlooking both Armies, and I can see the long lines of troops both Union and Rebel as they face each other and wait to begin their murderous work. The Batteries occasionally fire at each other and some of the Rebel shell reach our camp.

Mansfield, Va. near A.N. Bernard's House, June 11/63—Tuesday night just before dark the Rebels shelled our camp on the north side of the river. They did not do much damage except to a hill in our rear which was well ploughed with shot. Our Batteries soon got the range of the Rebel guns and compelled them to stop firing and seek cover. The wife of the Surgeon of the 10th Mass. is on a visit to her husband. She was sitting in a tent on a hill on the north side when a solid 30lb. shot struck very near to her. A shell burst in the air and a piece went whizzing through one of the tents. She went calmly to another hill and waited until the firing ceased, when she resumed her seat in her own tent again. Last night at 6 o'clock our Brigade crossed to the south side of the river, and for the third time we are near Fredericksburg. Our Regiment was immediately sent upon picket duty, way off to the left of our lines, and here we remained until morning without sleep. We arranged with the Rebels that neither side should fire unless an advance was made. On our right the firing was continuous through the night. We have just been relieved from picket duty and are resting inside of our works. The works are long and reach in a semicircle from river to river. I am well and happy.

Fairfax Station, Va., June 17th 1863—We are now five miles from Fairfax Court House and about twenty miles from Washington. Last Saturday night the Rebels opened fire upon us but were silenced by our Batteries. On a hill on the north side of the Rappahannock River our people had mounted a 100lb. rifle gun. It took several days to get the gun in position. Just before dark its only shot was fired. The recoil upset the gun, and as the Army was to move, the gun was sent to the rear. This shot passed over the river, over our heads, and into a Rebel fort on the hill near Fredericksburg. It burst and sent up a cloud of sand and dust. The noise it made was like that of a railroad train, and when it struck the whole army cheered. It rained, thundered, and lightened and in the midst of it the 6th Corps recrossed to the north side again. Here we rested until the next morning when we marched to Stafford Court House, which place we reached in the afternoon. Here we remained until 9 P.M. when we moved on and reached Quantico Creek at a place called Dumfries on Tuesday noon, almost dead from the heat. I never suffered more in my life than I did on this march. We rested at Dumfries until midnight when we started again and reached this place last night. It has been one of the hardest marches that we have ever known. Fairfax Station is on the railroad. We hear that the Rebel Army is in Pennsylvania. If this is so I trust we shall be able to catch them and end the war. Our address is 2nd Brigade, 3rd Division, 6th Corps.

Centreville, Va., June 25th 1863—Yesterday we left Fairfax Court House and marched to this place. We left Fairfax Station on the 18th and marched to Fairfax Court House where our Corps encamped about the town. Here we were ordered to reduce our baggage to the least amount possible to get along with. We are to travel light hereafter. Centreville is a queer old place, and this is the third time that we have been here during the last two years. Only a few buildings are now standing, and they are mere huts built of logs. The deserted Rebel works here appear strong. Every hill is crowned with a fort, and they are all connected by rifle pits and covered ways for Artillery to pass from one to another. The troops that have been stationed here have been ordered to the front, and it is rumored that we are to remain, but I do not believe it, for if the Rebels are in Pennsylvania the 6th Corps will be needed there.

June 26th 1863—We left Centreville this morning and passing through Herndon encamped at Drainesville at night.

June 27/63—This morning we broke camp and marched to Edwards Ferry on the Potomac River. Here we found a pontoon bridge and on it crossed over into Maryland again and encamped near Poolesville.

June 28th 1863—At daylight this morning we moved on and passing through Poolesville, Barnesville, and in sight, and in fact quite near to Sugarloaf Mountain. We encamped near a place called Percy's Mills.

June 29th 1863—Still on the move and after the Baltimore and Ohio Railroad we passed through New Market and a place called Ridgeway and camped at Mount Airy.

June 30/63—This morning we were detailed as rear guard, and as we have had rain and the roads were muddy, we had a hard march through Mount Vernon and Westminster to our camp near Manchester. The Rebel Cavalry hover in our rear all day.

Near Manchester, Md., July 1st 1863—We have been doing some fine marching for the past few days, making an average of twenty miles per day. We reached this place last night and expect to move this morning. We have not passed through the town as yet. It appears to be a fine little city, and as it is only two miles away I hope to be able to see it. Westminster is the finest place I have seen yet. We passed through its streets yesterday. The Rebel Cavalry moved out one side as we entered the other. The country is beautiful, and the people are very kind to us and appear glad to see us. Young ladies stand at the gates and furnish the men with cold water and loaves of bread as we pass. It has rained for a week and the roads are muddy. After marching for twenty miles it is not pleasant to lie down at night in the wet without any cover. I am tired—in fact I never was so tired in my life. But Hurrah! "It is all for the Union."

At New Market we halted for two hours and with a party of officers I went into town. Some ladies made us a lot of bread and show us much attention. It is entirely different from our treatment in Virginia. Pleasant farms are to be seen on every side, and the people stand on the roadside to see the troops pass. We are quite near to the Pennsylvania line, and it looks now as if we were to cross over. I am still in good health and spirits and have faith that God will guide us on the final victory. The Rebellion must be put down, and we are doing our best.

Middletown, Md., July 8th 1863—The great battle of the war has been fought and thanks be to God the Army of the Potomac has been victorious at last. But how can I describe the exciting events of the past few days? On the night of July 1st we were in camp near Manchester, Md. Rumors of fighting in Pennsylvania have been heard all the days, but the distance was so great to the battlefield that we knew little about it. The men were tired and hungry and lay down to rest early in the evening. At nine o'clock orders came for us to move and we in great haste packed up and started on the road towards Pennsylvania. General Hooker has been relieved and Gen. George G. Meade of Penn. assigned to the command of the Army of the Potomac. What does it all mean? Well, it is none of our affairs and we obey orders and march out into the road. We struggle on through the night, the men almost dead for lack of sleep and falling over their own shadows. But still we go on in the warm summer night. Little is said by any one, for we were too weary to talk, only now and then an officer sharply orders the men to close up. Sometimes the column would halt for a moment as obstructions were met in the advance, and then we would run to catch up. Daylight brought no halt and what little hard bread we had was taken from the haversacks and eaten as we marched on. On the morning of July 2nd we heard the firing in front and then we understood the reason for such great haste. I was taken sick upon the road and fell helpless to the ground. The Surgeon, Dr. Carr, gave me a remedy and a pass for admittance to an ambulance. I lay upon the road side until several Regiments had passed when I began to revive. I immediately hurried on and soon came up with my Co. "B." The boys received me well, and I went on without further trouble. The firing in our front grew loud and more distinct and soon we met the poor wounded fellows being carried to the rear. At a place called Littlestown we saw large numbers of our wounded men, and all kinds of carriages were being used to take them to the hospitals. At about 2 o'clock P.M. we reached the Battlefield of Gettysburg, Penn. having made a march of thirty-four (34) miles without a halt. The men threw themselves upon the ground exhausted, but were soon ordered forward. We followed the road blocked with troops and trains until 4 P.M. when the field of battle with the long lines of struggling weary soldiers burst upon us. With loud cheers the old Sixth Corps took up the double quick and were soon in line of battle near the left of the main line held by the 5th Corps. The 5th Corps were in reserve, but as we took their place, they moved forward and took part in the fight. Our Division was finally sent to the front and relieved Gen. Sykes' Division of Regulars. Picket firing was kept up until long after dark, when we were relieved and returned a short distance. The men threw themselves upon the ground, and oblivious to the dead and dying around us we slept the sleep of the weary.

July 3rd 1863—This morning the troops were under arms before light and ready for the great battle that we knew must be fought. The firing began, and our Brigade was hurried to the right of the line to reinforce it. While not in the front line yet we were constantly exposed to the fire of the Rebel Artillery, while bullets fell around us. We moved from point to point, wherever danger to be imminent until noon when we were ordered to report to the line held by Gen. Birney. Our Brigade marched down the road until we reached the house used by General Meade as Headquarters. The road ran between ledges of rocks while the fields were strewn with boulders. To our left was a hill on which we had many Batteries posted. Just as we reached Gen. Meade's Headquarters, a shell burst over our heads, and it was immediately followed by showers of iron. More than two hundred guns were belching forth their thunder, and most of the shells that came over the hill struck in the road on which our Brigade was moving. Solid shot would strike the large rocks and split them as if exploded by gunpowder. The flying iron and pieces of stone struck men down in every direction. It is said that this fire continued for about two hours, but I have no idea of the time. We could not see the enemy, and we could only cover ourselves the best we could behind the rocks and trees. About 30 men of our Brigade were killed or wounded by this fire. Soon the Rebel yell was heard, and we have found since that the Rebel General Pickett made a charge with his Division and was repulsed after reaching some of our batteries. Our lines of Infantry in front of us rose up and poured in a terrible fire. As we were only a few yards in rear of our lines we saw all the fight. The firing gradually died away, and but for an occasional shot all was still. But what a scene it was. Oh the dead and the dying on this bloody field.[31] The 2nd R.I. lost only *one* man killed and five wounded. One of the latter belonged to my Co. "B." Again night came upon us and again we slept amid the dead and dying.

July 4th 1863—Was ever the Nation's Birthday celebrated in such a way before. This morning the 2nd R.I. was sent out to the front and found that during the night General Lee and his Rebel Army had fallen back. It was impossible to march across the field without stepping upon dead or wounded men, while horses and broken Artillery lay on every side. We advanced to a sunken road (Emmitsburg Road) where we deployed as skirmishers and lay down behind a bank of earth. Berdan's Sharpshooters joined us, and we passed the day in firing upon any Rebels that showed themselves. At 12 M. a National Salute with shotted guns was fired from several of our Batteries, and the shells passed over our heads toward the Rebel lines. At night we were relieved and went to the rear for a little rest and sleep.

July 5th 1863—Glorious news! We have won the victory, thank God, and the Rebel Army is fleeing to Virginia. We have news that Vicksburg has fallen. We have thousands of prisoners, and they seem to be stupified with the news. This morning our Corps (the 6th) started in pursuit of Lee's Army. We have had rain and the roads are bad, so we move slow. Every house we see is a hospital, and the road is covered with the arms and equipments thrown away by the Rebels.

July 6th 1863—Today we have slowly continued the pursuit, passing through Fairfield and Liberty and encamping at Emmitsburg. Everything denotes that Lee is trying to cross the Potomac. I hope we shall catch him before he reaches Virginia.

July 7th 1863—We are still on the road and today passed through Franklin's Mills, Mechanicsville, and Catoctin Iron Works. Now the people stare at us as we march past.

July 8/63—We crossed the Catoctin Mountain this evening. It took us from dark until 2 A.M. on the 9th to reach the summit, a distance of about three miles. In some places the mountain was very steep, and we could only crawl along. Here we were obliged to halt our Brigade for the men were used up and could go no further.

July 9th 1863—We left the top of the mountain early this morning and marched down to Middletown, Md. where we are now resting for a few hours sleep in twenty-four for about three weeks. Again I thank God that the Army of the Potomac has at last gained a victory. I wonder what the South thinks of us Yankees now. I think Gettysburg will cure the Rebels of any desire to invade the North again.

Near Funkstown, Md., July 11/63—We arrived here today after crossing the South Mountain and passing through Boonsboro. Yesterday our Artillery had a fight with the Rebels, but it is quiet now. We are about fourteen miles from Hagerstown, where the Rebel Army is said to have halted. I do not see how they can escape us this time. Everybody except the Rebels are in good spirits, and they must feel lonesome after their defeat. Today I had a luxury. Some new bread and butter. It was very good. Our Army is very tired and ragged, but we know that if we can destroy Lee's Army now the war is over. This keeps us up to our work. Now is the time for the North to wake up and send men into the Army.

Line of battle near Hagerstown, Md., July 13/63—I have not changed my clothes for five weeks, but still I am happy, and we are doing good work.

Last night we had a skirmish, and the 2nd R.I. lost three men, one of them from my Co. "B." My poor little Company will soon be gone if we do not get recruits. We are now entrenched and are waiting for orders. General Meade is popular with the troops as all Generals would be if they would only lead us to victory. We are expecting a fight here as Lee's Army is not far off. I do not understand our movements but suppose them to be all right. Time will show however.

Boonsboro, Md., July 15/63—Yesterday the whole Army moved upon the Rebel's works near Hagerstown, but the enemy had fled. We followed to Williamsport, Md. where we caught about fifteen hundred prisoners who were unable to cross the river. It is said that we are to go to Berlin where we crossed last year and go into Virginia again. At last the northern soil is free from Rebels, and great must be the rejoicing at home. Good news again. Port Hudson has fallen. Well, now enforce the draft and we shall be all right. I wish they would send the 2nd R.I. to New York City. The riots in that city are a disgrace to the nation and ought to be suppressed at any cost of money or life.

Berlin, Md., July 17th 1863—Yesterday we again crossed the South Mountain and marching through the town of Burkittsville reached this place which is where we crossed the Potomac last year. A pontoon bridge has been laid, and we shall soon cross into Virginia.

Berlin, Md., July 19/63—I shall regret to leave Maryland, for the country is delightful. I am almost tempted to turn farmer and move to this state. We are busy today making out our muster and pay rolls. Some day we expect to be paid off. I hear that I have been drafted. Well

*Capt.
Thomas Foy*

this is a good joke after serving for over two years and an officer also. I hardly think I shall report as ordered. Some one in R.I. is very careless to put in the names of men already in the Army. I hope we shall get some recruits soon, for I want 37 in my Company "B." An incident of the Battle of Gettysburg should be told. A Colonel of a Georgia Rebel Regiment was found dead upon the field. Capt. Thomas Foy of our Regiment discovered in some way that the Colonel was a Mason, and with the assistance of some other Masons buried him. As I am not a Mason I do not understand the matter. While the burial was going on the skirmishers were constantly firing.

July 19th 1863—Again in Virginia. We crossed the river this afternoon and marched to this place which is called Wheatland. Here we shall camp for the night.

July 20/63—On the road again today, and tonight we are in camp at Phillemont.

July 22nd 1863—We have reached this place called Uniontown. But why Uniontown no one can tell. Here we expect to pass the night.

July 23/63—This day we marched to Rectortown and halted, but at 2 P.M. we started for Manassas Gap. The scenery was fine, and in spite of the heat I enjoyed the march.

Near Warrenton, Va., July 25/63—We arrived here yesterday rather used up. For two days we have had no food except berries. On halting last night we found high blackberries very plenty and everybody ate their fill. They were good, too, for we were nearly starved. It is reported that we are to remain here for a few days and receive clothing for the men, which is much needed.

Camp near Warrenton, Va., July 27/63—The notice that I was drafted has been received and has caused much merriment. I for the fun of the thing showed it to the Colonel (Rogers) and asked permission to report at New Haven. The Colonel said he "could not see it." Capt. William B. Sears, Lieut. Charles A. Waldron and Lieut. Charles F. Brown have been ordered to New Haven to take charge of drafted men. It is pleasant to be in camp again where we can sleep nights without expecting to be called out at daylight, as we have done for the past month. Warrenton is about two miles away and in sight. I have not visited the town yet. I enjoyed the trip to Manassas Gap very much. It is the most romantic place I ever saw. The mountains are very high and form a circle or basin in which is located the town of Markham. We only stopped there about two hours and then marched to this place. Our camp is in a valley between two very high hills, and the slopes are covered with fine blackberries. We live on them now, for we have had nothing to eat except hard bread and salt pork for several weeks. The weather is hot, and several men have been sun struck.

The 37th Massachusetts Regiment has lost several. This is a new Regiment in our Brigade and is called the "iron clads," because when they first arrived every man had a steel plate in his vest. But the first march disposed of the plates, for the men threw them away, and our men picked them up and used them to fry pork in. Some Mass. man presented them to the 37th.

Camp near Warrenton, Va., August 1, 1863—The following towns have been visited by the 2nd R.I. Vols. since leaving Fredericksburg June 13th 1863.

Fredericksburg, Virginia	
Mansfield, Virginia	
Falmouth, Virginia	
Stafford Court House, Virginia	
Dumfries, Virginia	Camped 1 night
Fairfax Station, Virginia	Camped 1 night
Fairfax Court House, Virginia	Camped 1 night
Centreville, Virginia	Camped 1 night
Herndon, Virginia	
Dranesville, Virginia	Camped 1 night
Edwards Ferry, Maryland	Camped 1 night
Poolesville, Maryland	
Bunker Hill, Maryland	Bainesville, Maryland
Indiantown, Maryland	
Hyattstown, Maryland	
Percys Mills, Maryland	Camped 1 night
Monrovia, Maryland	
New Market, Maryland	
Holly Bush, Maryland	
Plane No. 4, Maryland	
Ridgeville, Maryland	
Mount Airy, Maryland	Camped 1 night
Devesville?, Maryland	
Spring Mills, Maryland	
Westminster, Maryland	
Mexico, Maryland	
Manchester, Maryland	Camped 1 night
Mount Pleasant, Md.	
Unionville, Maryland	
Silver Run, Maryland	
New Tavern, Penn.	
Littletown, Pennsylvania	
Gettysburg, Pennsylvania	Battlefield
Cashtown, Pennsylvania	
Fairfield, Pennsylvania	
Millersville, Pennsylvania	

Emmitsburg, Maryland	
Franklinville, Maryland	
Catoctin Mountain, Md.	
Lewistown, Maryland	Camped 1 night
Orange Mills, Maryland	
Bellville, Maryland	
Middletown, Maryland	Camped 1 night
Boonsboro, Maryland	Camped 1 night
Bennevold, Maryland	Camped 1 night
Funkstown, Maryland	Camped 1 night
Hagerstown, Maryland	
Uniontown, Maryland	
Burkittsville, Maryland	
South Mountain, Md.	
Berlin, Maryland	Camped 2 days
Lovettsville, Virginia	
Wheatland, Virginia	
Pleasantville, Virginia	
Unionville, Virginia	Camped 1 night
Goose Creek, Virginia	Camped 1 night
Rectortown, Virginia	
Chester Gap, Virginia	
Manassas Gap, Virginia	
Markham, Virginia	
Darbies Four Corners, Virginia	Camped 1 night
Orleans, Virginia	
Warrenton, Virginia	

Camp at Warrenton, Va., August 1863—The month of August was passed very quietly in camp near the town of Warrenton. Clothing and camp equipage were issued to the troops and regular drills and parades that had long been omitted were held. Picket duty in the direction of Culpepper was performed, and as the season was warm the men enjoyed the life. One day Co. "B" while on picket discovered a cider mill in an orchard, and apples being plenty the mill was put into operation and the canteens filled with cider. At night I was ordered to retire the picket line to a more defensive position, and a new line was established some half mile in rear of the orchard, and the cider mill could be heard running for their benefit. My Co. "B" built me a fine house of stone and put on a canvas roof. I am now keeping house in good style. Visits to

Warrenton were frequent and the officers on Sunday attended church in that town. About the middle of August I received news from R.I. that my brother James D. Rhodes was seriously sick and liable to die. As he was constantly calling for me it was thought by the attending physician that my presence would be beneficial. I applied for a leave of absence for ten days which was granted August 19th. I went over to Warrenton early in the morning and rode down to Warrenton Junction on a locomotive, where I took the cars for Washington. My brother being pronounced out of danger I returned to the Regiment, reaching camp early in September. Nothing of special interest had occurred during my absence, and I at once assumed command of Co. "B." While at home I had little opportunity to visit my friends, being detained at the bedside of my brother. I returned with a thankful heart that God had spared his life.

Camp near Warrenton, Va., Sept 6th 1863— We are having considerable religious interest in our Regiment, and I pray God that it may continue. Soldiers are not the worst men in the world, but they are very careless in regard to matters of religion. We have had no Chaplain for many months and consequently no regular services. Our last Chaplain never did any good in the Regiment.

About three weeks ago three of our men who are Christians attended a religious meeting at one of the camps in Gen. Wheaton's Brigade. On the way home they kneeled down in the woods and prayed that God bless our Regiment. The next week six of them met for prayer, and last week about thirty were present. Tonight I was invited to join them. I accepted and made an address. About fifty men were present at first, but they soon began to come into the grove, and soon nearly every officer and man of our Regiment was listening to the service. I never saw such a prayer meeting before, and I know the Spirit of the Lord was with us. The Chaplain of the 1st R.I. Cavalry, Rev. Ethan Ray Clarke, came over and addressed the meeting. Colonel Rogers is a Christian man, and his words of council and advice are always welcomed. Frank S. Halliday (Son of Rev. S.B. Halliday) is one of our active men in religious matters. We have made seats by splitting long logs in halves and hewing them smooth, and our little grove arranged for service is I believe the "Temple of the Lord." May God help us and bless our Regiment. I have attended church today in Warrenton. The sermon was good but had a little too much treason in it to suit us Union men. I saw in the audience a Rebel Major in his gray uniform trimmed with gold. He is a surgeon on

Frank S. Halliday

parole and is in charge of the Rebel wounded. The ladies present did not seem to be particularly pleased with our party.

Camp near Warrenton, Va., Sunday Sept. 12/63—We have had a Sunday school this morning, and the Bible study was well attended by the men. We hope to have a Chaplain soon. Heavy cannonading can be heard in the distance, but we do not know what it means. It has rained hard all day.

Sept. 16th 1863—Yesterday we left our pleasant camp near Warrenton and moved to the vicinity of Culpepper Court House where we are now in camp.

Camp Sedgwick near Culpepper, Va., Sunday Sept. 27/63—This is a beautiful day with weather just right. We have had a quiet week with nothing of importance to report. Culpepper Court House is about four miles to the left of our camp while to the right and in front of us we have high ranges of mountains with deep blue peaks. Cedar Mountain is about five miles distant. Yesterday some Union Cavalry passed our camp carrying a Rebel flag captured in a fight the night before. Soon after a Rebel officer under a guard of blue jackets went past. On our march to this place we passed through the village or town of Sulphur Springs which before the war was a famous summer resort. Traces of its glory and beauty can still be seen in the ruined and blackened walls of its hotels. We did not stop long enough to visit the famous springs. This camp is named in honor of Major-General Sedgwick, the commander of the 6th Army Corps. He is very popular with the men, and whenever he appears loud cheers are given for "Uncle John" as he is familiarly called by the soldiers. He seems to like the title and always greets us pleasantly.

Saturday Oct. 2nd 1863, Bealton, Va.—Last night we left our camp near Culpepper and made a night march to this place which is on the railroad to Washington. It is raining and rather unpleasant marching.

Bristow Station, Va., Oct. 5/63—Saturday our Brigade under command of Brig. Gen. Henry L. Eustis (formerly Colonel 10th Mass. Vols.) left Bealton and marched to this place. We are now on the railroad and about thirty miles from Alexandria. It is reported that we are to guard the railroad. If this is true it will be the first duty of this kind performed by the 2nd R.I. Vols. I am busy trying to boss some men who are building me a house, or Shebang, as we call them.

Camp at Bristow Station, Va., Oct. 7th 1863—Our new Chaplain is Rev. John D. Beugless, formerly pastor of the Pawtuxet Baptist Church. It came about in this way: I have been urging upon the officers the importance of having a Chaplain. Some of the officers were opposed and were afraid that we might get another man like Jameson. The Captains or Company Commanders have the right under the law to elect a Chaplain and recommend that he be commissioned. A meeting was held at the Colonel's quarters on Sept. 7th, and after much talk I nominated Mr. Beugless. He is unknown to all the officers except myself, but they voted for him and the Governor has issued to him a commission. The Chaplain arrived while we were at Culpepper, and as he came after dark he found many of the men in a grove holding a

Chaplain
John D. Beugless

prayer meeting. I took him down to the woods and introduced him to the men. The Chaplain made a short address and then shook hands all around. At the first dress parade the Colonel introduced him to the Regiment. He has already made himself very popular, and I trust that God will bless his labors and that he will do much good. There are plenty of opportunities for Christian work in the Army, but the trouble seems to be a lack of earnestness. Many of the soldiers are good Christian men, but need some one to guide them. I feel greatly rejoiced over the prospect for the future.

Camp near Bristow Station, Va., Oct. 7th 1863—I have got the best hotel that a soldier ever lived in. Last Monday morning I took my Company and a six mule team and went into the country on a foraging expedition. After marching about three miles we came to the village of Brentville. I placed guards about the town to prevent being surprised by guerillas and then marched down the main street. Chaplain Beugless went on the trip with me. The town is deserted by all the white people and left to the care of the Negroes. One house in process of building is owned by the Rebel General Hunting. Here I loaded our wagon with boards, doors and windows and started back to camp. Since then the men have built me a house. It is eighteen feet long, ten feet wide and the peak is twelve feet high. On one side I have a window and another in the door with curtains for each. One of my men found me a desk, so I am living in style. All of the officers have built quarters, and it looks now as if we were to stay here during the winter and guard the railroad. I hope so, for this is the first easy duty we have ever had, and we need rest. There is some talk of sending the 2nd R.I. home for the winter. They will do so if one half of the officers and men will agree to stay in service three years after our present term expires. The U.S. offers a furlough of 30 days and a bounty of four hundred dollars ($400) to every enlisted man who will re-enlist. I hope that we shall decide to remain, for I could not be contented at home if mustered out and should rather be in the 2nd R.I. Vols. than seek service in any other regiment. I want to remain and see the end of the war. We had a very good meeting last night, and much interest was shown.

Bristow Station, Oct. 10/63—I have just returned from the camp of the 10th Mass. Vols. where the officers of the Brigade had a social meeting. Today there has been fighting on the Rapidan River, but we are too far in the rear to know much about it. It is rumored that our Corps (6th) has been engaged. We are all ready for a move. About one half of our Regiment is on picket daily, and we have more work to do than when we were at the front, but the danger is less. Capt. S.H. Brown and Company are guarding a bridge about four miles from camp, so for the present our mess is broken up.

Bristow Station, Va., Oct. 11/63—Still on guard duty. The enemy does not molest us. Only pretty girls with pies for sale invade our camp.

Line of battle, Chantilly Cross Roads, Oct. 16/63—The Army of the Potomac has again skedaddled to the rear, and we are now again near Centreville waiting for Lee's Army to come up and show fight. Last

Tuesday morning before light we left our comfortable camp at Bristow Station and marched to Warrenton Junction where we joined the First Corps who were covering the retreat of the Army trains. At dark we started with this Corps to the rear leaving the 2nd Corps as a rear guard. After marching all night we reached Catlett's Station, having made only five miles by reason of the roads being blocked with wagons. The night was bitter cold, and the men suffered severely. After sleeping two hours we moved on and crossed the Manassas Plain Battlefield and the Bull Run and arrived at Centreville more dead than alive. The 2nd Corps had a fight in our rear, and in our old camp at Bristow Station. They captured five hundred prisoners and five pieces of Artillery. We are now laying in rear of Battery "C" 1st R.I. Light Artillery as supports, and the men are building rifle pits. If Lee attacks us here he will meet another Gettysburg defeat. Nothing but Rebel Cavalry have appeared as yet in our front. Last night Capt. Fred. Barton, 10th Mass. Vols. and Acting Assistant Adjutant General of our Brigade was captured with several wagons while on the road to Fairfax. We have been short of rations and an ear of field corn roasted in the ashes tasted very good to me. Yet I am happy and feel well all the time. It is said that the 2nd Corps made a gallant fight and that Gen. Meade has issued an order congratulating them.

Camp near Warrenton, Va., Oct. 21/63—Last Monday morning the entire Army advanced, and today our Regiment reached our old camp with the stone house. Since we were here the 2nd and 11th Mississippi Regiments have occupied our quarters, and they made things look bad. They burned up the seats we used for church gatherings and destroyed all of our boards. The Rebels did not resist our advance except with Cavalry, and our Cavalry cleared the way for us. The people here seemed somewhat surprised to see us return. The game between Meade and Lee seems to me like a game of checkers, and Meade has had the last move. We do not know where the Rebel Army is, but I suppose Gen. Meade does, and that is sufficient. I have been sick for a few days, not sick in bed, but feeling badly. Surgeon Carr however will I reckon fix me up again.

Near Warrenton, Va., Oct. 24/63—I am well again. Quinine did it. I suppose I must have taken a cold, but why a soldier should take cold I cannot tell. Our Regiment received new overcoats today. They came in time, for the nights are getting cold. We have had rain today and life outside has not been pleasant. When the Rebels occupied this camp they cut down large oak trees and burned the trunks and used the branches for bed. A citizen told me that they were a noisy crowd and *yelled* all night. If pleasant tomorrow we shall have a Sunday school, the first in some weeks as our movements have prevented. Orders to move have just come, but they will probably be countermanded before morning.

Near Warrenton, Oct. 27/63—Still in camp. I hardly think that our Regiment will reenlist. While several of the officers (I for one) favor it, the men as a rule want to go home when their time expires. As one half must enlist again before they will send us home, I have no hope of going. It is growing cold very fast, and although our Regiment is in stone huts we find it difficult to keep warm. I have a huge fire of oak wood burning in my hut, but every time some one opens the blanket that serves as a door I imagine myself at the North Pole. I suppose one reason why it is so cold here is, we are so high up among the hills and mountains.

We have been expecting an attack from the Rebels, but so far they have only moved troops in our front. Yesterday the Rebel Army crossed to this side of the Rapidan and advanced to within five miles of our lines, but after a Cavalry fight retired again. Sunday we had our Sabbath school for the first time in three weeks. It was an interesting session. Chaplain Beugless preached a sermon to the Regiment. I have entirely recovered my health. One day I rode at the government's expense in an ambulance. I never was in one but once before and that was when I was a Sergeant Major on the Peninsular. Some of the officers ride quite often, but I prefer to walk with my men.

Near Warrenton, Va., Oct. 29/63—All quiet along the lines except a few stray shots fired at pigs that attack our outposts. Then down comes an order from brigade Headquarters threatening all sorts of punishment to men who persist in killing unoffending swine. Of course we promise if we should see any man killing a pig we would stop him, but officers are like policemen and are never around while mischief is being done. Gen. Terry reviewed our Brigade yesterday. He complimented the 2nd R.I. on their fine appearance and marching. Saturday we are to be mustered for pay. Chaplain Beugless is holding a meeting at the camp of the 7th Mass. Vols. tonight. He is very obliging and is sought after by other Regiments to preach.

Near Warrenton, Va., Nov. 1, 1863—Sunday and we had to postpone our Sunday as Gen. Eustis our Brigade Commander took a notion to review our Brigade. With six days in the week and nothing to do, I do not see why he should have selected Sunday. I doubt if he had any very good reason. Chaplain Beugless preached in the afternoon. After service I borrowed Surgeon Carr's horse and rode down to Warrenton. I called at the camp of Battery "G" R.I. Artillery and saw William and Gilbert Westcott. I see by the papers that 1st Lieut. Arnold Rhodes Chase (my cousin) has been promoted Captain in the New York Vols. He is a fine fellow and very popular in his Company and Regiment.

Near Warrenton, Va., Nov. 3/63—It is said that Captain William B. Sears is to be Major of the 14th R.I. Vols. The men are re-enlisting very slowly in our Regiment, and we cannot foretell the results. I have had a good hut of timber built, but it is very uncertain as to our remaining here any length of time.

E.H. Rhodes as Adjutant of the 2nd Rhode Island.

Nov. 5/63—A plan of forming a new Regiment in R.I. has been talked. Lieut. Col. S.B.M. Read is to be Colonel. Major Henry C. Jencks is to be Lieut. Colonel, Captain Stephen H. Brown to be Major. Lieut. Col. Read called upon me today and offered me a Captain's commission with the privilege of selecting my own commissioned and non-commissioned officers. I am pleased with the idea but have some doubts about its success. I shall soon have a Captaincy here if I wait, for I have commanded a Company for several months.

Near Kelly's Ford, Rappahannock River, Nov. 8th 1863—Thursday night before leaving Warrenton Col. Rogers sent for me and said that Adjutant William J. Bradford has been appointed an aide on General Wheaton's staff. The Colonel offered to make me Adjutant or Captain just as I pleased. As an Adjutant is allowed two horses and is a member of the Regimental Staff I decided in favor of the horses. So good bye sore feet for sometime to come. I am delighted with these new promotions. This brings Surgeon Carr, Chaplain Beugless and myself together now as staff officers, and Surgeon Carr and I tent together. Yesterday morning the 7th, we left our camp at Warrenton and marched to Rappahannock Station arriving at 3 P.M. Skirmishers were deployed from the First Brigade of our Division and the fight began. It was hot for an hour, and shot and shell flew lively. The 2nd Division of our Corps charged a Rebel fort and captured it with three cannon and over one thousand prisoners. Our Brigade only lost five or six men. The scene was fine, for the fight took place just at sun set and the fort was outlined against the sky. This morning we moved to this place. Address your letters to:

Lieut. E.H. Rhodes
Adjutant 2nd R.I. Vols.
2 Brigade
Third Division
6th Corps
Via Washington, D.C.

Kelly's Ford, Va., Nov. 10/63—We are now guarding the ford where we have two pontoon bridges down. The river is quite narrow at this point. Last night I took a ride into the country to try my horse. We found one house where they had milk for sale. The price was 35¢ per quart. We did not invest. In the fight at Rappahannock Station our Corps combined two thousand prisoners and four guns. The old 6th Corps is well thought of now. I am now in a mess with Col. Rogers and

Chaplain Beugless. I like it very much. It seems like civilization to have a tent to sleep in. Of course the Adjutant's office work keeps me busy, but I like it, and am happy.

Near Hazel Run, Va., Nov. 12/63—This morning we crossed the Rappahannock River at Kelly's Ford and moved to this place, which is about eight miles from Culpepper. On our march I had a chance to ride about the Rebel forts that we captured a few days since. These works were built in this way:

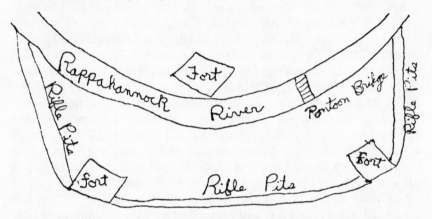

and were very strong. Gen. Sedgwick in his order states that the 6th Corps captured 600 prisoners: 130 commissioned officers, 2 Brigade Commanders, 4 cannon, 4 caissons filled with ammunition, 8 flags, 2,000 stands of arms, and one pontoon bridge. And all this with a less force than the Rebels had. In one of the forts are buried thirty five soldiers from the Maine Regiments of our Corps. Yesterday before leaving Kelly's Ford, Col. Rogers and myself took a long ride over to some deserted Rebel camps. Coming back we followed the course of the Rappahannock River, and it made me a little homesick, for it resembles the Pawtuxet very much. It is growing cold fast, and the ground is frozen hard.

Near Hazel Run, Nov. 15th 1863—Last night it rained, and as the weather is cold we are far from being comfortable. Heavy firing is going on in our front, but we do not know the cause, but are anticipating a battle somewhere on the Rapidan River. I bought me a fine bay horse with a white mark on his face, and he can run like a deer. I call him Old Abe. Our camp is called Camp Sedgwick again.

Camp Sedgwick, Nov. 17/63—Still in camp, and we have to keep huge fires burning in order to keep warm.

Camp Sedgwick, Nov. 19/63 Sunday—Today Capt. Samuel J. English and myself took a ride to Brandy Station located on a railroad. I have bought another horse—a Canadian. He is tough and just the kind of beast I need for rough work. I call him "Charley." This evening we held a prayer meeting. About one hundred and fifty men were present and we had a good time. Yesterday Chaplain Beugless and myself took a ride and called upon the Hon. John Minor Botts, the Virginia statesman and Unionist. The Rebels have persecuted him unmercifully and have put him in prison twice. He told us that a few days ago they arrested him again, but after taking him some miles allowed him to return home. We enjoyed our talk with him very much. He was one time a member of Congress. He owns 2200 acres of land. The Rebels destroyed his place, leaving only the house, which is large, with pillars in front. Mr. Botts told us that during the last fight the Rebel General Rodes posted a Brigade and a Battery in front of the house and notified him to move his family to a place of safety. Mr. Botts said he seated his family on the front porch and said to Gen. Rodes: "You have posted your troops so as to draw the Union fire upon my house and destroy it. This is my house and if any of my family are hurt I take the consequences and you take the responsibility." He said he added: "If you think you will be safer you may get behind my pillars." He told us that the troops were moved out of the range of his house. Mr. Botts treated us well and urged us to call again.

Camp Sedgwick, Nov. 24/63—Last night orders came for us to move and this morning we are all packed and ready. It is raining, and we all live in mud, sleep in mud, and almost eat in mud. We have no idea of where we are to go and can only surmise. I have fine times now when we are in camp and find the field and staff officers congenial spirits. The Colonel (Rogers) is very kind to me and we get on together in good shape.

2nd R.I. Vols. Dec. 3/63, Camp Sedgwick, Va., Thursday—We left our camp Thursday Nov. 26th and marched to Jacob's Ford on the Rapidan River and at dark crossed on a pontoon bridge without opposition from the enemy who withdrew as we advanced. Friday we followed the Third Corps, and a battle was fought. The 6th Corps acted as a reserve, and beyond some Artillery firing took no part in the fight. The Rebels moved on again during the night and the next morning,

Saturday Nov. 28th, we followed. Just before dark we came upon their line of defense at Mine Run and our Batteries were placed in position and fire opened. The Rebels replied in good style, and for a while there was "Music in the Air." Several English officers visiting the Army went up to the front to see the fight, but when the shells began to burst around them they went to the rear. I did not blame them, for I should have been glad to go myself. The boys had lots of sport out of this incident. We lay here in the mud all night, and the next morning (Sunday Nov. 29th) we moved to the left of the line. Our Division commanded by Gen. Terry was for a time attached to the 2nd Corps commanded by Gen. G.K. Warren. We marched past Robertson's Tavern and then took the plank road and moved to a position about ten miles from Orange Court House. Here we formed line of battle and waited events. The Rebel Gen. Stewart with his cavalry got into our rear and all of our Cavalry was sent in pursuit. This country is called the Wilderness, and it is well named, for it is all woods and swamp. Just at dark as the 2nd R.I. was getting into position the Rebels opened upon us with three Batteries, their shells passing over us. Here we lay down and tried to sleep.

Monday, Nov. 1st.—We were ordered to make an attack on the Rebel forts at 8 A.M. We advanced, and one hundred men from the 2nd R.I. were detailed as skirmishers. Before the Skirmishers could be deployed the Rebels came down upon the left flank of our Regiment, but we soon drove them back. Knapsacks, blankets were piled in heaps, and we waited all day for the order to attack, but it did not come. I had a good view of the Rebel forts and they appeared to be very strong. Bullets from the picket line of the enemy would at times sing over us, and the situation was not a pleasant one. Our mess servant found a house, and what was better, a *turkey*. This they roasted, and with sweet potatoes and new bread and butter they appeared to us about 2 P.M. Col. Rogers invited Col. Johns of the 10th Mass. to dine with us. The good things were spread upon a rubber blanket and we gathered around. The Chaplain began to say grace when bang went a gun, and a shell from the enemy howled over our heads. The Chaplain did not falter but went on with his prayer, when two more shells struck near our horses. We lay close to the ground until he had finished, when I called for my orderly to "Move my horse." The shells coming nearer and nearer we took the rubber blanket by its corners and moved under a knoll where we enjoyed a feast. Our Batteries soon got to work and our dinner was eaten while the Artillery duel went on. At dark our Division was again moved to a new position where we remained until Tuesday Dec. 1st, 9 o'clock P.M. when we started for the Rapidan River to return to camp. The weather was bitter cold, and to ride far was out of the question for one would fall off his horse, by reason of being sleepy. I missed the Colonel (Rogers) once during the night, which was moon-light and remembering that he had stopped at a brook to water his horse, I rode back to see him. I found him sitting upon his horse in the middle of a brook, and both horse and rider were fast asleep. I woke up the Colonel, and we rejoined the Regiment. The roads had been very muddy and much cut up by our wagon train. When the mud froze it left the roads in horrible condition for marching. However in order to keep awake I led my horse a good part of the night. Wednesday morning at daylight we recrossed the Rapidan at Ely's Ford and marched to within thirty miles of Brandy Station. This made a tramp of thirty miles from the battlefield, and the men are used up. Thursday Dec. 3rd we moved three miles to this camp. I do not understand the late movements, but I presume Gen. Meade does, and that is sufficient for me.

Camp Sedgwick, Va., Dec. 21/63—We are quiet in our winter quarters, and the men have built huts of logs, and we are very comforta-ble. At the Regimental Headquarters we have quite a village of huts arranged for comfort and convenience. I have a hut for the Adjutant's office and Sergeant-Major George F. Easterbrooks sleeps in the rear. Surgeon Carr and myself occupy a hut together while the Colonel and Chaplain Beugless try to keep each other warm. We drill when the weather will permit and sleep and smoke when it storms. We have received a number of recruits and about one hundred drafted men who look a little lonesome. Lt. Col. Read who was promoted from Captain of Co. "I" is absent on staff duty, and Major Henry C. Jencks is acting as Lieutenant Colonel. Tonight we have had a meeting of the officers to decide whether we are willing to remain in service after June 5th 1864. The following have agreed to stay: Captains Henry H. Young, Joseph McIntyre, John P. Shaw, Adjutant Elisha H. Rhodes, Lieutenants Edmund F. Prentiss and Thorndike J. Smith. Lieut. Samuel Russell will probably stay. I decided without hesitation. The United States need the services of her sons. I am young and in good health, and I feel that I owe a duty to my country. I entered the Army as a private expecting that the war would end in a few months. It has dragged along, and no one can tell when the end will come. But when it does come I want to see it, and so I am going to stay. I like a soldier's life and without egotism I

"Kate" from a painting by Mrs. Elisha H. Rhodes.

think I can say that I am doing some service. If I should go home I should be unhappy and want to come back. In fact I should seek service in some other Regiment. Our Regiment is a good one, and I prefer it to any other. So good bye homesickness. I am going, if God wills, to see the end of this wicked rebellion. Several of the men have already re-enlisted, and we shall have enough to form a good Battalion.

Camp Sedgwick, Va., Dec. 25/63—This is Christmas day and the third one I have passed in the Army. I have enjoyed a good long ride on my new horse *Kate*. I traded Old Abe for her and think I have one of the finest horses in the Army. She is a beauty and very fast, both running and trotting. I gave a dinner to a party of officers, and we tried to celebrate Christmas in a becoming manner.

Dec. 31/63—The year is ended. Good bye 1863, and may God grant that success attend our labors for our country in the year so soon to open.

Brandy Station, Va. — Camp Sedgwick, Va. — Wilderness — Spottsylvania — Noel's Station, Va. — Peake's Station Va. — Cold Harbor, Va. — Charles City Court House, Va. — Brandon, Va. — Petersburg, Va. — US Transport Peril — Camp Brightwood, Md. — Tennallytown, Md. — Orcutt's Cross Roads, Md. — Poolesville, Md. — Leesburg, Va. — Near Washington, D.C. — Hyattsville, Md. — Jefferson, Md. — Halltown, Va. — Petersville, Md. — Frederick City, Md. — Monocacy River, Md. — Harpers Ferry, Va. — Charlestown, Va. — Opequon Creek, Va. — Milltown, Va. — Middletown, Va. — Clifton, Va. — Winchester, Va. — Middletown, Va. — Kernstown, Va. — Camp Russell, Va. — Martinsburg, W. Va. — US Transport City of Albany — Petersburg, Va.

1864

Camp Sedgwick, Brandy Station, Va., Jany 1st 1864—The new year opens without any important events. The troops are in comfortable quarters, built of logs and covered with canvas. Drill takes place daily and an occasional review breaks up the monotony of our camp life. The men are still re-enlisting for the remainder of the war and I hope to be sent home soon on my leave of absence.

Jany 5/64—This is the last day for re-enlisting men, and we find we have nearly one hundred of the original men who are willing to stay and fight the war out. Eighteen of the officers have agreed to remain, but when the time comes I fear that some of them will back out. I shall stay however and see the end of the war if God spares my life. The following are the names of the officers who have signified their intention of remaining in the service:

Major Henry C. Jenckes	Did not stay *
Surgeon George W. Carr	Did not stay
Adjutant Elisha H. Rhodes	Remained
Captain John P. Shaw	Killed
Capt. Thomas Foy	Did not stay
Capt. John R. Waterhouse	Did not stay

Capt. Edward A. Russell	Did not stay
Capt. Joseph McIntyre	Did not stay
Capt. Henry H. Young	Remained
Lieut. Henry K. Southwick	Did not stay
Lieut. Edmund F. Prentiss	Remained
Lieut. Stephen West	Did not stay
Lieut. Thorndike J. Smith	Remained
Lieut. Samuel B. Russell	Remained

[*This column apparently pencilled in later. Of those officers listed under "Did not stay," Capt. Joseph McIntyre was killed in action before the end of his term of service and Lieut. Henry K. Southwick transferred to the 14th Rhode Island Heavy Artillery (Colored) where he served until the end of the war. All the others were mustered out on June 17th, 1864.]

If all of the above remain we shall have a nucleus of a good command.

Jany 7/64—The weather is cold, and the ground is covered with snow. The thermometer this morning was only 8 above zero. Some of the troops of the 6th Corps have been ordered away, and our Brigade has been transferred to the 2nd Division. We have been serving in the 3rd Division. Some of the troops that left today have gone to Sandusky, Ohio and others to Harpers Ferry. As soon as they left camp our boys made a raid upon the abandoned huts, and now have plenty of building material.

Jany 14/64—This is a sad day for the 2nd R.I. Vols. Our Colonel Horatio Rogers, Jr. who has had command since July 9th 1863 has resigned on account of ill health and is to go home. We are all very sorry to part with him, for he has endeared himself to both officers and men by his gallantry in battle and kindness in camp. His farewell order was read to the Regiment at dress parade. Lt. Col. Sam. B.M. Read is the senior officer, but as he is absent on staff duty, Major Henry C. Jencks will have command of the Regiment. Our Chaplain recently married a soldier of the 1st U.S. Sharpshooters. His name is S.J. Williams and his home is in Vermont. The bride is Miss Ellie P. West of North Carolina. This is the first wedding that we have heard of since going into our present winter quarters. I hear that the happy pair are to have a furlough and go to Vermont.

Saturday Jany 23/64—Mrs. Wheaton (Emma) the wife of General Frank Wheaton died at Harpers Ferry, Va. on the 16th inst. We all feel very sad, for she was well known to the officers and men of the 2nd R.I. having passed the winter of 1861 and 1862 in our camp at Brightwood. Tonight we dedicated our new chapel and in remembrance of R.I. and in recognition of God's goodness to us we have named it "Hope" Chapel. The building is made of logs hewn smooth on one side and built up cob fashion. Most of the hewing was done by Chaplain Beugless and Lieut. John M. Turner. The roof is covered by a large canvas, presented by the Christian Commission. Inside we have a fireplace and tin reflectors for candles on the walls. A chandelier made from old tin cans, or the tin taken from cans is in the centre.[32] The pulpit or desk is covered with red flannel, and the ground or floor is carpeted with pine boughs. We sent a detail of men in command of Capt. John G. Beveridge to a deserted church near by and took out the seats and placed them in our Chapel. Our boys had a fight with the guerillas but brought back the seats. The following is the order of service at the dedication:

Reading of Scripture	Chaplain John D. Beugless 2nd R.I. Vols.
Prayer	Chaplain Francis P. Perkins 10th Mass. Vols.
Sermon	Chaplain Ethan Ray Clarke 1st R.I. Cavalry
Prayer	Chaplain Daniel C. Roberts 4th Vermont Vols.
Benediction	Chaplain Norman Fox 77th N.Y. Vols.

Gen. Eustis and many other officers were present. We have organized a Union Church with chaplain John D. Beugless as Pastor. We have to start 26 members. We have also organized a Sunday School, and Adjutant Elisha H. Rhodes is Superintendent. Lieut. John M. Turner has a class of contrabands, mostly servants to the officers.[33] We hope to do much good in the Regiments and pray that God will bless our labors. The men have formed a society called the Rhode Island Lyceum which meets every Monday evening. Spelling school and lectures will be held every evening, so our time will be well occupied. Several ladies are now living in camp. Mrs. Henry C. Jencks, wife of Major Jencks, Mrs. Edward A Russell, wife of Capt. Russell, and Mrs. Amos M. Bowen, wife of Lieut. Bowen. This gives an air of civilization to our Headquarters.

Feby 4/64—A few nights since we had a very interesting lecture from Rev. J. Wheaton Smith, D.D. of Philadelphia. He lectured on his travels to the Holy Lands. The men were delighted with the new departure. The religious interest still continues, and we hope for good results from our labors.

Camp Sedgwick, Va., Feby 10/64—Hurrah! We start for home today. The following officers are in the party: Capt. John P. Shaw, Adjutant Elisha H. Rhodes, Lieut. Edmund F. Prentiss and Lieut. Thorndike J. Smith. We are to have thirty-five days leave of absence. Note. From Feby 10th to April 6th 1864 I was in R.I. on leave of absence. Our original was for 35 days, but Senator Wm. Sprague succeeded in getting our leaves extended until April 6th.

Above, Capt. John P. Shaw

Left, Lieut. Edmund F. Prentiss

Camp Sedgwick, Va., April 8th—Back in camp again. It seems quite natural to be with soldiers once more. We left Providence Wednesday evening April 6th on the shore line train for New York. About twenty of our men were on the train and as some of them were well supplied with liquor we had a lively time. Lieut. Thorndike J. Smith and myself stood guard at the doors of the cars nearly all night to keep the men from leaving. At daylight we arrived in New York. I chartered a horse car to take them down town, and on arriving at the City Hall Park marched them inside the fence for breakfast. After ordering breakfast for the men, Lieut. Smith and myself started for a hotel and had breakfast. We took a train at Jersey City at 9 A.M. and reached Washington at night. We went to the Metropolitan Hotel and stayed all night. This morning we came down to camp on the cars. Nearly all of the Officers were at the station to welcome us back, and I rode to camp on my mare Katie. I found the Regiment in the same old camp and have settled down to work again.

Sunday April 10/64—Rain and mud. Today I again took charge of my Sunday School and had a pleasant time with the boys. The Chaplain preached a good sermon this afternoon. Last night I received a box of good things and sent for the officers. We enjoyed the cake, cigars, etc. very much. No mail today, as the railroad bridge over Bull Run has been washed away.

April 12/64—Today our Brigade was reviewed by the Division Commander, Brig. Gen. Getty. Our Regiment wore white gloves and looked well. At dress parade tonight the Brigade band was present and gave us some good music. I have taken a long ride today, and in jumping a ditch my horse Katie pitched me off.

April 12/64—The weather is warm and delightful, although the distant mountains are still capped with snow.

April 16/64—Tonight we had a very interesting religious meeting, and about twenty took part in remarks or prayer.

Sunday April 17/64—Sunday School and church service today as usual.

April 18/64—Chaplain Beugless has gone to Washington to meet his wife. Surgeon Carr is to take a lot of sick soldiers to Washington tomorrow and will be gone ten days. Yesterday the 18th, the 6th Corps was reviewed by Lieut. Gen. U.S. Grant, and the display was fine and the weather delightful. The lines were formed near our camp, each Regiment in "Column of Divisions." All the Batteries and wagon trains were in line. General Grant is a short thick set man and rode his horse like a bag of meal. I was a little disappointed in the appearance, but I like the look of his eye. He was more plainly dressed then any other General on the field. After the review Generals Grant, Meade, Sedgwick, Hancock, Warren, Wheaton, Eustis and several others with their staffs rode through our camp. I had the pleasure of saluting for the first time the Lieut. General and received his acknowledgement. We are making our preparations for the spring campaign which cannot be delayed much longer. I have had a fine ride today in search of flowers.

April 21/64—The Regiment has been practicing at the targets today. The weather is delightful, and I have enjoyed a good long ride with Lt. Col. Read (now in command of the 2nd) and Chaplain Beugless. I called on General Wheaton. We are now in the 4th Brigade 2nd Division 6th Corps. I have been pistol firing from the back of my horse. She did not like it very well but soon became accustomed to the sound.

Sunday April 24th 1864—We have had a delightful day clear and warm until dark when it began to rain. After the usual guard mount and Sunday morning inspection the field and staff officers went out for a ride. In rear of our lines there is a small river called Hazel Run. It has run with blood on more than one occasion, for the Union and Rebel troops have fought for its possession. Today at 2 P.M. a more peaceful scene was witnessed, for in its waters four Union soldiers were buried with their Lord in Baptism. Our Chaplain Rev. John D. Beugless baptized two soldiers from Battery "G" 1st R.I. Artillery and the Rev. Francis Brown Perkins Chaplain of the 37th Mass. Vols. baptized two soldiers from his Regiment. The candidates wore their Army uniforms, but the Chaplains managed in some way to procure robes for themselves. The bank of the stream was covered with officers and men from the Regiments near, and the scene was solemn and impressive. In the evening our Chaplain preached in Hope Chapel, and the Lord's Supper was observed. I acted as one of the Deacons as did Lieut. John M. Turner, who is a Presbyterian. About 40 officers and men took part in the observance of the Lord's Supper, and all felt that it was indeed a Sabbath to our souls. May God bless us and keep us all in the paths of Righteousness for His name's sake, Amen.

April 26/64—Last night Chaplain Beugless preached his last sermon in our Chapel as the roof of canvas is to be taken off and sent to Washington. The subject of the sermon was "Our duty in the coming campaign." It was really a fine discourse and was listened to with much attention by the audience. We are getting ready to move, and fighting will begin soon. I hope Gen. Grant will be as successful in the East as in the West. Some of the officers whose time is up in June are already talking of home, but as I am in for the war I am not interested. I want to see the end of the war as I saw the beginning. Last night I called upon General Alexander Shaler and had a very pleasant visit with him.

April 28/64—A warm beautiful day. After dress parade Capt. Sam. J. English and myself rode over to the camp of Battery "E" 1st R.I. Light Artillery and took tea with my friend William B. Rhodes. Our church roof was sent off today, and we are nearly ready for a move.

April 30th 1864—I have just learned with much pleasure that my old friend and school mate William B. Westcott who has served faithfully and well as a sergeant in Battery "G" 1st R.I. Light Artillery has been promoted to be a Second Lieutenant. Well he is a good fellow and will make a first class officer. (One more officer from Pawtuxet.)

Camp Sedgwick, Va., Sunday May 1/64—We have had our regular service today, but it has not seemed much like Sunday, for we are preparing for a march, and the camp is in confusion. The officers are packing up and sending off their surplus baggage, and the ladies have left our camp for home. Our move means fight; may God grant us the victory.

May 2/64—We have had a furious gale today with clouds of dust filling the air, but at night a shower of rain gave us relief. My tent has been full of officers this evening singing and spinning yarns. My tent seems to be the favorite loafing place for the officers. Some of the troops have received orders to march, but we are still waiting.

May 3/64—Our turn has come. Orders have been received for our Division (Gen. Getty's) to march tomorrow morning at 4 o'clock. We shall probably cross the Rapidan River again and make another push for Richmond. While all are talking about the great battle in prospect I feel very calm, trusting in God that his protecting care will be over me. While I do not feel that I am more safe than others, yet I have a firm reliance upon my Heavenly Father and am willing to leave all to him.

May 4th 1864—At 4 A.M. we left our pleasant winter quarters near Brandy Station, and after a march of about twenty miles in the heat and dust we reached the Rapidan River and crossed to the south bank at Germania Ford. Here we rested for the night.

May 5th 1864—At daylight the Sixth Corps left the Rapidan River and struck into the country well called the Wilderness. We marched slowly until about noon when the advance found the Rebels posted in the thick and almost impenetrable underbrush and small trees. It was next to impossible to move Artillery, and the fighting was done by the Infantry. As our Brigade reached the line of fire we were formed in two lines with the 2nd R.I. and 10th Mass in front and the 7th and 37th Mass. in the rear line. We remained in line until between 3 and 4 o'clock P.M. when we were ordered to advance to the attack. The woods and brush were so thick and dark that the enemy could not be seen, but we knew they were in our front from the terrible fire we received. The Second Rhode Island was on the extreme right of the line and were harrassed by a flank fire from the enemy. Captain Joseph McIntyre of Company "E" was killed early in the fight, and as Chaplain John D. Beugless went to his aid he too was shot through the wrist. Our Chaplain is a brave man and has the warmest sympathy of the officers and men. The line surged backwards and forwards, now advancing and now retreating until darkness put an end to the carnage. Many men were lying upon the ground dead or wounded, and as darkness settled down we rendered such assistance as we were able.

May 6/64—We got a little sleep last night but not much, for the enemy kept up their fire, and the wounded were all about us. At daylight we were under arms and ready for the fight. We understood that we were to make another attack, but the Rebels anticipated our movement and advanced on the 5th Corps. The fight was a terrible one and was even worse than yesterday. The 2nd R.I. was soon engaged, and nobly did our men do their duty. In some parts of our Corps the lines were

Capt. Joseph McIntyre

*Assistant Surgeon
William F. Smith*

broken, and at one time our Brigade was driven back on the Germania Plank Road until we reached a redoubt built across the road and occupied by Battery "E" R.I. Artillery. As we fell back the Rebels seemed to be on three sides of us and were firing into our front and both flanks. A party of officers gathered about our colors, and drawing our revolvers we determined that the Rebels should not have our colors.

The lines were soon reformed, and we drove the enemy back to their original lines. Our Brigade charged into the swamp six times, and each time were driven out. Darkness again put an end to the fighting, and we lay down amid the dead and wounded. During the night the brush caught fire, and many of the wounded burned to death. Assistant Surgeon William F. Smith of the 2nd R.I. was in a road some mile or more to the rear when a cannon ball struck his horse in the head killing it instantly. Our losses during the battles of the 5th and 6th are 14 killed, 61 wounded and 8 missing.

May 7th 1864—Today we have had comparative quiet with only skirmishing going on in our front. We have entrenched ourselves the best we can with logs and earth and are waiting events. If we were under any other General except Grant I should expect a retreat, but Grant is not that kind of a soldier, and we feel that we can trust him.

[Letter:] *Wednesday morning May 4th we left our camp and crossed the Rapidan River at Germania ford and occupied the Rebel forts without opposition. Here we went into camp and rested for the night. Thursday morning May 5th we started at daylight and at 10 A.M. drove in the enemy's pickets in a dense forest of pine trees and underbrush. Our lines were soon formed, and our Brigade was ordered into action. Advancing in line of battle we soon met the Rebels and opened fire. The woods being very dark we could not see them, and they flanked our right, driving us back in confusion. We soon reformed and advanced again but were driven back leaving our killed and wounded on the field. The little birds sang sweet amid the scene of death and destruction. A third time we advanced and drove them about a mile when it became dark, and we halted for the night amid the dead and wounded. Such a night as I passed. No sleep and the wounded groaning on all sides. Daylight Friday the 6th we advanced again under a heavy fire of Artillery. Our men fell in all directions, but we kept on. (Yesterday a bullet struck me in my right fore finger but only hurt me a little.) Our lines were driven back and fresh troops sent in, but these shared the same fate. Soon we were ordered forward but had to return. A third time we tried it with the same result, losing many men every time. When we retreated the Rebels shelled us and added to the confusion. Officers with drawn swords and pistols were urging the men foward, but poor fellows it was no use, for it was certain death. Genl. Hays came galloping into the fight, but soon his white horse came out riderless leaving the Genl dead on the field. A fourth time our lines were formed and we advanced, but some troops on the left gave way, and the Rebels came into our rear and fired into us from three sides of a square. The way we did leave! Everybody travelled as fast as possible. Many were captured, but I came out all right. We formed new lines and rested for the night but had no sleep. Saturday our Regiment was sent on Picket on the plank road. We had two Regt's of Cavalry in front of us and when the Rebels opened fire they skedaddled through our Regt to the rear, but we stayed there and Genl Sedgwick drove the Cavalry back to the front. During the night the Rebels retreated to Spotsylvania and we followed. Our lines were formed in a piece of woods under a heavy fire. When the Rebels advanced our boys up and gave them a volley that sent them back. About two o'clock Monday morning 1st Inst, we were ordered to retire to the second line. Such a time as we had. We got lost and would go a little way when the Rebels would fire, and we would start in another direction. After hours of running about in the dark we found our way into our lines and worked all day fortifying our position under the fire of the Rebel Batteries. Battery E., R.I.L.A. came into position near our Regt and soon caused the Rebels to cease firing. Genl Sedgwick rode out to the front and was killed by a sharpshooter who shot him through the head. He was one of our best Generals, and his death was a great loss to the Army. Tuesday the 10th we remained in the forts all day and dodged shot and bullets. Wednesday the 11th was about the same as Tuesday, but at dark we the 1st and 2nd Division of the 6th Corps moved to the rear for rest. Up to this time we had been awake night and day. Thursday morning the 12th and 2nd Corps stormed the Rebel works and captured Genl Johnson and 6000 prisoners. I saw Genl Johnson as he rode past. At six A.M. our Brigade took possession of the Rebel works. The enemy advanced and tried to retake them. How the old Second R.I. did fire. I fired over a hundred rounds myself. Col. Read was firing when he was hit. At the same instant a bullet struck me in my right breast, tore my coat, glanced on my pocket book and bruised my right arm. It whirled me round, and I thought I was dead but soon found that I was all right. The ammunition was exhausted and the officers passed it up to the men in boxes. The New York Excelsior Brigade was driven out of the works on our Right which left us exposed to an enfilading fire, but our boys never moved. For three hours the Rebels were within twenty feet of our Regt. It seemed to me that the day would never pass away. A section of Battery "B" R.I. Artillery came down and opened on the Rebels with Canister, but they staid [sic] there.*

Major General "Uncle" John Sedgwick

About noon about one hundred and fifty Rebels through [sic] down their guns and ran into our lines unable to stand our fire. At four P.M. fresh troops came up and took our place after we had fought ten hours. Col. Edwards coming to our brigade said to Maj. Jencks, "Major, you may be proud of your Regt. this day." We laid down about twenty yards in the rear. To add to the horrors of the day it rained in torrents. All night the battle raged, and we had to lay there. Sleep would overpower us when we were not firing and such dreams as I had. I dreamt that I was home and so warm and comfortable sitting by the fire with mother and sister when some one says our lines are giving away. I jumped up wet

through, and we soon drove the Rebels back again. At daylight they retreated leaving all their dead and wounded and many prisoners. We captured a Rebel Captain and a 1st Lieut. May God save me from another such scene. The ditch to the rifle pit was full of dead and wounded blue and grey. Genl Russell estimated the number at 3000. Our men completely exhausted sank right down. I thought I should die of fatigue. I smoked most all day and so did we all we were so excited. The men did not mind shells any more then snow balls, they were so tired. They said it was death or Richmond, for they would never run. I never was so proud of my Regt in my life. The Rebels fell back to a new line, and we rested and made rifle pits until the morning of the 18th when we tried to storm their works but failed. Our lines advanced splendidly to within three hundred yards of their works when they opened their Artillery and mowed the men down in rows. We stood it for two hours and then fell back to our own works where we have fortified. Our loss is fearful. Two Captains killed and seven officers wounded besides over one hundred men killed and wounded. Yesterday I sent a list to Prov. which you will see in the papers. The advantages so far are with our Army, but we have more hard work yet.
[End of letter.]

May 8/64—Last night the 2nd R.I. was sent out on picket. We formed our lines before dark and I was ordered to go to the left of our Regt and find out if we connected with the troops of the 9th Corps. I rode out on a cart path, and before I knew it I was quite near the Rebel lines of pickets. I turned my horse quietly and rode into the swamp at a high speed and was glad to get back to our lines. About dark it was reported that the Union forces would move their position, and we were ordered to remain and keep up the appearance of a fighting front. We were told to save ourselves if we could, but that in all probability our Regiment would be captured. After dark I was sent out on to the picket line with orders for the men to put tin cups and canteens into their haversacks so that they would not rattle and to be ready to retire when the word was given. About midnight orders came for us to retire, and the men were silently drawn in and formed on the Germania Plank Road. We then moved down the road in the darkness until we reached the line of forts which we found deserted by our troops. I was ordered to ride in advance down the road and to endeavor to find Col. Joseph B. Hamblin, the Corps officer of the day. As the Rebel Cavalry were known to have passed the road in our rear I did not like the job given me, but knowing I must obey I drew my revolver, pulled the hammer back and rode on. About half a mile to the rear as I was riding in the shadow of the trees, some one put a pistol in my face and demanded "Halt." I quickly leveled my pistol and said: "Who are you?" A man replied "Give me your name, or I will fire." Knowing that my name could do no harm I replied "Rhodes." The man stepped out from behind his tree, and I saw that it was Col. Hamblin. He said: "Adjutant, I came near shooting you." I dismounted and led my horse into the woods, and we waited until the Regiment came along. We marched all night and at daylight caught up with the rear guard of the Army. They had in charge an immense number of Rebel prisoners. After a short halt for coffee we moved on again and joined our Corps near Spottsylvania Court House. Here we were formed in line of battle and with the 10th Mass. had a sharp fight with the enemy. Here we built a line of rifle pits and slept again with the dead and dying.

May 9/64, Spottsylvania—Today we have finished a heavy line of entrenchment, and the 2nd R.I. is supporting Battery "E" R.I. Artillery Capt. Wm. B. Rhodes. The guns are posted at wide intervals and we have Companies on the right and left of each cannon. The Rebels tried to form a line on our front but Battery "E" fired by Battery some six hundred rounds of solid shot, or shell with long fuses, and the Rebels gave up their plan. We have just learned that Major Gen. John Sedgwick commanding the Corps is dead, shot through the head by a Rebel sharpshooter. We are all sad for Uncle John, as he was called, was beloved by all the Army. Maj. Gen Horatio G. Wright has assumed command of our Corps.

May 10th 1864—Thank God I am still living. Our poor old Regiment has had a hard time since leaving our winter quarters, and we have lost seven officers and nearly one hundred men killed and wounded. We are still in our entrenchments facing the enemy.

May 11/64—Constant skirmishing going on in our front and both Armies are evidently preparing for another death grapple. Shot and shell are constantly passing over us, and we are fast adding to the roll of dead and wounded. Will it ever end. I hope for the best.

Line of Battle Near Spottsylvania Court House, May 13th 1864—Yesterday we had another fearful day of battle. Our Regiment behaved splendidly, and we are spoken of in the highest terms. Early in the morning we heard a terrific fire of musketry and Artillery at the front, and our Corps was sent forward. It turned out that the Second Corps under Gen. Hancock had charged the Rebel works and taken their entire line with several thousand prisoners. As we passed up to the front I saw two Rebel Generals as prisoners: Maj. Gen. Edward Johnson and Brig. Gen. George H. Stewart. They were talking with Gen. Wright and Gen. Wheaton. I heard Gen. Wheaton say: "How are you, Johnson?" and the reply was "How are you, Frank?" They shook hands very cordially, having been comrades in the Army before the rebellion. We did not go far before the bullets began to sing about us. The Second Corps was in the ditch of earthworks taken from the Rebels in the morning. We (the 6th Corps) relieved the 2nd Corps, and they were sent to another part of the field. The rain began to fall, and soon we were deep in mud and water. While we remained in the ditch we were sheltered from the enemy's fire, but if a head was shown above the works, bullets whistled immediately. On the right of our line the works formed an angle, and our Regiment found itself enfiladed by the enemy. Soon the horses and gunners of a Battery posted in the angle were killed or disabled, and the enemy charged with loud yells upon the guns. They came so near that they dropped a Rebel flag over into the ditch on our side, and as we opened fire they fled and left it there. One of our own Batteries stationed on a hill in rear of our line fired two shots which fell short and killed two of the 2nd R.I. One of these men was named Graves, and he had just returned from a Rebel prison. I was sent back to inform Col. Oliver Edwards 37th Mass. Vols. who had assumed command of the Brigade of the fact. I found the Colonel and asked him to have the Battery cease firing. He said that his staff were absent and asked me to ride over to the Battery with the message. As my horse had been left in the rear for safety, I mounted an orderly's horse, a great lumbering beast. As I reached a hill I was obliged to follow the ridge for several hundred yards. The Rebel sharpshooters opened fire upon me, and I tried to spur the horse into a run, but not succeeding, I threw myself upon the off side and held on by the horse's mane. In this way only my left leg was exposed. I lost my hat off, and as it was a new one and cost me seven and a half dollars I drew my sabre and ran the point through the hat and recovered it. I next lost my Navy revolver, but if it had been made of gold, studded with diamonds I would not have stopped for it. I reached the Battery and found the men lying upon the ground to escape the fire. I requested the Captain to elevate his guns, and after they were had fired a round from each and I saw that the shots went over our line, I returned to the Regiment running the guantlet of

Rebel sharpshooters again. In front of our line there was an open plain for perhaps two hundred yards and then there were thick woods. The Rebels formed in the woods and then sent forward a small party with a white flag. As we saw the flag we ceased firing, and the officers jumped upon the parapet, but as the party approached they were followed by a line of battle who rushed upon us with yells. Our men quickly recovered from the surprise and gave them a volley which sent them flying to the woods. From the woods a steady fire was kept up until after midnight. The guns which I mentioned above were still standing idle in the angle and neither party could get them. A Brigade of Jersey troops were brought up and attempted to enter the angle but were driven back. General Sickles' old Brigade (the Excelsior) were then brought up, but the men could not stand the terrible fire and instead of advancing in line only formed a semicircle about the guns. Capt. John P. Shaw of Co. "K" 2nd R.I. Vols. was standing upon a stump and waving his sword to encourage these men when he suddenly fell backwards. I shouted to Major Jencks that Shaw was down. I ran to him and found him lying with his head upon an ammunition box. I raised him up, and the blood spurted from the wound in his breast, and he was dead. As I had lost my pistol I took his and placed it in my holster and will, if I live, send it home to the Captain's father. Lt. Col S.B.M. Read was wounded in the neck and ear and left the field, and Major Henry C. Jencks took command of the Regiment. I took a position in the rifle pit, and the boys would load their guns and pass them to me to fire. I had just raised the gun for another shot when a bullet hit me in the breast, tore a piece from my coat, but glanced upon my pocket book and then struck me a glancing blow upon the right arm. I thought my arm was gone and hastily stripped only to find a slight flesh wound. On the 5th inst. I was hit by a bullet that took the skin from my right forefinger. We were very anxious to get possession of the Rebel flag which "was so near and yet so far." I called for volunteers to go with me and get it. Thomas Parker, a private of Co. "D" and several others came forward and offered to go, but before we could start Major Jencks came over and forbid what he called a foolish adventure. We expended all of our cartridges, and when a new supply arrived the officers broke open the covers and distributed the ammunition to the men. During the day and night the average number of cartridges issued to each man was nearly three hundred. Many of them however were wet by the rain. Just before dark the Rebels made a desperate attempt to retake their works, but we drove them back. And so the fight went on and continued until nearly 2 A.M. this morning (the 13th). We took many prisoners during the day, men who in the charges that the enemy made could not get away. I never saw even at Gettysburg so many dead Rebels as lay in front of our lines. I laid down to sleep about 3 A.M. today but did not rest much, for the wounded were all about us. As we were well protected by the earthworks our loss was not heavy, yet we had 12 killed and twenty one wounded.

General Wheaton complimented me upon my conduct in the fight and my name has been mentioned in an order issued by the Brigade commander. I thank God for his goodness to me and am glad that I have been able to do a little service to my country.

May 14/64—Today we were relieved at daylight by other troops, and we formed in rear of the 9th Corps. Here we remained until towards night when we moved to the left and formed in line two miles from Spottsylvania Court House. Our Battery and the Rebel guns have made a great noise today, but very little has been accomplished.

Sunday May 15/64—We have today finished the rifle pits that we began last night. It has been very quiet, as if out of respect for the day.

May 16th/64—Still in entrenchments keeping watch and ward. Artillery firing is kept up by both sides, but little real fighting has been done today.

Line of Battle Near Spottsylvania Court House, May 17/64—We have had no fighting for four days, and both Armies are building earthworks. So far we have been successful but at a terrible sacrifice of men. Our Division has lost about half its number. We had about nine thousand men when we left Camp Sedgwick. On the 12th inst. the Rebel dead were in heaps in front of our lines, and at one time the 2nd R.I. had one hundred and fifty prisoners. I am well and happy and feel that at last the Army of the Potomac is doing good work. Grant is a fighter and is bound to win. May God help him to end the war. We hope to see Richmond soon and humble the pride of the men who brought on this wicked war.

Line of Battle Near Spottsylvania Court House, May 19/64—Still fighting and digging. Our Regiment is very much reduced, and we have only nine line officers (Company officers) left on duty. Yesterday the old Sixth Corps had a grand fight. We started in line of battle before daylight and marched through the woods and brush towards the enemy. At daylight we came in sight of their line of forts and made a charge, but it was of no use, for their Artillery cut our men down in heaps. We reached the glacis in front of the Rebel forts, and here we were obliged to lay exposed to their fire. Lieut. Edmund F. Prentiss was severely wounded by a piece of shell which struck him in the groin. He had just been hit with a spent grape shot that struck him in the temple. I was near him and sent him to the rear on a stretcher.(Note: He recovered and lived for years after the war.) We sent our men back to the wood a few at a time until all were out of the direct fire. As I entered the woods I met Major George Clendennin, Asst. Adjutant on Gen. Wheaton's staff. He had his servant with him and invited me to take breakfast, which I did under fire. We had some hot bread and a broiled shad which some one had caught in one of the streams. Notwithstanding the Rebel shells I enjoyed my breakfast. We are now building earthworks about five hundred yards in front of the enemy. It is hot work, but the men are fast covering themselves. There will be sad hearts in R.I. when the news reaches home. We have had very little sleep for the past two weeks, and no one pretends to take off his boots. But I can stand it as long as the Rebels can, for we know we are causing them considerable trouble.

Line of Battle Near Spottsylvania Court House, May 20th 1864—A mail arrived today, the first in several days. I received eighteen letters as my share. We have finished our earthworks and now feel secure. Our works are strong and built of large trees covered with earth. Let the Rebels try to take them if they want to.

May 21/64—We remained in our rifle pits until dark when we withdrew and started towards Richmond again on the Bowling Green Road.

Sunday May 22/64—We marched nearly all last night but made slow progress. Today we passed Guiney's Station and after making a few more miles formed in line for the night.

May 23/64—Today we continued our march and in a short time reached the North Anna River. We could hear the firing in our front and on the south side of the river, but as our Corps now seems to be in the rear we did not do any fighting.

May 24/64—Before daylight we crossed the North Anna River and formed line near the 5th Corps. Here we built a line of rifle pits and rested for the night.

Line of Battle near Noel's Station, May 25/64—We have got out of the Wilderness and are now near Hanover Junction and only twenty five miles from Richmond.

May 26/64—Nothing of importance today. Still digging Virginia sand and making forts. At dark we recrossed the North Anna River and marched to within a short distance of the Pamunkey River.
(Our old friend of 1862)

May 27/64—We arrived in camp about daylight and received rations. Here we were allowed to rest. The Pamunkey is near.

May 28/64—We started early and crossed the Pamunkey River and marched to the vicinity of Hanover town where we were set to work building entrenchments. Great is the shovel and spade. Well I would as soon dig the Rebels out as to fight them.

May 29/64—We left our works sometime about noon and marched to Peakes Station where we found a part of our 6th Corps tearing up the rail road. We formed in line to defend them from the Rebels should they appear. Tearing up rail roads is an old trick of ours. The Rebel lines are in sight of us, but we hope to make them move on again soon. Our troops are at work destroying the rail road. The Rebels have retreated before us for the past few days but now seem to be waiting for our attack. I am well and happy but very weary having been in the saddle constantly for several days.

Peake's Station 15 miles from Richmond, May 30/64—Our column is resting for a short time at this place. The Rebels have retreated to the vicinity of Richmond. We are tired and hungry, as no rations have been seen for two days. Forty eight hours is a long time to go without food of any kind, but we expect rations tonight.

May 31/64—We are nearly seven miles from Mechanicsville and about fifteen miles from Richmond. Our advance to Peakes Station proved to be merely a reconnaisance and at 3 P.M. we retired. Just before we retired I was sitting on my horse in rear of the Regiment when I saw across the fields two bright spots in the woods. I knew at once that there were two brass cannon there looking towards us. Just then a surgeon of the English Army who is with us watching the course of the war rode up and said: "Lieutenant, Ah, his there anything hinteresting to be seen here?" I replied: "Just wait a moment, Doctor, and you will see something interesting." Just then both guns were fired, and the shells went screaming over our heads. The doctor turned and rode off, saying: "I will go to the 'ospital and see what is going on there." The boys shouted: "Is it hinteresting, Doctor?" I did not blame him, for he had no business to be at the front.

At 3 P.M. we started to retire, and our Brigade with a Maine Battery was ordered to guard the rear of the column. As soon as our pickets were withdrawn a body of Rebel Cavalry with a Light Battery attacked us, but we drove them back. We halted several times and our Battery opened upon them. They shelled us until nearly dark, when we reached this place and rejoined the Army. Our Regiment is now on picket duty, and I am writing as I sit on a gate under an apple tree. I have just had a good feast of ripe cherries. Last night our rations came up, and our two days' fast was ended. We have had much rain, and the roads are in a horrible condition. We are so weary that even when marching at night the men will go to sleep. One night last week I dismounted to rest and immediately went to sleep. Some one woke me up and said the Regiment had moved on. My horse was missing, and I followed on until I found her feeding by the road side. Part of the 2nd R.I. will go home in a few days, but as I have agreed to stay I shall remain. We do not know yet what will be done with the veterans. If the Regiment is broken up I have a promise of a staff position on the Brigade staff. The month of May has ended, and the Second R.I. has found it one of sorrow. We have lost since leaving our winter quarters Capt. Joseph McIntyre and Capt. John P. Shaw killed. Lt. Col. S.B.M. Read, Chaplain John D. Buegless, Capt. John G. Beveridge, Lieut. Charles A. Waldron, Lieut. Aaron Clark, Lieut. Edmund F. Prentiss, and Lieut. Patrick Lyons wounded, beside nearly one hundred enlisted men killed and wounded. Surely war is a cruel business, and what sorrow will be felt in R.I. when the sad news reaches our friends.

June 1st 1864—This morning our Corps started at an early hour and had a hard march to Cold Harbor where we arrived this afternoon. We were here in 1862 under McClellan, and some of the scenes are familiar. On arriving we formed in line of battle in the rear and in support of the Vermont Brigade. Artillery firing was kept up by both sides until dark, and then we went at our old trade of digging sand. Quite a respectable line of earthworks was made, and we lay down behind them for a little rest. Our Brigade just missed a share in the assault that our Corps made just before dark. We were formed in two lines, the 10th and 37th Mass. in the first line and the 2nd R.I. and 7th Mass. in the second line. Just as the line was ready to move forward a force of Rebels with a Battery appeared on our left flank and opened fire. Gen. Thomas H. Neill, now in command of our Division, rode up and ordered our Brigade to move to the left and protect the threatened flank. As we left the line the 2nd Conn. Heavy Artillery, a Regiment two years old but without active

Lieut.
Aaron Clark

service having been on duty in Washington, took our place. This Regiment numbered more men than our entire Brigade, and in their charge they lost their Colonel (Kellogg) and a large number of officers and men. Our Brigade charged front and advanced on the enemy and drove them from our flank. When we returned we found that the battle was ended, and but for the Artillery all was quiet.

Cold Harbor June 2/64—This morning some troops from the Second Corps relieved us, and we moved to a new position on the right where we relieved some troops of the 18th Corps. Here we covered ourselves with rifle pits and spent the days. Sharpshooters have been at work all day, and it has been anything but pleasant. This afternoon we had a heavy rain storm that seemed to dampen the ardor of both Armies. We slept under fire of the enemy.

Friday June 3rd 1864—We have had a terrible battle today, and the killed and wounded number in thousands. For some reason, perhaps because so many men go home tomorrow, the 2nd R.I. has been kept in the reserve. We saw the whole fight and only lost two men. Nothing seems to have been gained by the attack today, except it may be that it settles the question of whether the enemy's line can be carried by direct assault or not. At any rate General Grant means to hold on, and I know that he will win in the end.

June 4/64—We have remained quiet all day in our entrenchments with Artillery and picket firing going on constantly. As the men who have not re-enlisted will go home tomorrow, we have passed the days in preparing to say goodbye. Many letters have been written by those who are to remain and given to those who are to go home and deliver. I suppose the officers who are to leave us are happy, but I am glad to remain.

Cold Harbor, Va., June 5th 1864—Three years have passed away since I first enlisted. It seems a long time as I look back. If I had not agreed to remain in the service I should now be as wild with joy as those who are to go home. But I am happy and do not feel envious at all, for if God spares my life I am determined to see the end of the Rebellion. I cannot complain of my treatment since I enlisted. I have been a Private, a Corporal, Sergeant Major, Second Lieutenant, and Adjutant, and if everything works well I shall climb higher. It is not ambition that keeps me in the Army, however, for I trust I have higher and better motives for serving my country.

Wagon Park, 6th Corps, near Cold Harbor, Va., June 6/64—Today we have said goodbye to our friends who return home. Two hundred and sixty five men under command of Major Henry C. Jencks left tonight and are now on their way to R.I. Three hundred and twenty six men whose time has not expired, or who have not re-enlisted are left in the field. Capt. Henry H. Young, First Lieut. & Adjutant Elisha H. Rhodes, Asst. Surgeon William F. Smith, Second Lieut. Thorndike J.

Officers who returned to Rhode Island on June 6, 1864. Above left, Lieut. Stephen West; right, Capt. John R. Waterhouse. Below, right; Lieut. Henry K. Southwick.

Smith, and Second Lieut Samuel B. Russell remain with them. First Lieut. Edmund F. Prentiss is also on the rolls but is absent wounded. Capt. Young is on staff duty at Brigade Headquarters, and this leaves me senior officer and in command of the Regiment. We have one hundred and fifty men present for duty, and the balance are on detail or sick in hospitals. I have been offered a staff position, but if Capt. Young is to remain absent I prefer to command the Regiment. The responsibility will be great, and as I am but twenty-two years of age, the authorities may think me too young. But with God's help I shall try to do my duty by the men. Since the first of June the 2nd R.I. has lost killed and wounded twenty-five men. There is some talk of detailing the 2nd R.I. as Provost Guard at Corps Headquarters. I hope this will be done but cannot tell for we never yet had any safe duty to perform. We expect to go to the front tonight or tomorrow morning.

Veterans' Den, Underground, Cold Harbor, Va., June 7/64—This morning we are back in the trenches and I am no longer the Adjutant but the Commanding Officer. Gen. Wright commanding the 6th Corps says I shall have command of the Regiment and has directed me to reorganize it for future service. For the present I have made two Companies with Lieut. Smith in command of one and Lieut. Russell the other. My Sergeant-Major Geo. T. Easterbrooks is acting as Adjutant. I have just issued my first order: "General Order No. 1," assuming command and giving some advice to the men. Sergeants are acting as Lieutenants, and it will be several days before we can get our promotions. I have been already recommended by the general officers of the Brigade and Division for the Captaincy. We are in a large sandy field covered with forts and entrenchments. The men have burrowed underground to protect themselves from shells which the Rebels throw from mortars. Every few minutes a shell comes screaming over, and then we run to our holes. It is amusing as well as dangerous. We are covered with dirt, but still I am happy.

It appears now as if we were to make a regular siege of the enemy's works. Tomorrow we are to go into the front line for twenty four hours' tour of duty.

June 8/64, Front line, Cold Harbor, Va.—We are taking our turn at the front, and the Rebel line is only about two hundred yards from us. The men are well protected by bomb proofs. Constant firing of musketry and Artillery is kept up by both sides. Today we had a flag of truce sent into our line to bury the dead. This gave us a chance to get out of our holes and look at the Rebel works. They appear to be very strong. The Rebels who came with the flag were good natured and ready to talk with us.

June 9/64—At 2 o'clock this morning the 2nd R.I. was relieved from the trenches by a Mass. Regiment, and we are now a few hundred yards in the rear. I had rather be in the front, for here we catch most of the shells fired at the first line. But we are well sheltered. The weather is very hot and dusty, and as the men are obliged to stay in line and not move about, life is irksome. When we send for water the details have to run the gauntlet of the Rebel fire, and it is anything but pleasant. Mail should be directed to:

Lieut E.H. Rhodes
Comdg 2nd R.I. Vols.
4th Brigade 2nd Division 6th Corps
Via Washington

June 10/64—I have recommended Second Lieut. Thorndike J.Smith to be promoted First Lieut. and shall make him Adjutant of the Regiment as soon as I can get some officers. I have recommended Sergeant Major George T. Easterbrooks and one other Sergeant to be Second Lieutenants and shall promote from the ranks as fast as possible. I saw Capt. Wm. B. Rhodes of Battery "E" R.I. Artillery and Capt. George H. Rhodes of the Cavalry today.

What a strange scene meets the eye on every side. Forts on the plains and in the woods. Constant roar of Artillery and bursting of shells. Even as I write I saw one poor fellow shot down as he left his shelter. May God forgive the men who brought about this war. I fear that I shall yet hate them.

Headquarters 2nd R.I. Vols, Near Charles City Court House, Va., June 14/64—When will wonders cease. Thirty six hours ago the Army of the Potomac was within nine miles of Richmond, and now we are forty miles distant. Sunday night June 12th we left our works at Cold Harbor under cover of the darkness and took the road towards the James River. We marched all night and all day Monday the 13th, crossing the Chickahominy River at Jones bridge about dark. Here we encamped tired and sleepy. I became so sleepy that I could not ride my horse and so walked to keep awake. This morning at 4 o'clock we started again, and we are now near Charles City and about three miles from the James River. The men are used up by the intense heat and fatigue of the past week. As soon as my tent was pitched I lay down and slept for four hours. It is said that we are to cross the James River and attack Richmond from the south side. Either side suits me if we can only win.

James River near Brandon, Virginia, June 16/64—This morning we left Charles City and marched to this place on the James. Our Corps is in line along the river bank. We are enjoying the scene very much. My shelter tent is within a few feet of the river, and I have been lying in the shade all day watching the gunboats and transports pass up and down the river. The river is about half a mile wide, and a pontoon bridge has been laid. The wagon trains are passing over the bridge while some of the troops are crossing in steamers. The 5th Corps is now crossing, and we expect to take our turn tomorrow. We have enjoyed a good bath in the river, and the men are washing their clothes, having been deprived of this privilege for a long time. One of the darkey servants has never seen a river before and called it a "Right smart brook." While watching a steamboat sail by he said, "Does dat dar wheel turn on de ground?" He also asked "How they got dot boat out of the water nights." We have had much fun with him. This morning we heard heavy firing up the river from General Butler's lines. I suppose we shall attack Petersburg or Fort Darling next. The 7th Mass. Regiment left our Brigade yesterday for home, their time having expired.

Near Petersburg, Va., June 17/64—Last night we crossed the pontoon bridge over the James River to Windmill Point and marched all night halting this morning a short time for breakfast. We then continued on and made about twenty-five miles to this point which is about three miles from the city of Petersburg. Here we ran against the enemy line of forts and went into line of battle for the night.

June 19/64—Yesterday morning we found that the Rebels had abandoned their first line of works, and we took possession. In the morning I had some rifle practice at the Rebels in a line of works in our front. About noon I was standing with Lieut. Thorndike J. Smith on a little knoll in rear of our works when we saw his father who is a private in the Regiment and acting as Postmaster coming across the plain in our rear. Our cook carrying some pork, hard bread and coffee was with him, and as the bullets whistled past his head would duck and dodge. I was laughing at his strange antics when Lieut. Smith asked me to tell his father not to come to the front again until dark. Before I could reply I heard a *thud* and saw Lieut. Smith falling. I caught him in my arms and called for a stretcher. He was shot through the back, the bullet penetrat-

Lieut. Thorndike J. Smith

ing his lung. I sent him to the hospital, and we fear he will die. He is a fine fellow and a brave man and is to me like my own brother. I pray God that his life may be spared. His father dropped the letters on the ground and went to the rear with his wounded son. The bullet has since been taken out of Lieut. Smith's breast having passed through his body. At 4 P.M. our Division was ordered to charge and leaving the shelter of our works we rushed across the plain for the second line. But we could not take them, but did succeed in holding a new line half way between the two, which our men are now fortifying. The Second R.I. behaved splendidly, and I am very proud of them. We lost seven men. A division of colored soldiers charged over the same ground but were driven back. They fought well and left many dead on the field. During the night the Rebels fired into my Regiment from a rail road cut on my left flank, but after some confusion we drove them back. Half of the men stood in arms while the other half slept a little. It was a hard night for us. Even as I write the bullets are whistling over my head, but my men have scooped out a place in the sand for me, and I write in some degree of safety. I have not been much in favor of colored soldiers, but yesterday's work convinced me that they will fight. So Hurrah for the colored troops! Shot and shell, canister and bullets, all the time. Petersburg is only about two miles away, but yet it is afar off.

Near Petersburg, Va., June 20/64—Last night at 9 o'clock our Brigade was relieved from the front line where we had been under fire for thirty six hours and ordered to the rear a short distance for a rest. About midnight I got the Regiment into camp and then had a good sleep under a peach tree. This morning the Rebels began to shell my camp from Batteries on the other side of the Appomattox River and made it so warm for us that I was obliged to move the Regiment to the shelter of a hill. Some of the shots came from heavy guns and would strike the ground and ricochet for a long distance. One shot struck a barn near and made the splinters fly. The 10th Mass. Vols. go home today their three years having expired. This leaves only the 2nd R.I. Veterans and the 37th Mass. Regiment left of the old Brigade. Yesterday Sergeant Major George F. Polley, 10th Mass. Vols. showed me a board on which he had carved his name, date of birth and had left a place for the date of his death. He had re-enlisted and was expecting a commission as Lieutenant in the 37th Mass. Vols. I asked him if he expected to be killed and he said no, and that he had made his head board only for fun. Today he was killed by a shell fired from a Rebel Battery. Petersburg must be a warm place to live in just now, judging from the amount of iron we have thrown into it. Last night our mortars opened upon the city, and we watched the shells as they rose in the air and fell into the Rebel forts. I am often asked the question "Are you not sorry that you agreed to remain in the service?" I answer "*No*, I want to see the end of the war."

June 22/64—The 2nd R.I. has not been engaged today, as we are at work building rifle pits and guarding the Jerusalem Plank Road on the left flank of the Army. Yesterday President Lincoln paid us a visit. I did not see him, as I was at the front.

June 23/64—Last night just as we finished our rifle pits we were ordered to move, and my Regiment is now supporting Battery "G" 5th U.S. Artillery on the Jerusalem Plank Road. The 6th Corps has been fighting all day, but we have had very little firing on our part of the line, only skirmishing. Lieut. Smith has been sent north and the surgeons have hopes that he may recover.

June 25/64—Still in our rifle pits covered with dust and watching the enemy. A new move is to be made, but of course we do not know the particulars. We shall find out soon enough. I hear that our late Chaplain, John D. Beugless is to go into the U.S. Navy. I am glad for him, for he is a brave man and a good soldier.

June 26/64—Hurrah! My commission as Captain in the 2nd R.I. Vols has arrived, and I was this day mustered into the U.S. service.
Direct: Capt. E.H. Rhodes
                       Camdg 2nd R.I. Vols.
                   4th Brigade 2nd Division
                       6th Corps

Captain E.H. Rhodes

June 27/64—We are now having an easy time on our line, nothing to do but watch the Rebels. Fighting is going on every hour on some part of the line, and our turn will come again soon enough. Yesterday some of my men discovered an ice house full of ice, and we have been having a luxury in the way of iced water. Yesterday being Sunday I attended service at the camp of the 37th Mass. Vols.

June 28/64—Governor James Y. Smith of R.I. has written me a very kind and complimentary letter which cheers me very much. I called today on General Wheaton and met General Wright, General Russell and others. Last night I called on Capt. Wm. B. Rhodes of Battery "E" R.I. Artillery. We have found a supply of lemons and have iced lemon aid in abundance. Yesterday I saw my valise long enough to get out a change of underclothing. The weather is very hot.

June 29/64—This is the first letter that I have written with ink for nearly two months. This morning my headquarters wagon came up and I had my tent pitched, but just as I commenced writing came the order: "Captain, have your Regiment ready to move at a moment's notice." The tent will have to come down, and we shall be off to a new point. I suppose we having had a rest will have to take our turn at siege work. Last night the air was full of shells, and the roar of the cannon was not calculated to make us sleep soundly.

July 1st 1864—Before I could finish my letter of the 29th in ink our Corps moved, and I will finish it in pencil.

The 6th Corps marched to Ream's Station, and while a part built rifle pits the other tore up the rail road track. I made my headquarters in a house near the rail road track and procured some vegetables and ice which helped our Army rations very much. After destroying the road we returned to the lines, and the 2nd R.I. is now supporting Battery "E" R.I. Artillery, and are ready for a fight.

July 2/64—We are back in the lines again, and I have an arbor of green boughs to shield me from the sun. The thermometer stands today at 124, and the men are suffering severely. During our recent raid the 6th Corps caused great destruction, but it's the penalty that Virginia must pay for treason. When we reached Ream's station we found quite a village with a good depot, fair dwellings, work shops and well cultivated gardens and fields fenced in. When we left nothing remained but smoking ruins, trampled fields and a rail road useless for some days.

July 4th 1864—The glorious fourth has come again, and we have had quite a celebration with guns firing shot and shell into Petersburg to remind them of the day. This day makes four 4th of Julys that I have passed in the Army. The first at Camp Clark near Washington, the second at Harrisons Landing, the third at Gettysburg and today at Petersburg. I had a party of officers to dine with me today, and we gave what seemed to me, by way of contrast a fine dinner. This was our bill of fare:

> Stewed oysters (canned)
> Roast turkey (canned)
> Bread pudding
> Tapioca pudding
> Apple pie (made in camp)
> Lemonade
> Cigars

Tomorrow if we march, hard tack and salt pork will be our fare.

The siege goes on, and tons of iron are poured into the city. Rebel prisoners say we can never take the city, but we think differently. Our heavy guns are doing much damage, and we hope to see the end. A good story is told about President Lincoln, which may be true or false. The President unattended walked up to Major General Wright's Headquarters and was stopped by the guard who said: "We do not allow citizens to pass, especially you sanitary fellows." The President sent in the word that Mr. Lincoln would like to see General Wright and was admitted.

Last night I attended church service at the camp of the 37th Mass. Vols.

July 6/64—The 4th Brigade 2nd Division 6th Corps has been broken up, and the 2nd R.I. and 37th Mass. Vols. have been transferred to the Third Brigade, First Division, 6th Corps. The Brigade will be commanded by Col Oliver Edwards, 37th Mass. Vols and the Division by general David A. Russell, formerly Colonel of the 7th Mass Vols. The Regiments in the Brigade are as follows: 37th Mass., 2nd R.I., 49th Penn, 82nd Penn, 119th Penn. and 5th Wisconsin Vols.

We now wear a red cross upon our caps and hats. The Greek cross is the badge of the 6th Corps. The first Division wears *red*, the second *white*, and the third *blue*. Yesterday I had charge of a large detail and built a heavy fort across the Jerusalem Plank Road. This work will be mounted with heavy guns. [Note: This work was afterwards called Fort Davis.] We expect to move soon and join our new Division. The weather is hot, and the men are allowed to wear straw hats when they can get them, but the regulation cap is used on parade, I am wearing a large soft white felt hat which I received by mail. It is not very military but is very comfortable. The Army presents a rather motley appearance now, as little regard is paid to dress and all are dirty and ragged. Still I am happy and probably the best contented man in the Army of the Potomac.

July 8/64—Yesterday we moved our camp and joined the 1st Division. We are now in rear of the main line, and my camp is in a fine oak grove. We enjoy the shade very much. It is a little lonely, for we have little to do. Our Batteries at the front keep up a constant fire, but we are too far away to see the result. We have been mustered for pay which we hope will come soon, for not an officer has any money. General Grant has issued an order for the Companies to issue rations to the officers the same as to the enlisted men, and the value of the rations will be charged to us on our pay rolls. But for this we should starve. The 4th R.I. Vols. has joined the Army of the Potomac and are in the 9th Corps. We have just heard of the destruction of the Rebel Steamer *Alabama* by the Yankee *Kearsage*. Hurrah![34]

On board U.S. Transport Peril, James River July 11/64—Will wonders cease. Saturday night the 9th, we left camp with the 6th Corps at 11 o'clock and marched to City Point. Here we remained until dark on Sunday the 10th when the 2nd R.I. and 37th Mass Vols. embarked on the Steamer *Peril* and started down the James River. Our steamer is a fine large propeller, and in conversation with the Captain I found that he used to be acquainted with my father. The men are rather crowded, but the officers have fine staterooms in the saloon, and we are more than enjoying ourselves. It is very early in the morning, but altogether too pleasant to sleep.

6 A.M. We are now fifty miles from City Point. We had to anchor two hours during the night for some reason. The river banks are very beautiful, and we are enjoying the scenery. Many vessels loaded with troops and Batteries are sailing with us. I suppose we are bound for Maryland where Early's Rebel Army is making a raid. Well, this suits me, for I shall prefer Maryland to Virginia. Many of the officers like myself are busy writing letters to be mailed when we reach Washington.

8 A.M. We are just passing Fortress Monroe and the scene is a grand one. Hampton Roads is full of shipping, including war vessels. I was interested in seeing a three turreted Monitor called the *Roanoke*. She looks as if she could do good service. One large French man-of-war is anchored near the fort, and as we passed her yards were manned by

sailors in white uniforms, and at the firing of a gun all the sails were set. I never saw a more beautiful sight. After passing Fortress Monroe the officers were invited to take breakfast.

2 P.M. We have just dined and notwithstanding the style displayed we have enjoyed a good dinner. Our ship rolls a good deal in Chesapeake Bay, and some of the officers look very pale, but I being something of an old salt, rather enjoy it. The transport *Rebecca Clyde* came along side of our ship, and our Brigade band gave them some music, which was returned by the band of the 2nd Connecticut.

4 P.M. We have had a very heavy shower, but it is now pleasant again. We are just entering the mouth of the Potomac River. The scenery is fine. 6 P.M. Supper is over and we are telling stories and smoking. 9 P.M. This has been a delightful day. Life on a transport is certainly very pleasant, and I wish we could prolong it for a month. I shall have a good sleep tonight without any cannon accompaniment which we have had for more than two months past. We shall arrive in Washington sometime tomorrow.

Steamer Peril, Potomac River, July 12/64—4 A.M. I am up early this morning, for it is altogether too pleasant to sleep. The steamer anchored again last night and has just started.

6 A.M. The river begins to narrow, and the banks can be more plainly seen. We are now near Acquia Creek and sixty miles from Washington. Then for the old life again, dust and heat.

10 A.M. We are passing Mount Vernon, and our band is playing a dirge in memory of the "Father of his country." Fort Washington is in sight, and a party of ladies are waving a U.S. flag. Our band played the "Star Spangled Banner." The Capital is in sight, and soon we shall go on shore and learn the news.

12 M. Here we are at the 6th Street Wharf in Washington, and we can hear musketry which does not sound far off. We do not know what it means.

Brightwood near Washington, D.C., July 12/64—Well, this has been a queer day. We landed from the steamer at 12 M. As I stepped upon the wharf and heard the firing in the distance I supposed that it was troops drilling. An officer approached me and said: "Who commands these troops?" I replied: "I command one Regiment." He then said: "Have your men form, and I will send a guide to show you the way to Brightwood, and do not wait for your horses." I told him that I knew the way and did not require a guide. While the men were disembarking the staff officer informed me that the Rebel General Early was near Bright-wood, and an attack was expected immediately. I marched up Sixth Street, and then up Pennsylvania Avenue, and followed Sixteenth Street to Brightwood. The people in Washington seemed to be very happy to see us and were much frightened. Many citzens had guns in their hands, and the Treasury clerks were drawn up in front of the Treasury Buildings. One young man had on a straw hat, linen duster, kid gloves, well polished boots and eyeglasses. He also had a full set of equipments and a musket. Wishing to be polite to me as I passed he "Presented Arms" with the barrel of his musket to the front. Our boys cheered him in great style. Several citizens fell into our ranks with guns in their hands and seemed to be full of fight. The ladies brought water to the men and some passed to the soldiers packages of tobacco as we marched along. On arriving at Fort Stevens I formed my Regiment in the old camp of the 7th and 10th Mass Vols. in rear of the fort. In 1861 and early in 1862 our Brigade then composed of the 2nd R.I., 7th and 10th Mass. and 36th New York Vols were camped at this place. Fort Stevens was then called Fort Massachusetts and was built by the 7th and 10th Mass. Regiments, while the next fort to the right was called Fort Slocum and was built by the 2nd R.I. Vols. We did not expect in 1861 that these forts would ever be of service, but now we are glad that we helped to build them. We remained in line until about 6 P.M. when with a picked force the 2nd R.I. and 37th Mass. went to the front. Fort Stevens was firing shell into the Rebel lines while Fort Slocum was sending its shots with fearful screams after Early's men. Our column passed through the gate of Fort Stevens, and on the parapet I saw President Lincoln standing looking at the troops. Mrs. Lincoln and other ladies were sitting in a carriage behind the earthworks. We marched in line of battle into a peach orchard in front of Fort Stevens, and here the fight began. For a short time it was warm work, but as the President and many ladies were looking at us every man tried to do his best. Just at dark I was ordered to take my Regiment to the right of the line which I did at a double quick. I never saw the 2nd R.I. behave better. An old gentleman, a citizen in a black silk hat with a gun in his hand, went with us and taking position behind a stump fired as cool as a veteran. The Rebels at first supposing us to be Penn. Militia stood their ground, but prisoners told me that when they saw our lines advance without a break they knew we were veterans. The Greek Cross of our Corps told the story, and the Rebels broke and fled. I lost three men wounded. It was a fine little fight but did not last long. A surgeon standing on the fort beside President Lincoln was wounded. We slept upon the field, glad that we had saved Washington from capture, for without our help the small force in the forts would have been overpowered. Early should have attacked early in the morning. "Early was Late."

July 13/64, Tennallytown, Md.—The Rebels retired last night, and this morning we followed to this place where we are in camp.

Orcutt's Cross Roads, Md., July 14/64—We moved to this place today and are now waiting for orders.

Poolesville, Md., July 15/64—We reached this place today and find that the Rebels are all across the Potomac River and on their own soil in Virginia. I have just returned from a ride through the village and have enjoyed the kindly greetings of the people very much. It is not like Virginia at all. The people are all glad to see us. The country is charming and is in marked contrast with that of Virginia. As we entered the village of Poolesville this morning a staff officer told me to turn right on reaching the Common and march across it. We did so, and much to our surprise and horror we saw a man dangling by the neck at the end of a rope attached to a scaffold. He proved to be a soldier named Hymes who belonged to the 65th New York Vols. who had been acting as a spy for the Rebels. Being detected he was tried by a Court Martial, promptly found guilty, sentenced to die, and hung. He had on part of a uniform and was a miserable looking fellow. I understand that he had made several visits to the enemy before he was captured.

July 16th 1864—This morning we marched to White's ferry on the Potomac. A Regiment of Rebel Cavalry fired at us with carbines from the Virginia shore as soon as we came in sight. Battery "C" 1st R.I. Artillery went into position and soon with their shells sent the Rebels flying behind the hills. It was fun for us to see them urge their horses into a run to escape the shells. Our Division then forded the stream and again landed in Dixie. The river was wide at this point and about three feet deep, and we were very wet when we landed in Virginia. About dark we arrived in the vicinity of Leesburg and encamped for the night. The men were wet and uncomfortable and glad to gather about the fires to dry themselves.

Near Leesburg, Va. Sunday July 17/64—Today we have remained quietly in camp, and I have enjoyed the rest very much. The view of the mountains is very fine.

Monday July 18/64—Today we left Leesburg and crossed the mountains at Clark's Gap, passing through the village of Hamilton. Greatly to our surprise we were welcomed by the ladies of this village with waving Union flags and handkerchiefs. Such loyal demonstrations in a Virginia town were never seen by the 6th Corps before. We then passed the village of Purcellville, an unimportant place. We found in the road many broken down and burned wagons which the Rebels had abandoned in their retreat when hard pressed by our Cavalry. Just before dark we arrived at Snickers Gap in the Blue Ridge Montains and commenced the ascent. The grand view from the summit repaid us for our hard work. On one side we could see the valley of the Potomac with the blue hills of Maryland in the distance, while on the other side the fertile valley of the Shenandoah stretched out like a map as far as the eye could reach. The Shenandoah River rippled and glistened in the setting sunlight at our feet. Soon the booming of cannon and the sharp rattle of musketry warned us that our old enemy was near. Hurrying down the slope we found that a part of General Hunter's Army had crossed the river and had been driven back, losing many men. A Rebel Battery discovered us and opened fire but fortunately did no injury to our Brigade, but several were killed and wounded in our 3rd Division. Batteries "C" and "G" 1st R.I. Artillery soon made it so uncomfortable for the Rebels that they ceased firing. As soon as it became dark the 2nd R.I. was sent out to picket the bank of the river. I have forty of my men armed with Spencer Repeating rifles that will hold seven cartridges at one loading. I borrowed these guns from the 37th Mass. who are armed with them and have used them for some time. We marched silently down to the river, and I posted ten men under cover within forty yards of the enemy before they discovered us. When they found our position it was too late for them to drive us away. The balance of my Regiment I held in reserve. We could hear the Rebels talking and speculating upon the chances of being driven back by the Yankees at daylight.

Tuesday July 19/64—We passed a very uncomfortable night with very little sleep. At daylight this morning four wounded soldiers who had remained on the Rebel side of the river all night attempted to cross to our lines. A Rebel officer ordered his men to fire upon them, which they did, but the men reached us in safety. I had forbidden my men to fire when on picket as it is murderous business, but when I heard this officer order his men to shoot wounded men I ordered my line to open fire which they did with much spirit. The Rebels supposing we had the muzzle loading muskets would leave their shelter as soon as we fired and shout some insulting message. But they soon found that the fire was kept up, my forty men doing the work of perhaps five times as many. One Rebel called out: "I say, Yankees, what kind of guns have you got?" Our only reply was another volley. All day we kept up our fire, but as the Second was behind banks of earth no damage was done to us. We saw the Rebels carry off seven wounded men. In order to get to the river for water to drink the enemy would sometimes expose themselves when they would pay the penalty by a wound. I made the acquaintance of a Union family near by and took tea with them. The lady was very kind to our wounded and even carries water to them on the field. Her house was struck several times by shot and bullets, but she was as cool as an old soldier.

Wednesday July 20/64—This morning the 2nd R.I. and the 37th Mass were ordered to cross the river. We dashed into the stream and gained the opposite bank, to find that it was an island. We took to the water again and soon landed on the Rebel side. The enemy retreated. I found some good chickens however at a house near by. We marched to the village of Berryville where we remained until dark and then started back towards Washington.

Thursday July 21/64—We reached Leesburg today after a march of thirty miles without sleep. Leesburg is a very pretty town. We passed through and camped at a place called Goose Creek. Soon after passing Leesburg, Mosby's Rebel Cavalry attacked our trains and captured a number of sick and wounded men. Five of these captured belonged to my Regiment.

Friday July 22/64—Today we marched to this place which is called Difficult Creek and shall remain over night.

Tennallytown, D.C., July 23/64—This morning we crossed Chain Bridge and are once more in the District of Columbia. We are under orders to move, and I expect we shall take transports back to Petersburg. Our campaign has been brief but successful.

Near Washington, D.C. July 24/64—Today I received a First Lieutenant's commission for 2nd Lieut. Thorndike J. Smith and Second Lieutenant's commissions for Sergeant Geo. T. Easterbrooks and Sergeant Charles W. Gleason. This will give me four officers. Governor James Y. Smith wrote me that he wanted me to do all in my power to retain our Regimental organization. I have no doubt now but what we shall soon have a full Regiment. We may remain here for a few days, as

Sergeant George T. Easterbrooks

we need supplies, and then we shall probably return to Petersburg. Some of my men need shoes and suffered much during our late march. The five men captured by Mosby from the Second R.I. have made their escape and are now in camp again. Our camp is near Fort Reno and Fort Gaines on the Maryland side of the river. Our camps are filled with visitors, ladies and gentlemen who seem to take great delight in talking to the veterans of the 6th Corps.

Sergeant
Charles W. Gleason

Tuesday July 26/64—We left camp about noon and marched through Rockville to this camp which is about five miles beyond the village. The Rebel General Early is again moving upon Maryland and instead of going back to Petersburg we are to try another campaign in this state. Yesterday I rode into Washington and enjoyed a good dinner at a hotel. It was quite a treat to meet my friends there. We have marched twenty miles today, and the heat has been intense.

Near Hyattsville, Md., July 27/64—Today we marched to this village which is twelve miles from Frederick City where it is said we are bound. We are near Sugar Loaf Mountain, and the scenery is very fine.

Jefferson, Md., July 28/64—Today we marched through Frederick City, a fine large town and are resting for the night at or near Jefferson.

July 29/64, Halltown, Va.—We left Jefferson this morning and marched to Harpers Ferry where we crossed the Potomac on a pontoon bridge and are now in camp four miles beyond. Harpers Ferry is delightfully situated in the mountains, and the scenery is very picturesque. All of the government buildings are in ruins having been burned by the U.S. troops in 1861 to prevent them falling into the hands of the Rebels. Halltown is a small village and not of much account. We are now at the opening of the Shenandoah Valley and the Shenandoah River is not far away.

Petersville, Md., July 31/64—Yesterday we made a long and hard march into the mountains near Harpers Ferry, Virginia and then recrossed the Potomac and reached this place at 3 o'clock A.M. The poor old Sixth Corps has been on its feet for a long time, and we are very weary. But it is all for the Union, and I trust we are doing good work that will help the boys we left at Petersburg, Va.

Near Frederick City, Md., Monday August 1/64—Several men were overcome by heat on our march to this place. Yesterday the thermometer marked 130 in the sun. Yesterday we passed through the town of Jefferson again. As it was Sunday all the people were out in their good clothes. It must have been a queer Sabbath for them.

August 2/64—We remained in camp today, and I paid a visit to the city and enjoyed it very much. The people were kind, and I was much pleased with the neat appearance of the streets and houses. We shall probably move from here tonight or tomorrow morning.

Monocacy River, Md., Aug. 4/64—This morning we left Frederick City and marched to this place. My camp is in a wheat field on the bank of the river, and we have enjoyed a good bath. It is cloudy, and we hope for rain to cool the air and lay the dust. The wagon train has arrived, and as we have not seen our baggage in many days we were glad to get our fresh clothing. We hope to remain in this camp for a few days for rest.

General Russell commanding our Division has said some kind things about me, all of which is pleasant for a soldier to hear. Buckeystown is the nearest settlement to our camp, and we send our letters there to be mailed. It is quite a village for this part of the country.

Near Monocacy River, Md., Aug. 4/64—This morning I received an order from Headquarters 6th Corps detaching the 2nd R.I. from the 37th, recognizing it as a Regiment and ordering me to report to Colonel Edwards commanding our Brigade. I reported and received this reply: "Captain, if you will handle your Regiment in the future as well as you have in the past I shall be satisfied." I am much elated over this order, as steps were being taken by certain parties to consolidate the 2nd R.I. with some other command. Now we are all right, and as soon as I can get recruits we shall have a full Regiment.

Aug. 5/64—Major Ellis, a Division staff officer, died yesterday from the effects of wounds received at Spottsylvania. The entire Division was under arms and saluted the remains as they were bourne past our lines. The President's fast day was generally observed in the Army. We held services at Brigade Headquarters.

Near Harpers Ferry, Va., Aug. 7th 1864—Friday night at 9 o'clock we received orders to march and as we were waiting for the final orders I lay down on the ground holding the bridle of my horse in my hand and went to sleep. The officers and men did the same. At daylight yesterday (Saturday) I awoke feeling cold and found that it had been raining all night. As I had no blankets or covering of any kind I was wet and uncomfortable, but a cup of hot coffee warmed me some, and at 9 A.M. we started and forded the Monocacy River and passed for the third time within a week through the town of Jefferson. After dark we halted for supper and then continued on to Sandy Hook on the Potomac River. My Regiment was detailed as rear guard and marched some distance in rear of the main column picking up the stragglers. We passed under the canal through a culvert and marched upon the tow path of the canal with the Potomac River on one side and the canal on the other. The towpath was about eight feet wide, and the marching was not good. About midnight a staff officer came back and said that if I wished I could halt until daylight. We tied our horses to the brush and went to sleep. The staff officer could not find the way back to the Brigade and so stayed with me.

Harpers Ferry, Va., Aug. 7th/64—This morning we started along the towpath and arrived at Harpers Ferry where we crossed the Potomac on a pontoon bridge. This made twenty-five times that I have crossed the Potomac since I entered the Army. We are now in camp with our Brigade. Major General Philip H. Sheridan has arrived and has taken command of this Department. This looks like work before us with little prospect of going back to Petersburg at present.

Near Charlestown, Va., Wednesday Aug. 10/64—We left Harpers Ferry this morning and marched to this camp passing through Charlestown. This is the place where John Brown was hung and we had each band and drum corps play "John Brown's Body Lies Mouldering in the Grave." "But His Soul Goes Marching On" as we passed through the streets of the town. The men joined in singing the hymn much to the disgust of the people. I saw at Harpers Ferry the engine house where John Brown was captured and at Charlestown the spot where his execution took place.

Near Opequon Creek, Va., Thursday Aug 11/64—This morning we continued our march and are now in camp for the night. We are not far from the city of Winchester which I hope to visit, for it is a famous place in the Shenandoah Valley and said to be a fine little city. Several battles have been fought there during the war.

Milltown near Winchester, Va., Friday Aug. 12/64—This morning after starting on our march our Brigade was detached from the Division and ordered to Winchester, there to await the arrival of our wagon trains and then escort them to the front. The Brigade with the exception of the 2nd R.I. remained in the city. We were ordered to Milltown, a little village one mile south of the city on the Strasburg Pike. On arriving I formed line on a creek running across the road and posted my pickets. I then arrested some of the citizens who were spying about and sent them under guard to Winchester. There is a large flour mill here owned by a Mr. Hollinsworth who lives in a fine brick house with pleasant grounds. Mr. Hollinsworth and wife offered me the use of a room, but I preferred to sleep under the trees. The family were strong Union people, and I have arranged to take my meals with them. I have taken a ride into the city and found many Union people. In fact we were very much surprised to be treated so kindly. Winchester is an old fashioned sort of place, inclined to be aristocratic but its glory departed on the advent of the war. This evening myself and officers passed the evening with Mr. and Mrs. Hollinsworth and Mrs. H. gave us some good music on the piano.

Near Middletown, Va., Aug. 14/64—Yesterday the wagon trains arrived at Winchester, and our Brigade took charge of them and escorted them to this point. We are not far from Cedar Creek, and the Rebel Army is on the south side of the Creek. This valley is very beautiful, a perfect garden.

Aug. 15th & 16th 1864—We remained quietly in our camp near Cedar Creek.

Near Charlestown, Va., Aug. 19/64—Well here we are again back in the vicinity of Harpers Ferry. Wednesday night we left our camp near Cedar Creek and began to fall back. All night we marched and the next day also until dark when we reached the Opequon Creek where we crossed and then halted. After riding twenty four hours I was very weary and so sleepy that I could not sit in my saddle. As soon as we halted I lay down in a clover field and went to sleep. Just as I was getting comfortable an order came for us to take position on a bluff overlooking the river, as the enemy was supposed to be coming. Here we built a slight breastwork of rails and waited for the enemy, but he did not appear. At daylight we resumed the march, and at dark yesterday we reached this place. Today we are getting a little sleep and rest. I shall try to get a leave of absence for five days to go to Philadelphia.

Aug. 20/64—Hurrah! My leave of absence for five days has just been granted, and I am off for Philadelphia.

Aug. 21st 1864—I rode over to General Custer's Cavalry camp and requested an escort of Cavalry to go with me to Harpers Ferry. He told me if I would wait until tomorrow morning that he would send one with me but could not do so today. Being anxious to go on I armed my orderly and meeting a soldier mounted and going to Harpers Ferry I pressed on. We narrowly escaped capture at the cross roads beyond Halltown, the guerillas leaving a sutler's wagon that they were plundering as we approached. Arriving at Harpers Ferry I took a freight train to the relay house and a passenger train from there to Philadelphia where I arrived on Monday morning Aug. 22nd and went to the Continental Hotel. I passed five days in Camden, N.J. and then returned to camp. During my absence the Rebels attacked the line held by the 2nd R.I. and one of our men was wounded.

Harpers Ferry, Va., Aug. 27/64—I arrived back to my Regiment at 3 P.M. today and found everything in good condition.

Charlestown, Va., Aug. 30/64—Sunday we left camp at Harpers Ferry and moved to this place again. Yesterday the Rebel Cavalry attacked our lines and we expected a battle, but the enemy withdrew. I am expecting a lot of recruits now in a few days. This will give me a larger command.

Picket line, 1st Division 6th Corps near Charlestown, Va., Sept. 2/64—Today I am on duty as Division Officer of the Day and in charge of the picket line. I shall be relieved at dark today, as I went on duty last night. Last night I was in the saddle most of the time riding along the line in the darkness. It was not very pleasant work, as our line runs through the woods, and there is much fallen timber. The country in this vicinity is very fine, and the farms are well cultivated. The people seem to be well disposed towards us, but it may be from policy or even force of habit. One gentleman kindly sent me some iced water by a servant as I passed his house. The nights are getting cold, and we find our overcoats to be very comfortable.

Near Clifton, Va., Sept. 3/64—Today we left our camp near Charlestown and moved up the valley to this point. About dark the enemy attacked the line held by Gen. Crooks command (the 8th Corps) but were repulsed. Our Corps did not get into the fight. Only a few men were injured. An officer has just called and said: "Captain, you will have your command under arms at 4 A.M. tomorrow, as an attack by the enemy is expected." Well let them attack, we shall be ready for them.

Sept. 4/64—We were in line at 4 A.M., but the enemy did not put in an appearance.

Sept. 5/64—The Second R.I. had quite an adventure yesterday which I will try to describe. After standing under arms until it was ascertained that the enemy were not in our immediate front, I was ordered to report to the Brigade commander, Colonel Edwards. The Colonel told me that I was to proceed with the 2nd R.I. and 5th Wisconsin Volunteers out on the road and establish an outpost about one mile from camp. The Colonel supposed that I was the senior officer and would have command, but we found out that the Captain commanding the 5th Wisconsin ranked me by date of commission, and he therefore took charge. A Company from the 37th Mass. Vols. commanded by Captain Chamney was attached to my Regiment for the day. We marched out for a mile across the open plain until we reached a high hill with a thick hedge surrounding three sides of it. Here I suggested that we halt and entrench, leaving the main body of the troops while a Company or two be deployed as skirmishers and sent into the woods in our front. But the Captain commanding the 5th Wisconsin, a German and brave man, over ruled me and insisted upon forming line in the woods. We found the woods filled with large rocks, while the trees stood so thick as to render it impossible to see far in any direction. The 2nd R.I. formed line of battle with the Company from the 37th Mass. on the left flank while the 5th Wisconsin went through the woods for perhaps a quarter of a mile and deployed as skirmishers. I had with me a mounted orderly from Brigade Headquarters, and he asked permission to look for some chickens. I gave him permission but cautioned him to be on the watch for the enemy. About noon as I was writing a letter I heard some shots, and the orderly bareheaded leaped his horse over a rail fence and landing near me shouted: "The Rebels are coming!" I immediately formed my men and ordered Captain Champney to deploy his Company of 37th Mass. on my left flank and then sent word to Captain Charles W. Kempf commanding the 5th Wisconsin. The Captain came back in great excitement and turned over the whole command to me. I requested him to remain in position while I sent the 2nd R.I. back to the hill mentioned above, where the men soon threw up a breastwork of rails. I went out on to the picket line and found that the attack came from a body of Rebel Cavalry.

The firing was heard in camp, and General Russell commanding our Division with Captain Henry H. Young (2nd R.I. on the Brigade staff) came out. In the meantime I had withdrawn the skirmishers and had posted them behind the hedge mentioned above. The General approved of my plans and ordered me to hold the position until dark and then retire to camp. After he retired Captain Young rode out to the front and was fired upon by some Rebels in a house. The Captain rode off at great speed followed by bullets and losing his hat. The Rebel Cavalry rode around to our rear and cut us off from camp, but not having any Artillery they could not drive us from the hill. If I had had a gun I could have made it rain for them with shell. As soon as it became dark, I commenced sending the men into camp, a Company at a time. Silently a Company would leave the hill, march for quite a distance up the line of woods and then cross the plain guided by the camp fires. The mounted officers remained until the last Company had left, and then we rode up along the edge of the woods until we had got beyond the Rebels when we put spurs to our horses and soon reached our lines. It was reported in camp that we were prisoners. Our men were scattered along the entire line of the Army, but are now coming into camp. Our losses, being well sheltered, were few, but we had what they call in this section of the country "A right smart time."

Clifton, Va., Sept. 6/64—We have fortified our camps, building rifle pits in front of each Brigade. But the enemy have retired and have marched up the valley in the direction of Winchester. The weather is cold, and we have had two days of hard rain.

Sept. 7/64—Still in our works at Clifton waiting. I am well and happy and enjoy life as well as most people do. Plenty to do and plenty to eat.

Sept. 9/64—I have heard from Lieut. Smith. He is recovering from his wound and will rejoin the Regiment as soon as the surgeons will allow. I have appointed him Adjutant and shall be glad to see him.

Near Clifton Sept. 11/64—Today I am on duty as Division Officer of the Day and have remained on the picket line. I shall be relieved at 4 P.M. I did not have my tent brought out, as it bid fair to be pleasant last night. About midnight I lay down under a tree, but a violent storm came up, and I got wet. It thundered and lightened in fine style. Three officers of a Pennsylvania Regiment were crowded into a shelter tent, and they tried to make room for me. I crawled in, but it rained so hard that our tent leaked like a sieve, so we had to stand and take it. At daylight this morning it cleared off, and we are feeling better natured in the sunshine.

Sept. 12/64—Last night our Brigade had a dress parade commanded by Colonel Edwards. General Russell and other officers were present. The roads are now very muddy, and our movements may be delayed. The Rebels are now on the line of Opequon Creek, about six miles from our camp.

Sept. 15/64—We have laid out our camps in fine style, and one would suppose from appearances that we were to remain here, but I don't believe it. We have regular drills now, and I drill my Regiment for one hour and a half every afternoon. Dress parade ends the day's work. My mare Katie is a beauty, and I enjoy the rides both on duty and for pleasure which I take every day. Katie is a little wild, but I rather like to have her cut up antics. She is fast and a good jumper as well. It rains nearly every night, but the days are pleasant.

Near Clifton, Va., Sunday Sept. 18/1864—This is a beautiful Sabbath day, and I have enjoyed it very much. Now that we are performing regular camp duty we can make a distinction between Sunday and other days, but when we march this is impossible. A foraging party has been out and returned with a large quantity of things, such as sheep, geese, turkeys, chickens, etc. So just now we are in clover and living on the fat of the land. As it will not last we make the most of it. I selected one lamb from our flock, and we are to make a pet of it. We have named him "Dick" and he is already a great favorite. We may remain here for some time yet.

Headquarters 2nd R.I. Vols. Winchester, Va., Wednesday Sept.

21/64—Thank God my life has been spared and I have been permitted to share in one of the most decisive victories of the war.

Sunday night the 18th we received orders to be in readiness to march at a moment's notice from our camp near Clifton. We knew that the order meant fight, and the men prepared themselves for the coming struggle by throwing away all that might impede their free movements. Ammunition was inspected and the cartridge boxes were filled. Before daylight on the morning of Monday, the 19th, our Division left camp and took the road to Opequon Creek. We marched slowly along, and it was 8 o'clock before we reached the Creek. On the opposite bank our Cavalry were deployed across the plain, and white puffs of smoke here and there showed that the enemy were contesting the advance of the Union horsemen. We crossed the river, and our Brigade was formed in column of Regiments on a sandy plain. The 3rd Division of our Corps was sent forward to attack the Rebel lines partly concealed in the woods and groves, but did not succeed in their efforts, and soon many stragglers were seen coming to the rear. Artillery was freely used on both sides, and after the repulse of our 3rd Division it was generally thought that we would wait until dark and then retire to our fortified camps at Clifton. But we did not know Phil Sheridan. A Rebel Battery enfiladed our Brigade and a shot striking the horse of Captain Kempf commanding the 5th Wisconsin Vols., then bounded down the line of his Regiment and wounded several men. The horse, a large white animal, had a part of his flank shot off and started on a run with his tail hanging by a piece of flesh. The Captain jumped to his feet and shouted: "There goes my ..... horse, my ..... haversack, my ..... blankets, my ..... canteen" and he also named over all of his traps that went off on his horse. (The blank spaces above may be supplied with adjectives.) Notwithstanding the fact that shot and shell were plunging into our Brigade, the group of officers including myself who witnessed this scene rolled in the sand convulsed with laughter. We had to change our position, for the Rebels seemed to have the exact range of our line. About noon our Division was ordered in, and we drove the Rebels back towards the city. The 2nd R.I. reached a little knoll near a house, and finding a heavy stone wall in my front I formed behind it and opened fire. While in this position the 37th Mass, one of the best Regiments I ever saw, and armed with Spencer Seven Shooting Rifles, had advanced well to the front and could be seen about a mile to my right, laying upon the ground exposed to the rife of the Rebel guns in a redoubt. Colonel

Edwards rode up to me and pointing to the 37th Mass. said: "For God's sake, Rhodes, take the 2nd R.I. and go and help Montague." (The Lt. Col. commanding the 37th Mass. is George L. Montague.) I withdrew my Regiment from the hill and moving at a run along the rear of our line of battle tried to gain the cover of a small piece of woods in rear of where the 37th was located. The Rebels seeing my movement shelled us unmercifully, but we kept on and were soon in the woods. Behind this grove I saw the ammunition train and on one wagon in large letters "37th MASS." As they use a copper cartridge, a special wagon is provided for them. Suspecting that the 37th was out of ammunition I hastily caused several boxes to be opened and then had our boys fill their pockets with cartridges. I then deployed the Regiment as a skirmish line and instructed the officers and men to move to the front at a double quick, form on the right of the 37th, have their men lay down and then close intervals to the left by creeping on the ground. The plan worked well, and we reached our position with the loss of only two or three men. I reported to Colonel Montague who was the only man on his feet, and he said: "You can do no good, for I have no ammunition." I told my story, and the cartridges were distributed to his men. The Rebel guns in the earthwork were about four hundred yards off, and a white guidon showed above the parapets. I had my Regiment rise, fire a volley, and then lay down and load again. We did this until the Rebel guns were silenced. We remained here until the main line advanced to our position. General David A. Russell commanding our Division was killed by a shell, and General Frank Wheaton assumed command.

The country for, say, three miles each way about the city is open and covered with farm houses and orchards. In rear of the city as we faced are a line of hills and on the hills are forts. One of them called the Star Fort appeared to be the strongest. Our lines were formed with the 19th Corps on the right and the 6th Corps on the left, while the Cavalry Corps held the extreme right with the 8th Corps in reserve. About 5 P.M. General Sheridan rode down the line hat in hand, and the whole Army cheered and shouted itself hoarse. An order for a general forward movement was given and away we went. Col. Edwards our Brigade commander, rode up to the 37th Mass. and seized the colors and shouted: "Forward!" Away we went, the 37th Mass. and the 2nd R.I. heading for the Battery that we so need. The Rebels limbered up their guns, but we pressed them so hard that they cut the traces and ran off with the horses, leaving two cannon in our hands. The Rebel line broke and fled. Bugle calls were now heard on our right, and soon the Cavalry was seen coming over the rolling ground. With loud shouts they dashed into the mass of fleeing Rebels. Friend and foe mingled together cutting and slashing right and left. The Infantry stood still and looked on. The plain was covered with fleeing Rebels and soon three Batteries on the hills ceased firing and limbering up the guns joined in the flight. All was confusion, and our Batteries galloped to the front, unlimbered and sent their shot and shell into the Rebel mass. Down through the streets of Winchester fled the Rebels, and our Cavalry pursued, and firing up and down the streets took place. Darkness came on and put an end to the fight. Around one house, surrounded by a picket fence, I counted 16 dead Cavalrymen shot off their horses by Rebels in the yard. The Rebels left their dead and wounded on the field as well as one piece of Artillery and several caissons. After the fight the men were wild with joy. I could have knelt and kissed the folds of the old flag that waved in triumph. We captured several Rebel flags which were displayed along the front of our line. I cried and shouted in my excitement and never felt so good before in my life. I have been in a good many battles but never in such a victory as this. "Hurrah for Sheridan!" After the fight our Brigade commander rode up to the 2nd R.I. and called me out and said many complimentary things about us. He also informed me that he had recommended me for a Brevet Major's commission. All of this is very pleasant to me, for the Regiment behaved very finely. The Second lost nine men killed and wounded and seven missing. These may be killed, or they have been taken prisoners. We have captured a large number of Rebel prisoners, and the city is full of wounded. We slept at night on the field.

The next morning the 20th we marched through the city with our Corps, but on arriving on the south side of the town our Brigade turned into a field and formed in column of Regiments. General Sheridan rode up and made a little speech. He praised the Brigade for its good work of yesterday and said we were to be left in Winchester as a garrison. So here we are. Our first duty was to bring in such of the wounded as were not found last night. The Taylor house and the Virginia House, the two principal hotels are used as hospitals and are full of wounded, while the churches as well as private houses are put to the same use. I rode out to the field to superintend the burial of the dead. I found the body of my friend Major James L. Rice 2nd Conn. Vols. and had it buried by itself and shall try to send it home to his friends. He usually wore a fine Masonic pin, but some one had taken it from his coat. In fact he had been robbed of everything of value. I cut a square and compass with his name, rank and Regiment upon an ammunition box cover and placed it at the head of the grave. Poor Rice, he was much older that I, but we were intimate, knowing each other as Masons and comrades.[35] Yesterday one of my men, Private Henry Bromly of Co. "B" captured a Rebel Colonel and turned him in to the Court House yard with other prisoners. We have several hundred officers and a large number of enlisted men as prisoners. I visited the Court House today and talked with some of the Rebel officers. They were much depressed in spirits, for their defeat was a great surprise to them. While on the field I met several ladies from Winchester caring for the wounded of both sides, giving them water. It will take two or three days to finish the burial of the dead. It is a sad duty to perform. I never was in a battle where I felt so comfortable in my Army experience. It did not seem possible for me to be killed or even injured, and for once I rather enjoyed a fight. Perhaps it was because everything was in our favor.

Winchester, Va., Sept. 23/64—We have glorious news today. General Sheridan has again defeated the Rebels at Fisher's Hill, twenty-one miles from here and has taken 16 cannon and a large number of prisoners. We have sent off most of the prisoners, and the wounded are being taken care of. My Regiment is camped on Kent Street, one of the main streets of the city. From a house near I have borrowed some chairs, tables, etc. and have a very comfortable headquarters. Some of the people are very kind to us, but others have a rebellious spirit. No one, citizen or soldier, is allowed to leave the city, and martial law prevails. Some of the ladies, or so-called ladies, are inclined to be saucy and will leave the sidewalk if they meet a Yankee officer and take to the street. When they do this we raise our hats and pass on.

Yesterday I was Officer of the Day and had to ride through the city several times. Winchester is a pretty place. The main street is Loudon Street, while Kent, Market, and Braddock Street run parallel with it. The cross streets are Cork, Water, Piccadilly, etc.

Sept. 27th/64—The city is becoming more quiet, and we are getting used to our new duties. The Army is now one hundred miles away, near Harrisonburg. Last Sunday, Sept. 25th, I was ordered to escort a wagon train to Strasburg, twenty-one miles up the Valley. We had a fine march, passing Milltown, Kernstown, Bartonville, Newton, and Middletown, arriving at our destination at dark. Here we remained over night, and the next morning we started to return to Winchester. I found

Strasburg full of Rebel wounded in charge of Rebel surgeons on their parole. On our way back (Sept 26th) my orderly, Corporal Zacheus Chase, who is armed with a Spencer Seven Shooting Carbine (a present to me) took a ride into the woods looking for chickens. As he did not return I became alarmed and was about to send out a Company to look for him when I saw him riding across the field with four Rebel soldiers in front of his horse. The Corporal held his carbine in hand and as their party came up halted them and reported. Two of these men had brass instruments, having belonged to a Rebel band, but the others were soldiers. I made them retain the instruments and marched them into Winchester and delivered them to the Provost Marshal. The Corporal rode upon them as they were sitting under a tree and explaining that he had seven cartridges in his carbine demanded their surrender, so they came in quietly.

At Newtown a Negro told me that Mosby and some of his men were in town and would attack us as we passed through. I caught a citizen and sent him to Colonel Mosby with my compliments and told him to get out of the town or I would burn it. The citizen asked me if I had orders to burn the town. I told him we would have the fire and get the order afterwards. The Rebels left, and we could see them on the hills, but not near enough to fight. I did not propose to have them attack me from the houses. I sent some skirmishers into the town and then followed with the Regiment. We posted pickets about the outskirts and then cooked our dinner in the street. We found plenty of milk, peaches and grapes which the people gladly sold to us. One lady invited me into her house and gave me a good lunch. Two young ladies present turned their chairs and sat facing the wall, but this did not take my appetite away. I dined at a house near Kernstown and then returned to Winchester arriving late in the afternoon. We made the entire march of 42 miles inside 48 hours, and I did not have a straggler. I passed last evening with some young ladies in the city, and today I am invited to dine with one of the residents. I hope we shall be allowed to spend the winter in Winchester, for it is great fun.

One young girl told me that when the Union and Rebel troops were fighting in front of her house, she ran out on the front steps in her excitement. She also said when she saw the Union flag she cried for joy. All of our supplies come now from Martinsburg by wagon train.

Sept. 29/64—Today I had a present from a citizen in the city of a beautiful bouquet. A Company of recruits, numbering three officers

Capt. James A. Bowen

and eighty men arrived last night. This makes a fine addition to my command. The Company will be known as Co. "E." Company "D" is on the road. The officers of Co. "E" are Capt. James A. Bowen (formerly a Lieutenant in the 12th R.I. Vols.), 1st Lieut. Frank S. Halliday, promoted from Sergeant at the 2nd R.I., and 2nd Lieut. John K. Dorrance, a recent graduate of Brown University.

Oct. 2/64—Today Captain Bowen, Surgeon Smith and myself attended the Episcopal Church, it being the only one in use, the others having been taken for hospitals. This church has a fine organ and a choir. The music was good, and we enjoyed it, but the sermon was a little rebellious. The rector was trying to prove that people should receive all afflictions as from the hand of God and stated that no matter how diabolical the agents sent might be, the people should remember that the Lord sent them. (How are you diabolical Yanks?) He prayed for all Christian rulers. I hope this included Jeff Davis, for he certainly is in need of prayer. There were several Rebel officers present who belong in prison, but were paroled for the day in order that they might attend church. I wonder if the Rebels would do as much for us, if we were prisoners. The sacrament of the Lord's Supper was administered, and one Union soldier (a Private) partook. Most of the ladies were dressed in black, and it seemed almost like a funeral. Several families lost friends in the late battle, and the whole city is in mourning. It made me sad to see the people so sorrowful and weeping, but when I remembered that they brought their troubles upon themselves and that the women encouraged the men to make war on the Government, I could not help feeling that their punishment was just. When the contribution box was passed the Rebels put in Confederate money, but the Union soldiers deposited U.S. money. I saw one citizen take out a roll of Confederate bills, take one off without looking at it and put it in the box. He had better put in a *New York Herald*, for that would have sold for a price here. As we were walking back to camp two young misses in front of us were talking about the service. One said: "Did you see our boys there? I suppose they let them out of prison to attend church." "Oh, you little Rebels!" said Surgeon Smith as we passed on. Yesterday it rained all day, and it was quite cold, but today it is warm and pleasant again. A few nights since while spending an evening with a family in the city a Miss Virginia Wall told me that she knew a Rhode Island man in the Rebel Army, that his name was James R. Sheldon, and that he was a Sergeant in Kershaw's Division and belonged to a Georgia Regiment. This is my old schoolmate and neighbor of Pawtuxet. I have written to his family, as this news is only about two weeks old.

Oct. 4/64—I have taken a walk through the cemetery near the city, and my heart was sad as I passed the newmade graves of Confederate soldiers and saw the wreaths of flowers which mourning hands placed there. I have seen more sad scenes of the war since coming to Winchester than ever before. I met a lady a few days since who has had three brothers killed and one maimed for life since the war began. She is still very bitter and desires to have the war go on. As we walked around some trees we came upon a party of ladies and paroled Rebel officers burying the body of a Rebel Colonel. It was too late for us to retreat, and so we removed our hats and stood near the party. A Rebel officer in uniform read the burial service. The scene was a sad one, and the people looked at us as if we were intruding, but I did not feel it would be right to leave and so remained. The dead man was Colonel Funk of Winchester.

Wednesday Oct. 5/64—Today I took the 2nd R.I. Vols. and the 5th Wisconsin Vols. and went into the country to search the houses for arms. The people are honest farmers during the day, but at night they arm themselves and mounting their horses are guerillas and fire upon our pickets and destroy our wagon trains if they can overpower the guards. The work was not pleasant, but we had to perform our duty. The people were often wild with rage, but we found that those who professed their innocence the loudest had the most contraband arms. At one house, after putting the family under guard in a room, we found in various places all the equipments of a soldier except the gun. This after much searching we found in the grain room, hid in a barrel which was filled with grain. We loaded a six mule wagon with arms, equipment and sadles and returned to camp. A gentleman from Massachusetts went with me looking for the grave of his son, killed on the 19th. He found it in the woods and was almost heartbroken as he knelt beside it. Yesterday myself and officers dined with a family in the city.

Oct 7th 1864—Two more of my men have died from the effects of wounds and will be buried today. I am Field Officer of the Day and shall be busy riding about the picket line all day.

Sunday Oct. 9/64—I have attended church today at the Episcopal Church. The sermon was a rebellious one as usual, and I fear, did me little good. After the service the rector gave the following notice: " A Chaplain of a New York Regiment will hold service in this church this evening at early candle light, but as we have no way of lighting up perhaps he will not want this notice given." The Rebels smiled as if it was a good joke, but after service we decided that the church would be lighted if each of us had to hold a candle in our hand. But the people are not all Rebels by any means. Last night a boy came to my tent with a beautiful bouquet and said: "Captain, here are some flowers which Sister sent to you." It is rumored that Gen. Sheridan is to retire down the Valley, and we may have to leave. But I hope not, for I like this place very much. It is quite cold now and our overcoats are in demand.

Oct. 11/64—Yesterday the Army at the front had a fight and General Sheridan captured 11 more cannon. The loyal people in Winchester rejoice, and the Rebels are downhearted. It is funny to sit in my tent and receive applications from the people for guards. We always ask this question: "Are you loyal to the U.S. ?" The majority immediately go into a long argument to prove that the South is right and the North wrong. We do guard all property whether belonging to loyal or disloyal parties. Colonel Edwards is in command of the city, and the 37th Mass. Vols. are doing Provost Guard duty with Lieut. Col. Montague as Provost Marshal. It would be hard work to tell what kind of duty the 2nd R.I. are doing. We have to guard the picket line, furnish guards to trains, look after property, etc. My pet lamb "Dick" survived the battle

*Major General
Philip H. Sheridan*

and is well known in the city. He follows me or my horse wherever I go.

Oct. 13/64—Rumors are about that the 6th Corps is to return to Petersburg. I hope not, for I rather like this place. The weather is cold, and we have had a hard rain.

Oct. 14/64—I am again Officer of the Day and in charge of the picket line. Colonel Mosby with his Rebel Cavalry have been hovering about the city all day but did not attack us. He is in Virginia what the *Alabama* was on the ocean. We never know when or where to expect him. When I have been out with the 2nd R.I. I have tried to bring on a fight with him, but have never succeeded as yet.[36] I had a long hard ride today, as our picket line surrounds the city, and of course the circuit is large. But the day was fine, and I rather enjoyed it after all. In fact, hot or cold, rain or shine, I enjoy myself and am happy.

Sunday Oct. 16/64—Attended church this morning, but I can hardly say "worship" for at the only church (an Episcopal one) the minister is a regular old Rebel. I hope we shall have another one opened soon.

Our men are putting fireplaces into their huts and getting ready for winter. It is so cold that I am writing in a house near my camp. The man has a wife and one child, but how they manage to live is a mystery. His wife bakes bread for us, and our cook uses their stove. Several sutlers have opened stores in the city for sales to soldiers, but citizens cannot purchase except on a permit signed by the Provost Marshal. It is very amusing to see the people apply for permits. Hoop skirts and shoes, hairpins, ribbons and laces seem to be in demand by the fair ones of Winchester. The soldiers sometimes buy these articles for the people, but it has been forbidden.

Oct. 18/64—The house occupied by Colonel Edwards, the Post Commander, is on Braddock Street, corner of Piccadilly Street. The rooms are furnished in good style. The music room is used by the Asst. Adjutant General as an office. This morning a party of officers including myself met there and had a sing and music on the piano. Yesterday we made up a party of ladies and officers and with a Cavalry guard took a ride out into the country. One young lady of Winchester rode my horse, Katie. We had a pleasant time and hope to repeat at a future day.

A few days ago I happened to find two Rebel soldiers in a house just out of town. We arrested the men, and I placed a guard over the house. The lady living there sent me a very insulting message and demanded that the guard be withdrawn. She claimed that she would not have a Yankee soldier in her house, but she did. I sent word back that as she had no choice in the matter, that the guard would remain. It is amusing sometimes to hear the remarks made about us.

Oct. 20th 1864—Yesterday was a day of intense excitement in this city. At daylight we heard the sound of cannon at the front, and it appeared to draw near. I turned out and had my Regiment form and soon received orders to report in person to Colonel Edwards commanding the post. He told me that there was a big fight going on at the front and that General Sheridan who had been his guest the night before at the Logan Mansion (Post Headquarters) had gone to the front. I was ordered to take command of the 2nd R.I. and 5th Wisconsin Volunteers and look out for the north part of the town. I formed my Brigade and sent out a line of skirmishers. During the morning our wagon trains came into town pell mell. The other four Regiments of our Brigade were posted on the south side of the city and took charge of the stragglers who came down the Valley Pike by the hundreds. We stopped the wagons and where the drivers were demoralized we put soldiers on the teams, and by night I had some two thousand wagons parked on the plains north of the city. The Union people were filled with dismay as rumors of a defeat to our Army reached the city, while the Rebels were jubilant, and I was told several times during the day as my duty caused me to ride through the city that General Early would send us flying out of Winchester before dark. At one time it looked very much as if he might do so, but we kept up our courage. The Rebel Cavalry were all about the outskirts of town, and I had all I could do looking after the pickets. Many Rebel families prepared food for the expected Rebel Army, but they did not come, and at night we received the news of Sheridan's glorious victory. Hurrah for Sheridan! He is the man for me.[37] After it became quiet I rode into town and called upon some Rebel acquaintances who had taunted me in the morning with talk about our leaving and told them the news. Our Army is now pursuing Early into the mountains. I hope they may catch him and use him entirely up.

General Ricketts of our Corps was wounded and brought to Winchester. I with other officers helped to take him from the ambulance and carry him into the Logan House. I suppose all of the wounded will be brought here tomorrow. General Bidwell of our Corps was killed. The old Sixth Corps has again covered itself with glory. For once the 3rd Brigade has missed a fight. Yesterday a man insulted Colonel Edwards on the street, and the Colonel promptly knocked him down and sent him to the guard house. I believe he is the landlord of the Virginia Hotel. We hear that our Division, the 1st, has suffered severely. This morning we were under arms at 3 o'clock but all was quiet. Capt. Henry H. Young (2nd R.I.) has been made Major of our Regiment, but I am not sure whether he will take command or not. Another Company is on the way to the 2nd. R.I.

Oct. 23/64 Sunday—All is quiet, and we are doing our routine duty. Today I attended (for a change) the Lutheran church which has just opened. The minister prayed for peace and unity and then preached a rebellious sermon. There is not much difference in the ministers of this town. The Rebel citizens do not feel as happy as they did last Wednesday when they thought General Early's Army was coming. The Rebel General Ramseurs body was brought into Winchester today escorted by two Rebel Majors. Both Armies suffered severely in the battle of the

19th Inst., but it was a victory for the Union and a defeat for the Secessionists. Since the 19th of September we have captured from the enemy seventy pieces of Artillery. Jeff Davis must keep his guns at home if he does not want to lose them, for General Sheridan claims everything that comes into this Valley. Well, a few more victories like the two we have had in the Valley and the war will be over. No one will rejoice more than myself, for I am tired of bloodshed. But God has been good to me, and I hope I shall live to see the end as I saw the beginning of the Rebellion.

Oct. 25/64—We had another scare today. General Alfred N. Duffie (formerly Col. 1st R.I. Cav.) left our lines on the north side of the town today in an ambulance, bound to Martinsburg. Soon a soldier came back and reported that the General had been captured and that the Rebels were coming in force. The troops were formed, and I sent out some men to investigate. They found that the General had been captured by Gen Mosby's Guerillas, and this ended the scare. My sheep "Dick" is a character and has been taught many tricks by the men. He is belligerent in his disposition, and woe be to any who is not on his guard when Dick approaches. I think I shall send him to Barnum as a curiosity in the sheep line.

Headquarters 2nd R.I. Vols., Near Middletown, Va., Nov. 1/64— We have left the delights of Winchester and are now at the front with our Division and Corps. Last Friday night (Oct. 28) I was ordered to report to the Post Commander. As I was on duty as an Officer of the Day I thought it was another Mosby scare, but I was told by the Colonel commanding to relieve all pickets belonging to our Brigade with troops that would report to me and to be ready to march the next morning to the front. We did not sleep much for we had much to do and many goodbye calls to make. But it was of no use to feel badly about it, for I am only too grateful that we have had such a fine rest in Winchester. I called on several friends and then made my preparations for departure. My men had just built me a fine house, and this I turned over to Lt. Col. Snyder of the 9th New York Regiment who relieved me. Saturday morning I left Winchester with our Drum Corps playing "O Carry Me Back to Old Virginny," and "Glory Hallelujah." The Union people applauded and the Rebels scowled. Colonel Edwards remains in command of Winchester, with the 37th Mass. as Provost Guard. Colonel Isaac C. Bassett commands our Brigade. We arrived at the front about 3 P.M. and found the Army encamped on the line of Cedar Creek and on the battlefield of Oct. 19th. General Wheaton who commands our Division, rode over to see his "old boys," as he calls the 2nd Rhode Island. The fields look more like a cemetery than a camp, for they are covered with graves. Mountains enclose us on three sides, and the scenery is very beautiful. It is very cold, and we keep huge fires burning in front of our tents day and night. The Rebels have entirely left our front, and we perform our regular drills as if we were in a permanent camp. Near the camp there are two caves formed in the solid rock. One is about 30 yards long and quite high. I went into it yesterday and fired my pistol to hear the echo.

Major Young (2nd R.I.) has been detailed as Chief of Scouts on General Sheridan's staff. This leaves the command of the Regiment in my hands. Several officers have been commissioned in the Regiment. Second Lieut. Easterbrooks is to be First Lieutenant, Adjutant Smith is to be Brevet Captain, Quartermaster Sergeant Robert Small to be First Lieutenant, Second Lieut. Gleason to be First Lieutenant, Sergeant David Small and William Perry to be Second Lieutenants.

Sergeant Robert W. Small

Near Middletown, Va., Nov. 6/64—A train of wagons came through from Winchester yesterday. They had a hard time, one man killed and four captured by Mosby's men. A mail came with the train. This morning we had another scare, and the whole Army was on line at daylight, but the enemy did not appear. The ground was covered with snow this morning, and the mountains are white on their summits. Today I took a ride over to the camp of the 1st R.I. Cavalry and saw several of my friends. It is very cold, and the men hover over their fires. It is rumored that this Army will winter near the city of Winchester, but I have some doubts about it. But something will have to be done soon or the men will suffer much from the heavy snows that will come soon.

Near Middletown, Va., Nov. 8/64—Today we have held an election for President under the law that allows soldiers to vote. Lincoln of course is the favorite with the soldiers. For three days it has rained and we have been under arms every morning at daylight waiting for the enemy to appear, but he does not show up. I have had a log hut built for my quarters, but I trust we shall not have to stay here for the winter, for it is a bleak, desolate sort of a camp. If we don't go back to Petersburg, I hope we shall move either up or down the Valley.

Near Kernstown Nov. 10/64—The band at Brigade Headquarters is playing the "Star Spangled Banner" in honor of the re-election of President Lincoln.

Yesterday the entire Army fell back to this little town or village which is only three miles south of Winchester. The location is pleasant, and we are camped in a fine oak grove with plenty of wood for fuel. This morning a large party of officers including myself rode into Winchester. We had a fine time and returned this evening. It seemed quite homelike to me to meet my friends again. A few nights since our sheep "Dick" took his place in line with the officers when they came up to salute at dress parade and marched with them. It made lots of fun for the boys.

Near Newtown, Va., Nov. 13/64—Here I am three miles from camp and in charge of the picket line. I am quartered in an old log house, occupied by one of the natives. Yesterday the Rebels attacked our Cavalry in sight of our camps but were driven off with the loss of three of their cannon. General Torbert was in command of our Cavalry, and the fight was sharp for a few minutes. It is Sunday, but nothing would indicate it here. Our men back in camp are building a line of rifle pits.

Near Kernstown, Nov. 13/64—Our line of fortifications is finished, and I should not be surprised if we remained here for some time. The weather is growing cold very fast.

Camp Russell, near Kernstown, Nov. 18/64—Our camp has been named Russell in honor of General D.A. Russell killed Sept. 19th at Winchester. An order came in just now and said: "General Wheaton sends his compliments and would like to see Captain Rhodes at Division Headquarters." I immediately reported to the General and found that he had received a new Division flag, a present from the ladies of Providence. The flag is a fine one, and the General well deserves the compliment. It is raining, but I am quite comfortable. My Quartermaster sent me up a tent, and I have had a fireplace put in. Yesterday our Brigade was reviewed by the brigade commander. The officers of the 2nd R.I. were complimented on the manner of their salutes.

Camp Russell, Nov. 20/64—Still raining and I fear the grand review by General Sheridan which is down for tomorrow will have to be postponed. I have an invitation to dine at Brigade Headquarters on Thanksgiving Day.

Martinsburg, West Virginia, Nov. 26/64—Last Tuesday our Regiment was detailed to guard a wagon train to this place. Just at dark we left camp and marched to Winchester and halted on a hill without tents or fuel. It was one of the coldest nights I ever knew. As soon as the ranks were broken the men rushed into the city, and the people allowed them to sleep in their houses. I went to the Provost Marshal's Headquarters and slept in a good bed. Wednesday morning it was bitter cold, but we started with the wagon train and reached this place at dark. Not having any friends here we slept in the fields and suffered much from the cold. I called upon the commanding officer, General Littlefield of New York, and found him very kind and obliging. This little city is on the Baltimore and Ohio Railroad, and at the end of each street strong stockades are built to keep out the Rebel Cavalry. I stopped at the hotel as I passed by, and a citizen asked me: "Are you from the front?" I replied: "Yes." "Do you know how far it is to the camp of the 2nd R.I. Volunteers?" I said: "Oh yes, it is about one eighth of a mile." "No," said he, "they are near Winchester." I then told him that I belonged to the Regiment and that they were just outside the gates of the city. He introduced himself as A. Crawford Green of Providence and told me that he had a load of cooked turkeys for our Thanksgiving dinner. I took him out to camp and introduced him to the Regiment. He made a little speech, and we gave him three cheers and three for Rhode Island. We had turkeys enough to give one to every three men in the Regiment. The 18th

Connecticut Regiment was camped near us, and we invited them to share our turkeys which they gladly did. In the evening I attended a meeting of a Masonic Lodge (I being a member of Harmony No. 9, Rhode Island) and met officers of all ranks. A Rebel Major on his parole took a degree.

Martinsburg, West Va., Sunday Nov. 27/64—Lieut. Halliday, Asst. Adjutant, and I attended the Methodist Church today, and I enjoyed the service and felt that we were worshipping our Master. The pastor announced that "This is a loyal church" and invited all Christians to remain for the communion service. We remained and partook with the others, both citizens and soldiers. The pastor prayed for the President of the United States and for the success of the Union Armies.

Camp Russell, Kernstown, Va., Nov. 30/64—Home again in camp with a cheerful fire blazing and very happy with my comfortable surroundings. We left Martinsburg early yesterday morning and marched to Winchester where we remained over night. This morning we came to camp. I found that a new Company "D" with three officers and eighty men had arrived during my absence. Captain Stephen Thurber is in command with First Lieut. Benjamin G. West and Second Lieut. Jeremiah Tourgee promoted from the 2nd R.I., Captain Thurber is on picket, and I have not met him yet. Tomorrow I am going to move my camp to a better location where I expect to make the best camp in the Army and hope to remain during the winter.

Capt. Stephen Thurber

2nd Lieut. Jeremiah Tourgee

U.S. Transport City of Albany, James River, Va. Dec. 4/64—About midnight Wednesday Nov. 30th orders came for us to move at daylight Dec. 1st. We (that is our Corps) took cars and reached Washington about noon Dec. 2nd. We took our pet sheep with us, but on reaching Washington, the field and staff officers found themselves without money, so we sacrificed our sentiment and sold poor Dick to a butcher for $5.00 and invested the proceeds of the sale in bread and Bologna sausage.

The 2nd R.I. and 82nd Penn. Vols. were embarked on the sidewheel steamer *City of Albany*, and we are bound for Petersburg. After leaving Washington we sailed as far as Alexandria and anchored for the night. At daylight Saturday morning, the 3rd, General Wheaton came down on the steamer *Idaho* and the fleet got under weigh and sailed down the Potomac. The officers have the use of the staterooms and cabins, and we are very comfortable, but the men are crowded on the decks. Last night we anchored in Hampton Roads and started again this morning and shall probably arrive at City Point tonight. I was sorry to leave the Shenandoah, for we have had a fine campaign, but duty is duty, and I do not complain. If it will end the war I am satisfied to go to any point they choose to send me.

Headquarters 2nd R.I. Vols., Entrenchments before Petersburg, Va., Dec. 4/64—Here we are again in the trenches before Petersburg after our five months' absence in Maryland and the Valley of the Shenandoah. We left the steamer at City Point on Dec. 4th and rode in the cars to Parke's Station 12 miles. Here we remained overnight. As it was dark when we left the cars there was some discussion as to how near the front we were. This question was soon settled by the sharp crack of rifles as the pickets near us began to fire. We decided that we were quite near enough. Yesterday Dec. 5th we moved to this camp. The 5th Corps was stationed here, but they marched away to a new position, and we occupied their trenches and forts. We are near the Weldon Rail Road and our Brigade is in line with Fort Wadsworth on our left and Battery Twenty-six on our right. In front of my camp we have a high and very strong line of earthworks. The enemy are nearly two miles in our front, but the picket lines are very near to each other. To our right and in front of the 9th Corps, constant firing is kept up, but there seems to be an agreement on our lines not to fire. The 5th Corps left some very good log huts. The one that I am living in has a good fire place and is quite comfortable. The Army camp looks like a great city, and several large buildings have been put up, while sutler's stores are very numerous. But the change from the Valley is great, and it will take some time to get accustomed to siege work, which we dropped so suddenly in July last. Little progress has been made since we left here, but we know the war will end in our favor sometime.

Dec. 7th/64—Today I am Division Officer of the Day and have charge of the picket lines. This morning I rode along the entire line in full view of the Rebels, but not a shot was fired. The Rebel works are very strong, and I could see their men walking about and could count the guns in their forts. Yesterday the Rebels shot one of our Union soldiers on the picket and got possession of his cap. Their idea was to tell by the badge on the cap the number of the Corps to which he belonged, but it did not happen to be a 6th Corpsman. I shall be on duty on the picket line for *three* days. I have detailed Capt. Stephen Thurber as an acting field officer and he is now living at my Headquarters. I think he will prove to be a good officer.

Friday Dec. 9/64—This morning General Wheaton came out to the picket line, and he and I crawled out to the front as far as we could without passing the Rebel pickets. With glasses we could see the Rebel works, and we made our observations and retired. After noon I was relieved and ordered back to camp where I found the 6th Corps ready for a march.

Dec. 12/64—At 4 P.M. on the 9th we left camp, and the Corps marched in a cold storm on the Squirrel Level Road to the vicinity of Hatcher's Run. It was so cold that riding was an impossibility, and as the snow turned to rain the men's clothes became stiff with ice. We halted about midnight in a swamp filled with water and fallen timber. After many failures we managed to start a fire, and soon the swamp was blazing with camp fires. We had no tents, and if we had they would have been of no use for the ground was covered with snow, ice, and water. We hovered over our fires half frozen until daylight the next day (the 10th) and then moved to the edge of the woods and built a line of breastworks. The Rebels attacked our skirmish line but did not reach our earthworks. Here we remained until 5 P.M. when we marched back to our camp in front of Petersburg, almost dead with cold and fatigue. We had just settled down in our huts before the fire when orders came for us to move again. We started off in the mud and water a foot deep and marched about five miles to near Fort Sedgwick (called Fort Hill) on the 9th Corps front. Here we put the men into huts without roofs. Myself and staff crowded into a hut with some soldiers and sat by the fire all night. Sunday, the 11th, we passed in this camp trying to keep from freezing and had just gone to sleep when we were ordered to return to our old quarters. We reached camp about midnight, and I turned in and did not get up until 11 A.M. today. Two nights without sleep has a tendency to make me sleepy. Winter campaigning is cold work, but it is all for the Union, and I will not complain. I thank God that I have such good health and can stand it.

Dec. 14/64—We are very comfortable in our camp and have resumed drills and parades. It is said that the campaign is over for this winter, but I hardly think so, for we are so near the Rebels that we can watch their daily drills and hear the noise of their camps, and it does not seem possible that two such large Armies can lie still so near each other for any length of time.

General Wheaton has been promoted Brevet Major General U.S. Volunteers. We are all delighted with this compliment to our old Colonel. Last night we had a fine sing and enjoyed the music made by ourselves very much. First Lieut. Easterbrooks is now Captain. I made fifteen officers since I took command of the 2nd R.I. six months ago. I suppose my time for promotion will come sometime.

Dec. 16th/64—The Rebels shelled the camps on my right today, but for some reason they let us alone. I am very much obliged to them. My camp was officially inspected yesterday, and we received many compliments.

Dec. 20/64—The weather is cold, but we keep up our drills believing it is to be better for the men. My log hut is very comfortable with its fireplace made of sticks and mud with a barrel for a chimney. On the walls are numerous pictures of Generals and battles taken from *Harper's Weekly*, while a carbine and my sabre and spurs hang on the wall. My Library is not extensive, only some dozen books on a shelf with a rude table beneath. Several chairs made of cracker box boards with a bed of poles and boughs complete the furniture. The hut on my right is occupied by the Adjutant and Quartermaster, while Captain Thurber and the Surgeon occupy a hut on my left. In the rear of our quarters we have an office, cook house and a tent for our servants. Besides we have a hut where three times per day we meet to try the quality of Uncle Sam's hardtack, etc. We had a Brigade dress parade tonight, which attracted some attention.

Dec. 21/64—A wet stormy day and nothing going on to report. We are glad to stay in our huts and keep dry and warm.

Dec. 22/64—The weather is too cold to get up our usual scare on the picket line. We do not fear the result of an assault by the enemy on our works, for they are very strong. The forts and batteries, as they are called, are within range of each other and are connected by curtains or rifle pits. In front of our works are deep ditches now filled with water and in front of this an abatis made of limbs and trees driven slanting into the ground and with the points sharpened. Then we have wires stretched about in every direction about six inches or a foot above the ground. And still in front of all this the trees are slashed and are piled up in great confusion. I wish the Rebels would try to take our lines. It would be fun for us.

Sunday Christmas Dec. 25/64—This is the birthday of our Saviour, but we have paid very little attention to it in a religious way. Last night a party of officers from the 49th Penn. Vols. came to my quarters with the band and gave me some fine music. Just as they left a party of officers from the 37th Mass. Vols. came and gave me a serenade. I invited them in and entertained them the best that I could. About midnight Company "F" (a new Company) arrived in command of Capt. John A. Jeffreys. This gives me six full Companies, and I now have one of the largest Regiments in the Brigade. About two o'clock this morning I turned in for a sleep. This morning it being Sunday as well as Christmas we held our usual inspection, and then I took a ride and dined with some friends. It does not seem much like Sunday or Christmas, for the men are hauling logs to build huts. This is a work of necessity, for the quarters we have been using are not warm enough. This is my fourth Christmas in the Army. I wonder if it will be my last.

Dec. 26/64—My Adjutant, Thorndike J. Smith, arrived to see me last night in camp, and I was delighted to see him. He came on business and is to return for duty soon.

Dec. 27/64—We have been busy all day building quarters for the new Company "F." Yesterday we received the news of the capture of Savannah, and this morning a grand salute was fired in honor of the victory.[38] Since Christmas it has been quiet with very little firing on the lines.

Dec. 29/64—Our camp is finished and looks well. The huts are all of one size, and the six streets are graded. The Medical Inspector of the Corps took a look at our camp yesterday and said in his report that the appearance of the camp was highly commendable. Tomorrow we shall commence new huts at Headquarters.

Dec. 31/64—Goodbye old 1864. Your departure is not regretted, as it brings us so much nearer the end of the war. May God grant us success in the year about to open.

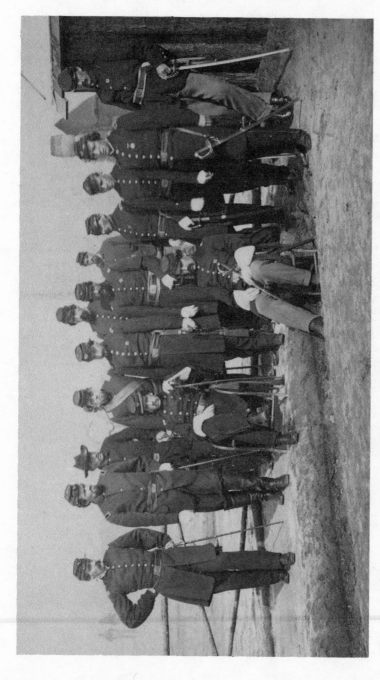

The officers of the 2nd R.I.V. in the lines before Petersburg, Winter, 1864-1865. Seated in chair on left, Col. E.H. Rhodes; in chair on right, Capt. James Bowen. Standing, from left to right; Capt. Geo. Easterbrooks, Capt. David Small, Lieut. Elisha Arnold, Lieut. Frank Halliday, Capt. Stephen Thurber, Capt. Charles Gleason, Capt. John A. Jeffreys, Corporal Maurice O'Hern (Color Bearer), Lieut. Benjamin West, Lieut. Jeremiah Tourgee, Lieut. Robert Small, Lieut. James McKay.

Petersburg, Va. — Home on Leave — Back to Camp — Weldon Railroad — Sayler's Creek, Va. — Appomattox Court House Va. — Burkesville, Va. — Wellsville, Va. — Petersburg, Va. — Manchester, Va. — Hanover Court House, Va. — Fredericksburg, Va. — Camp near Fairfax Court House — Hall's Hill, Va. — New Haven, Ct. — Groton, Ct. — Providence, R.I.

1865

Trenches before Petersburg, Va., Sunday Jany 1st 1865—New Years Day again and this is the fourth that I have passed in the U.S. Army. The war drags along, but we feel that we are gaining all the time, and when Petersburg and Richmond fall, as they must soon, the war will end. I am grateful to God for all his mercies toward me and that I am spared in health and strength to do my share towards restoring the Union. Colonel Amos D. Smith III of Governor Smith's staff arrived today at noon with a new set of colors and marker for the 2nd R.I. Volunteers. One flag is the regular U.S. pattern, while the other is a blue state (R.I.) flag with the state coat of arms upon it. One of the Guidons is blue and the other red, with "2nd RIV " on each in gold letters. Tomorrow will be a grand day, and the presentation will take place. The weather is very cold.

Monday Jany 2/65—This has been a grand day in our camp, and we have had many visitors. At 2 o'clock P.M. the Regiment was formed with the Brigade band on the right. The ranks were opened, and I took my station in front of the center of the line. When the colors appeared escorted by the guard and Col. Smith I gave the command "Present Arms," and the drums sounded the "March." I then returned my sabre, and Col. Smith presented the new colors with a fine speech, to which I replied. I then presented the colors to the noncommissioned officers selected to carry them, saying a few words to each. The colors were then escorted to their proper place in line, the band playing the "Star Spangled Banner." After this we held a dress parade. Our Brigade commander and staff and the staff of our Division commander, General Wheaton, were present. Gen. Wheaton was absent by reason of sickness, but he sent me a fine letter. In the evening I had a party of officers at my quarters and we enjoyed the evening very much.

Tuesday Jany 3/65—This morning Col. Smith and myself took a ride and called upon Brevet Lt. Col. John G. Hazard and Brevet Major T. Fred Brown 1st R.I. Light Artillery. At noon we dined at Corps Headquarters with Col. Charles N. Tompkins 1st R.I. Light Artillery, Chief of Artillery 6th Corps. It is now snowing hard, and it looks like a severe storm, which if it continues will interfere with our plans for tomorrow.

Thursday Jany 5/64—I had a queer affair today. One of our new men was taken sick and showed some signs of insanity. Some of his comrades tried to hold him, but he broke away and made an attack upon me, tearing my uniform. I had him properly secured, and an investigation found that he had been discharged from the 1st R.I. Vols. for insanity and had boasted that he had played a good trick upon his officers and would repeat the same game in the 2nd R.I. After satisfying myself that he was a fraud I ordered him to be punished. Sometime during the day he got away and attacked me again. I happened to be near a wood pile, and picking up a club I used it upon him until he begged for mercy and owned up that he was not crazy. He is now in confinement and living on bread and water for a few days. This man is a regular "bounty jumper," and the men are pleased to have him exposed.[39] Col. Smith left our camp for Rhode Island today. We enjoyed his visit very much and shall long remember the grand time we had at the flag presentation.

Friday Jany 6th 1865—Today I have witnessed a sad sight—the execution of a soldier who deserted from a Jersey Regiment. The condemned man first rode about the camps in an ambulance and seated upon his coffin. A Chaplain was with him and an escort of soldiers had him in charge. As he passed my quarters I had a good look at him and made the remark that if they would let him alone he would die from fear, but my prediction did not prove true, for he died bravely. Our entire Division paraded to witness the execution. I tried to get excused from attending but did not succeed. As we arrived at the place of execution the lines were formed on three sides of a square with the grave on the fourth side. The coffin was placed near the grave and the condemned man was seated upon it with his eyes bandaged. A firing party was drawn up in front of him, and after the prayer by the Chaplain, the Provost Marshal gave the commands: "Ready, Aim, Fire." I made up my mind that I would not look at the scene, but when I heard the commands given I almost involuntarily looked towards the firing party and saw it all. As the reports of the muskets were heard the man fell back dead. The body was placed upon the top of the coffin and the Division marched by in column of Companies, and as each Company approached the grave the Captain gave the command "Eyes right," and each soldier was obliged to look at the body. I was glad when it was over. The man rightly deserved his fate, but I prefer not to see justice meted out even to rascals. I had rather read the accounts in the papers. The troops returned to camp, and the scene was the topic of conversation during the balance of the day.

Sunday Jany 8/65—The Brigade band are now in front of my quarters giving me a serenade. We have had a splendid day but not much of a Sabbath. After inspecting the troops I took a long ride. The Rebels in our front are quiet, and we enjoy life after a fashion. Some days we are in a state of great excitement expecting an attack every moment, but for a few days past there has been very little firing on our lines. This evening I called upon General Wheaton. Captain Steven Thurber, who has been acting as a field officer, has returned from his leave of absence.

Jany 12/64—Life in our entrenched camp has been dull for a few days past, but we now hold regular drills in a field in rear of our line of works. This with picket duty serves to keep us awake. Today a deserter from one of the Regiments of our Brigade (not the 2nd R.I. Vols.) was drummed out of the service and then sent to prison for two years at hard labor. The entire Brigade was paraded, and the man under arrest passed down the line with the drums playing the "Rogue's March."

I hear that Col. George E. Church, formerly of the 1st R.I. Vols. has been appointed Colonel of the 2nd R.I. Vols. Well, aside from the injustice to me, I think Governor Smith has made a mistake, for Church has not the least chance of ever being mustered as Colonel of the 2nd R.I., and the Governor has incurred the displeasure of our Regiment and the censure of my commanding officers from the Brigade to the

Corps Headquarters. I have served for more than three and a half years and have commanded the Regiment for six months with rank below other officers who have smaller commands, and it does not seem right to have the Governor send a man from R.I. to take command. I might resign, to be sure, but I hope I am serving my country honestly and not for personal ends, and I shall try to see the end of the war. God willing, I think it will come out all right, as I am assured by those in high command that I shall not be superseded by any appointee of the Governor.

Jany 16/65—Hurrah! I have been promoted Brevet Major U.S. Vols. by the President for gallant conduct at the Battle of Winchester Sept 18/64, and the promotion has been confirmed by the Senate. This entitles me to the rank and uniform of a Major, but I shall still receive the pay of a Captain unless I am assigned to duty by the President under my Brevet commission. I am very proud of this new grade, for it will prove to the governor of R.I. that I am appreciated by the officers under whom I serve. I am somewhat indignant at the Governor for treating me as he has and feel that after my long service and command and the flattering recommendations that have been sent to him, that he ought to treat me better. But it is all for the Union. Yesterday I was detailed to inspect the 82nd Penn. Vols. and had a hard day's work, as the Regiment is a large one. We have just received the news of the capture of Fort Fisher, N.C.

Jany 17th 1865—I have today received an order from General Meade commanding the Army of the Potomac granting me eighteen days' leave of absence, and I am directed to proceed to R.I. on business connected with my Regiment. This business is to try and get promotions for the enlisted men of the Regiment and to persuade the Governor to send no more citizens to the 2nd R.I. as officers.

Note: I left camp in front of Petersburg on Jany 18th 1865 and proceeded directly to my home in Providence, R.I. After visiting my friends I called at the office of Governor Smith who received me kindly and after making several inquiries in regard to the 2nd R.I. asked me: "What can I do for you, Major, in the way of promotion?" I replied that I was not in R.I. for the purpose of securing promotion for myself but desired that some ten or twelve sergeants should receive commissions and that he would officer all new Companies raised for the Regiment from the veteran sergeants in the field. After the Governor had explained in regard to the political pressure brought upon him for appointments and we had discussed the various questions at length, he agreed to my proposition, and I gave him a list of names of veterans that I desired to have promoted. This list he sent to the Adjutant General's office, and I took the commissions back to the field with me on my return. The Governor insisted that something should be done for me, and I then suggested that if he would promote Major Henry H. Young (serving as Chief of Scouts on Gen. Sheridan's staff) to be Lieutenant Colonel I would be satisfied to take the position of Major and retain command of the Regiment. This he refused to do, claiming that Young had agreed when promoted Major to return to the Regiment but had failed to do so. I endeavored to explain this matter by stating that Gen Sheridan would not relieve Major Young from duty upon the staff and that as Young was a gallant veteran, he ought not to lose his promotion. I left this matter as stated above, but a few days before leaving home I was surprised to receive from the Adjutant General's office a commission as Lieutenant Colonel for Elisha H. Rhodes in the 2nd R.I. Vols. I immediately called upon the Governor and urged him to give the commission of Lieutenant Colonel to Young and to make me a Major. This he refused to do and stated that if I did not accept as Lieutenant Colonel, Young could not have the rank. I then proposed to take the commission, see Young, and if he would return to the Regiment, to send it back to R.I. and have one sent to Young as Lieutenant Colonel. I did see Young on my return, and he declined to take the command of the Regiment, and I was mustered into service by Captain & Brevet Major A.M. Tyler as Lieutenant Colonel 2nd R.I. Volunteers. This promotion was of great service to me as it gave me rank in proportion to my command. Young and I remained good friends until his untimely death.[40]

Friday Feby 3rd 1865—I left Providence at night on my return to the Regiment.

Sat. Feby 4/65—This morning I arrived in New York, and after taking breakfast I crossed the Hudson to Jersey City and took the cars for Baltimore where I arrived at 3:30 P.M. I found that the river was frozen and no steamers could leave for City Point, so at dark I continued on to Annapolis. Here I found the steamer *River Queen*, formerly of Providence, about to sail, and after some trouble I got passage on board of her.

Sunday Feby 5th—We arrived this morning at Fortress Monroe and I transferred myself and baggage to the transport *George Leary* [?] and

Colonel E.H. Rhodes

we started for City Point, Va., where we arrived about dark. At City Point I found a train just going to the front over a military railroad and took cars for camp where I arrived at 10 o'clock P.M. As I approached my Headquarters I was met by the sharp challenge of the sentinel with: "Who goes there?" I answered "Friend," and quickly added: "Sentinel, have the camp guards orders to challenge?" knowing as I did that it was not the custom of our troops inside the line of fortifications. He recognized my voice, and as I approached I found the headquarters hut dark and no lights to be seen in camp. On my asking for an explanation the servant told me that the 2nd R.I. with the other troops of the Brigade had marched from camp at an early hour today for Hatcher's Run and that a battle was probably to come off tomorrow. I found my man, Solomon D. Hatch, who has charge of my horses in his hut and gave him orders to have Katie saddled at 3 A.M. tomorrow morning. I then sent for the Sergeant of the Guard, and after giving him directions to call me at 3 A.M. tomorrow I turned in for a sleep.

Monday Feby 6th 1865—About 3 A.M. I heard some one pounding upon my door and supposing it to be Sergeant of the Guard I called out "All right, Sergeant." But a voice replied: "How are you, Captain?" and I recognized the voice of my Acting Adjutant, Lieut. Frank G. Halliday, who had left the Regiment during the night and had ridden to camp hoping to find me. He was much pleased to find that I was a Lieutenant Colonel and not a Captain. We mounted our horses and started for Hatcher's Run five miles distant where we arrived just at daylight. I found the Regiment at their old trade, digging rifle pits, and as I crossed a little bridge that divided the main road from the line the boys discovered me and dropping their shovels and picks gathered around and gave three cheers for the Captain. Some one quickly discovered the silver leaves upon my coat, and as the news of my promotion became known cheers were given for the Colonel, and I dismounted and shook hands with the officers and men as they marched past me. This demonstration of respect and esteem was very pleasant for me, and I felt very happy to know that I had the love of my men. The men returned to their work of digging, and I rode over to Brigade Headquarters to report my arrival, and here received many hearty congratulations upon my promotion. I then called upon Frank Wheaton commanding our (First) Division and was warmly congratulated by him. He advised me to be mustered into service at once and sent for his mustering officer, Captain A.M. Tyler, but he could not be found. Orders came for us to move across the river, Hatcher's Run, and as I left General Wheaton to return to my Regiment he said: "Goodbye, Rhody. Take good care of yourself today, for if you are wounded it will only be a Captain's pension." We immediately crossed the run, and the 2nd Brigade went into action, but our Brigade (the 3rd) with the 1st Brigade of our Division were placed in a fort as reserves. It was hot work for a short time, and our troops were driven back to our fort but soon regained the lost ground. The fight continued all day until darkness put an end to the battle when we were relieved and recrossed the river and went into a piece of woods for the night. Just before midnight I found Capt. A.M. Tyler, our mustering officer, sleeping near a fire, and after some growling at being disturbed he mustered me out of service as a Captain and then mustered me into service as a Lieutenant Colonel.

Tuesday Feby 7th 1865—This morning when I awoke I found as did all the troops that I was covered with snow and ice. It had snowed during the night and then turned to rain which froze as it fell. I never felt more uncomfortable in my life, and we started fires to try and dry our clothing. To make it still more uncomfortable the Rebels opened fire upon us and pitched one shell almost into my fire. We again crossed Hatcher's Run and formed line of battle in a field. The rain continued, and so did the rebel fire, and we passed a very unpleasant day. The fire of the Rebel Batteries was so severe that the troops were placed in the rifle pits for protection. The 5th Corps was in our front, and at 5 P.M. orders came for our Division to relieve them in the rifle pits and for the 5th Corps to advance on the Rebel lines. The fire for a season was severe, and one shell passed through our rifle pit and struck into Co. "D" of the 2nd R.I., but fortunately it did not explode. My new men behaved well, it being their first experience under fire. After the fighting ceased we made fires and tried to dry our clothing.

Wednesday Feby 8/65—This morning at 1 o'clock we received orders to recross Hatcher's Run and return to our old camps. We had a hard march in the darkness and reached camp about daylight, tired, wet and hungry. I am glad I arrived back in time to be with my men under fire yesterday, for I wanted to see how the new men would stand it. I am just delighted with their conduct and shall go into the next fight with perfect confidence in them.

Before Petersburg, Va., Friday Feby 10/65—When I arrived back at camp I noticed that our Headquarters huts had been changed, but I asked no questions. On our return from our trip to Hatcher's Run the Surgeon, Dr. William F. Smith, invited me to inspect a new hut that had been built during my absence in R.I. I took a look at the new house and expressed my admiration of it when he said: "Colonel, please consider this hut as yours for the future." I am very grateful to the officers and men who planned this pleasant surprise for me, and I know I shall enjoy the new habitation. It is made of logs with a canvas roof, sides lined or covered with white cloth and a good board floor and door. At one end I have a fireplace with a mantel and the boys have put in some ornamental work on the chimney.

The late move was to extend our lines towards the South Side Rail Road, which is with the exception of the rail road to Richmond, the only road leading from Petersburg that is now in the hands of the Rebels. The officers and men to whom I brought commissions are very happy. General Wheaton sent for me today, and we have talked over the 2nd R.I. affairs. Lt. Col. James W. Miller 82 Penn. Vols. made me a present today of a fine pair of silver leaves for my fatigue coat.

The weather is fine today and as warm as spring. We are enjoying it after the snow and ice of a few days ago. I am very well and happy as a man ought to be.

This evening the band from Brigade Headquarters came over and gave me a serenade in honor of my promotion. I have received so many congratulations and compliments that I fear that I shall yet be proud. Well, I am proud. Proud to command such a gallant body of men as the 2nd R.I. Vols.

Sunday Feby 12/65—No church service today near enough for me to attend, so I have remained in camp. Attended inspection, dress parade, etc.

Last night a glee club from one of the Regiments near gave me a fine serenade. I am much favored by the musical talent of the Army. Well, it makes this life pleasant and even enjoyable, and we are better men and soldiers for cultivating a taste for fine things.

Tuesday Feby 14/65—We now have a new Brigade Commander, Brevet Brig. Gen. (Colonel) Joseph E. Hamblin. I am well acquainted with him, having first met him when he was a Major. He is a gentleman and a fine soldier and will do honor to our Brigade.

Today I have taken my first pleasure ride since returning from R.I. I rode over to the camp of Battery "B" 1st R.I. Light Artillery, but finding that they had been ordered to Hatcher's Run, I continued my ride to that place. Our new lines of works extend to that point now. For miles the men were at work building rifle pits and cutting down the timber. The Rebels were in sight across the fields, but no firing was going on. I found Lieut. William B. Westcott Battery "B" after a two hours' ride and had a pleasant visit with my old schoolmate. The trees are splintered by shot and shell, and in one tree I counted sixteen bullets. One week ago I was at this place and in the fight. I rode my horse Charley on this trip, and on my return to camp attempted to exercise Katie, but she has been in the stable so long that she is wild and almost unmanageable.

Thursday Feby 16/65—We have had a lively time today, both sides doing their best to shell out the other. On the 9th Corps front, to the right of our line, the air has been full of shot and shell, and the roar of cannon has been heard all day. All quiet on our front however. Our Rebel neighbors are good natured.

Friday Feby 17/65—Today I have been at work in charge of a detail of six hundred men at work on a fort called Fort Fisher which is built across the Weldon Rail Road. It rained all day, and we worked in the mud and water. This fort will be a strong one, and as it is in sight of the Rebels we shall have music before it is finished.

Sunday Feby 19/65—A very quiet day and a very pleasant one. I inspected my Regiment this morning and General Hamblin, our Brigade Commander, was present. After dinner I took a long ride on my horse Katie, and since returning I have entertained callers at my house, or "shebang," as Army huts are called.

Tuesday Feby 21/65—We have been busy all day improving our camp and my headquarters. We have built a fence in rear of the line of tents and put white sand in all of the streets. This gives a very clean and cheerful appearance to our camp which we think is one of the best in the Army. We are having delightful weather and quite warm, and I take a long ride every day. This afternoon I made a trip to General Meade's Headquarters. We have today glorious news—the fall of Charleston. Salutes have been fired along the entire line, and the troops have cheered themselves hoarse. Thank God for the victory, for I hope it will help to end the war. The enemy still continues to desert to our lines. Last night ten came. They all tell the same story—that the Southern cause is hopeless. I begin to feel that the war is really drawing to a close, but we shall have some severe fighting yet. Great apprehension of an attack by the enemy on our front is felt, and the troops are constantly drilled in the manner of manning the earthworks. Each Company has a space marked off for it in the line of breastworks, and the letter of the Company is painted on a board and nailed to the cap log of the rifle pit. When an alarm is sounded each man seizes his gun and equipments and runs to his place in the works and then puts on his equipments. It takes the 2nd R.I. just *two* minutes to get into line after the alarm is sounded.

The indications are that something is about to happen, but just what no one seems to know. If the Rebels attack our ranks they are going to get whipped, for our lines are strong and protected in front by all sorts of contrivances including wires stretched along the ground. But we still go on improving our camp, and I have just had a fine fence built in front of my Headquarters. I see that the U.S. Senate has confirmed my appointment as a Brevet Major U.S. Vols. Well, it comes late, but it is a compliment that I appreciate very much.

Thursday Feby 23/65—Yesterday was Washington's Birthday and we celebrated in fine style. At 12 o'clock noon I was invited to the camp of the 119th Penn. Vols. Lt. Col. Gideon Clark commanding, where we found a fine collation spread to which we did ample justice. Music by the band and a glee club followed. A flag was raised at this camp, and the hour was much enjoyed. In the evening myself and staff were invited to Brigade Headquarters where we were entertained by General Hamblin. The grove in front of Headquarters was illuminated, and the band was stationed there. After an hour passed in talking, smoking, walking about and some dancing we were invited into a large hut where we found a splendid supper ready for us. The supper was followed by speeches, recitations and singing. About 11 o'clock, right in the midst of our fun and frolic, an order came for the troops to be ready to repel an expected attack on the 6th Corps front at daylight. Of course this broke up the party, and we left for camp to make ready for the expected fight. I had the trench guards doubled in my camp and at one o'clock this morning went to sleep.

At three o'clock this morning the Regiment was formed very quietly in a rain storm, but at daylight we were dismissed, as the Rebels did not appear. Perhaps they may try it tomorrow morning. It was rather an anxious night for us. A Rebel Colonel and thirty men deserted last night and came into our Brigade lines. We get now about one hundred Rebel deserters every night. I hold an officers' school every evening, and we are improving on our drill.

Saturday Feby 25/65—If the news of today be true the Rebels are preparing to evacuate Petersburg. Gen. Meade ordered all Batteries on the 9th Corps line (to our right) to open on the enemy's works, and as I write the cannon are booming, and the air is full of bursting shell. The Rebels are replying, and we have "Music in the air." It is raining tonight, and it is very dark, but the firing keeps up, and we can see the lighted fuses of the shells as they cross each other in the air. I am on duty as Division Officer of the Day, and this morning I took a ride along our picket line. The Rebels were quiet and did not fire at me. Last night one hundred and sixty Rebels deserted and came into our lines. We have some circulars printed offering to pay each Rebel deserter for his musket and equipments and to give him a free passage to the North. We send men out in the night and place these circulars on the stumps of trees, and the Rebels find them and so distribute them to their men. It is said that the Rebels have sergeants detailed to watch their picket lines, but many succeed in getting away. Tomorrow night I shall sleep upon the picket line, and shall have a chance of seeing some of the prisoners. The war is certainly drawing to a close, and I am thankful to God for it, for although I love a soldier's life, yet I love my home better and want peace.

Picket line 1st Division 6th Corps, Weldon Rail Road front of Petersburg, Monday Feby 27/65—I am still Division Officer of the Day. I have a hut on the picket line built of logs and supposed to be bullet proof. A guard is stationed near my hut, and the reserve pickets are in front. About fifty yards in front of the hut are the pickets sheltered by rifle pits with trees slashed (or cut down) in front, while about three hundred yards from our lines we can see the Rebels. Last night the bullets whistled over our heads quite merrily, and we were constantly on the alert. I made a trip down the line and saw that everything was right and about midnight lay down in the hut for a sleep. The Officer of the Day has a *three* days' tour of duty and of course must sleep. The other officers and men only remain on duty twenty-four hours and are not allowed to sleep. I told the sergeant in charge of the guard at the hut not to allow any deserters to enter until he had called me. After sleeping a short time I heard some one say: "Colonel," and looking up saw four Rebels standing in the hut. My first thought was, upon waking up that I was captured, and reaching down into my boot leg (My boots were on.) I pulled out my revolver and drew the hammer back. The sergeant said: "Hold on, Colonel," and recognizing his voice I woke up fully and realized the situation. The four Rebels were deserters and belonged to the 37th North Carolina Regiment. I examined them and took down their answers to certain questions on paper and then after taking the cartridges from their boxes, sent them with the memoranda to the Provost Marshal at Corps Headquarters. The object of sending questions and answers in writing to Corps Headquarters is to see that they tell the same story twice alike. Before they left one of them told me the name of his friend who would try to desert. Soon after firing commenced on the line, and the Rebels shouted to some one to halt and come back. Our men shouted "Come in, Johnny," and soon a Rebel soldier came crashing through the brush in our front and landed unhurt in our lines. He was brought to me, and remembering the name given by the first party, I at a venture addressed him by it. He looked somewhat surprised but admitted that I was right. I then told him his Captain's name, the letter of his Company, number of his Regiment, Brigade and Division and also the name of the officer in command of the Rebel picket line (of course I had obtained this information from the first lot.) The man said I was right and seemed somewhat dazed at the information I gave him. I ordered the guard to take him to Corps Headquarters, and just as he left he turned and said: "I know you Yankees are smart, but I cannot see how you found out so much about me." I replied: "Oh, that is all right, we have ways of getting the news that you people know nothing about." He left believing that there was some mystery about the Yankees, and then we had a good laugh. Last night we only got five deserters on our front, a smaller number than usual. We sent out a large number of circulars last night. We use them as bait and some times catch our fish.

Before Petersburg, Va., March 1st 1865—Yesterday I was relieved from duty as Division Officer of the Day on the picket line and returned to camp.

The scare about a Rebel attack has subsided, but the general impression is that the Rebels are preparing to leave Petersburg. Well I hope they are, for we have had a hard time trying to persuade them to leave. General Joseph B. Hamblin and staff called upon me today and expressed himself much pleased with my camp. I also called today upon General Wheaton who has just returned from Rhode Island.

Before Petersburg, Va., March 3/65—Very quiet in camp and nothing to do but drill and study tactics. We practice fencing every day and a little pistol firing. The enemy keep up their firing on our right in front of the Ninth Corps, and of course our forts reply, but we seldom have to dodge Rebel shell on our part of the line.

Before Petersburg, Va., March 5/65 Sunday—Yesterday the storm which has lasted for a week cleared away and today the weather is fine. Major Zenas C. Rennie [?] Allotment Commissioner for Rhode Island, is visiting me in camp. About three P.M. yesterday we started for a ride and did not reach camp until near midnight. We made a number of calls, and by the time we reached Division Headquarters, where we finished our visits, our party had increased to about twenty officers. The

Major will leave tomorrow and will take home for the officers and men a goodly sum of money, as we were paid off today. Although the day is Sunday, yet the payment of the troops went on. It is not customary to pay Sundays as a rule, but the excuse today was that the Army is liable to move, which is true. Our 6th Corps is trying to raise the sum of twenty thousand dollars for a monument to Maj. General John Sedgwick to be erected at West Point, N.Y. I have no doubt of the success of the scheme. My Surgeon, Dr. Smith, has gone to R.I., and as he lives in my hut I miss him very much. He is to be gone fifteen days.

Before Petersburg, March 6th 1865 Monday—We have received no mail for several days and do not like it. A soldier can do without hard bread but not without his letters from home. All quiet in our lives.

March 7th 1865 Tuesday—The weather is delightful and warm as spring in R.I. Yesterday I had a picture (photo) taken of all the officers that could be spared from duty taken in a group. A part of the Regimental Headquarters is shown in the picture. Gen. Wheaton and staff were also photographed at his Headquarters in rear of my camp. The Brigade band gave me a serenade last evening. The 2nd R.I. have subscribed about two hundred dollars towards the Sedgwick Monument. We have received good news again from General Sheridan's Army in the Shenandoah Valley.

March 8/65 Wednesday—It has rained hard all day and everything looks desolate, and I feel very lonely and homesick. The news from Gen. Sheridan came through Rebel deserters, and we hope it is true. No news of a move yet, but it cannot be delayed long. If Lee stays in Petersburg General Sherman will catch him from the south. I hope so, for I am tired of fighting and want the war to end. But I am going to see it through.

Before Petersburg, Va., March 9th Thursday—We have taken to poetry, that is the officers have, and we meet evenings for study and then read Longfellow. My last effort was the "Courtship of Miles Standish." One of my Lieutenants reads "Shakespeare," and we have lots of fun at his recitations.

This morning the Rebels attacked our picket line and made it lively for a short time, but they did not attack the main line of works. The scare was over in a short time. The weather today is very fine.

March 11/65 Saturday—Today I made a visit to City Point going and coming on the railroad. The distance is only sixteen miles, but we were three hours on the way back. General Grant came today with a large party of officers and ladies to hold a review. City Point is now a city indeed. Several large buildings have been erected, and the James River is full of vessels. I had no special business at City Point and only went down for a change of scene. It is rumored that Gen. Grant will soon review the 6th Corps.

First Division 6th Corps Picket line near Petersburg, March 12/65 Sunday—Here I am again near my old friends the Rebels doing duty as Division Officer of the Day. Gen. L.A. Grant of the Vermont Brigade is Corps Officer of the Picket, and we have just taken a ride along the line. The day is fine and warm, and but for the danger picket duty would be fun.

Before Petersburg March 14/65 Tuesday—Back from picket duty and find everybody excited with orders to move. Well, I am ready, and may God give us victory.

Before Petersburg, Va. Wednesday March 15/65—Well, we have had a queer experience today. Last night I received a letter from Col. Benedict, the R.I. State Agent in Washington, that he and Dr. Richard Browne of R.I. (a dentist) with a Miss Lena Lunt of Chicago (a cousin of Col. Benedict) would pay me a visit from City Point. We put everything in fine order, decorated my Headquarters, and then a party of officers in full dress uniforms went over to the depot called "Mead Station" to receive the party. They came all right, and we escorted them to our camp. Just as we entered my hut the Rebels attacked our pickets in front of my camp. I hastily told Col. Benedict to take the lady to a deep hollow in rear of our camp and then started for the Regiment which had formed in rear of the parapet as soon as the attack began. The firing in front was furious for a while, and some of the bullets came over our works. Much to my surprise I soon found Miss Lunt behind the works with the men clapping her hands in great glee. I tried to send her away, but she would not go, and so I had her keep below the parapet where she would not be hit. It was all over in a few moments, but the lady seemed to enjoy the novelty. After dinner we started for a ride. I borrowed a side saddle from Lt. Col. Clendennin's wife at Division Headquarters, and Miss Lunt rode my mare Katie. After tea we went over to the railroad station and found that the last train had left for City Point. A good natured engineer however agreed to let Col. Benedict and Miss Lunt ride to City Point on the engine which he was to run down.

Before Petersburg, Va. March 17th Friday, Saint Patricks Day—Dr. Browne accepted my invitation to remain with me for a few days. We attended the celebration at the camp of the Irish Brigade (so called). The

Lt. Col.
James Benedict

sports were rough, and after seeing one Colonel and two enlisted men thrown from their horses and injured so that they will probably die, I returned to camp satisfied the Irish celebrations are dangerous amusements. Hurdle races and ditch jumping were the principal features of the games. I like a good horse and a good run, but such sport as I saw today is not to my liking. The enemy opened fire, but ceased when they found it was a celebration.

Sunday March 19th 1865—After inspection today accompanied by my Surgeon, Dr. Smith, and my visitor, Dr. Browne, I rode over to the 9th Corps line and called at Fort Sedgwick (or Fort Hell as it is called). The 4th and 7th R.I. Vols. are on duty in this fort. The Rebel and Union lines are only a few feet apart on this line. As we looked over the parapet we saw a party of Rebels looking over the works within a few feet of us. It seemed queer. This was one of the good days, and so no firing was going on. We were not allowed to talk with each other. I went back to my pleasant camp well satisfied that there was more space between us and the Rebels. Last night about nine o'clock the air was full of shells on our right. The firing was kept up from cannon and mortar nearly all night. It was a pretty sight to watch the fire from the shell fuzes as they crossed each other in the air, but it was death for many poor fellows. After dress parade I took a walk over to the Corps Headquarters and then called upon Gen. Oliver Edwards who has just returned and taken command of our Brigade relieving General Hamblin.

Another new Company has arrived from R.I., and I have made 1st Lieut. Charles W. Gleason Captain and placed him in command. Assistant Surgeon William F. Smith has been made Surgeon with the rank of Major. We are still under orders to be ready to move at a moment's notice.

Monday March 20th 1865—Today our Division (1st Division 6th Corps, Brevet Major Gen. Frank Wheaton commanding) was reviewed by Major General Meade, Major General Wright and Admiral David B.[D.] Porter of the U.S. Navy. I have never seen a finer review. The day was fine and warm, and officers and men appeared neatly dressed and in good form. Our Division feel that a compliment was paid us by selecting our Division to show the Admiral.

We have in our Regiment a Council of the Union League of which I am President. Tonight we initiated six new members. My hut was decorated with flags and sashes for the purpose, while crossed swords were suspended from the walls. It made us feel a little solemn as the sound of the guns on our right was borne to our ears.[41]

Tuesday March 21/65—This is my birthday. Twenty-three years old today and I have been in service nearly four years. God has been very good to me, and I am grateful for his protecting care. Dr. Browne left for home today. I was sorry to part with him. Charles Slocum of the 4th R.I. Vols. sent me a mortar made from Rebel bullets fired in Fort Sedgwick. It seems to be a suitable birthday present for a soldier. Slocum and I were boys together in Pawtuxet. We are having a rainy day.

Before Petersburg Wednesday March 22/65—All quiet and nothing to do but drill and watch the enemy, but business will soon be brisk enough to suit us all. This siege must end soon.

Thursday March 23/65—We have had a heavy gale today accompanied by a sand storm. The sun shone bright, but the wind howled and whistled, unroofing our huts and tearing up the trees. The air was full of sand which entered our huts and covered everything. The woods on the Rebel picket line in our front caught fire, and they had to retreat to their main line of forts. Of course we could not take advantage of this, as the fire prevented.

President Lincoln is at City Point and is to review some part of the Army. It may be our Division, for we think we are about the best.

Sunday March 26th 1865—We had a very exciting day yesterday. At daylight the Rebels charged upon Fort Stedman on the 9th Corps front and got possession. Our Division was ordered to march to the relief of the 9th Corps. The distance was about five miles, and we made it at a double quick most of the time and arrived in season to see a Division commanded by Gen. John J. Hartranft of Penn. recapture the fort with many prisoners. We got a good shelling as we passed the Rebel forts and lost two horses from our Division. We then returned to camp and were immediately ordered to the left of the 6th Corps line near Fort Wardsworth on the Weldon R.R. Here we found Mr. & Mrs. Lincoln, Gen. & Mrs. Grant and Gen. Meade. The object of the movement was to drive in the enemy's picket line and extend our own. My Regiment happened to be the extreme right flank of our Division, and as we charged the enemy made a countercharge through a Rebel camp and caught me in a right flank. I quickly threw to the right and rear my right wing and opened fire which broke their line, and many surrendered, being unable to get back to their lines. Our whole line then rushed forwards and drove the Rebels from their works. I caught two Rebels myself and turned them over to a guard. The firing was heavy until dark when we began to throw up rifle pits. The line was finished about midnight, and then we were relieved and returned to camp. We had neither breakfast nor dinner yesterday and were half starved when we reached camp at 3 o'clock this morning. After a cup of hot coffee I turned in and did not get up until 9 o'clock this morning.

Picket line, 1st Div. 6th Corps before Petersburg, Tuesday March 28th 1865—Again I am on duty as Division Officer of the Day in command of the picket line. I came out yesterday morning and shall return tomorrow. Our picket line was advanced on Saturday last and drove the enemy from their rifle pits, and we are now occupying them. One officer and thirty men from the 2nd R.I. took part in the advance and were highly complimented by Brevet Brig. Gen. Issac C. Bassett, the Corps Officer of the Day. He said to me: "Colonel, you may well be pleased with the conduct of your men, for I never saw a skirmish line do better." Last night the Rebels planted a Battery in front of my line and massed a force of Infantry. Expecting an attack I reported the fact to Gen. Wheaton commanding our Division, and he sent me as reinforcements three Regiments of Infantry which with my pickets gave me some two thousand men. A deserter came in this morning and explained the reason for massing the Rebel troops in my front to be this: They were expecting an attack from us. I have sent the extra troops back to camp with orders to report to me again early tomorrow morning. Gen. Wheaton and staff with a party of citizens from New York and Rhode Island came out to see the lines. As we did not dare to ride, we walked along such parts of the line as were safe. The battle of last Saturday turns out to have been a rather brilliant affair for our Corps. The enemy appear to have suffered severely and lost much ground. Gen. Edwards has complimented the 2nd R.I. very highly upon their conduct. We were placed in a very trying position. We are still under orders to be ready to move, and no doubt a few days more will settle the fate of Petersburg. I shall be glad to welcome the dawn of peace, for I am tired of bloodshed. But if God wills I am going to see it through. I started in with this idea, and if I live I will see the end of the rebellion. Gen. Sheridan with the Cavalry Corps has rejoined the Army, and it looks as if work was to be done. Peach trees are in blossom near our camp, and the air is springlike.

Picket line, Wednesday March 29/65—Still on picket and very quiet, although every man is on the alert. Something is about to happen. We are all ready to move, and if I did not know our leaders I should feel that we were in trouble and about to retreat. But I feel sure that the enemy are about to leave Petersburg, and we are held in readiness to pursue them. I shall be relieved from picket tonight, and I am glad, for I have not slept for two nights.

Before Petersburg, Va. Thursday March 30/65—It is raining hard, and far to our left towards Five Forks and Hatcher's Run we can hear the boom of cannon and rattle of muskets. We are waiting to hear the result of the fight, and it is said that our movements will depend upon the said result. Gen. Sheridan with the 5th Corps and the Cavalry are on this expedition. We are still packed up and simply waiting—waiting for orders. Last night I went to bed and slept for the first time in two or three days, but as soon as I dropped off the long roll sounded, and I had to turn out and see that the forts were manned. Away off to our right the air seemed to be full of bursting shells. They looked like meteors as they crossed and recrossed in the air. We remained in line until midnight and then dismissed until 4 o'clock A.M. After daylight I managed to get a short nap. Well, I have endured this life for nearly four years, and I sometimes think that I enjoy it. Great events are to happen in a few days, and I want to be there to see the end. The end of the war will be the end of slavery, and then our land will be the "Land of the free."

Before Petersburg, Friday March 31/65—Great times may be expected. Last night all the Regimental commanders were ordered to report to Brigade Headquarters where we were told that the 6th Corps must attack Petersburg this morning at 4 o'clock and that we must not fail, but that we must take the enemy's work no matter what it costs. We returned to our Regiments in a solemn frame of mind and made preparations. The canvas roofs were taken off from the huts, knapsacks and haversacks packed and finally muskets loaded, bayonets fixed, and the Regiment stacked arms to wait for the order to move. No lights were allowed, and not even a lighted match was seen. About midnight a staff officer rode up and told me that the order was countermanded. We felt quite relieved, although we know that it must take place soon. The rain was falling steadily, and as our roofs were off we had no shelter. I lay down however for a nap, but at three o'clock this order was soon countermanded, and we remained in line until daylight. The fight has raged all day on the 2nd Corps front to our left, and we have been under arms waiting for something to turn up. It means fight within a few hours, and may God give us a victory. Grant knows what he is doing and I am willing to trust him to manage Army affairs. I have written letters to be sent home in the event of my being killed and given them to the Surgeon. I have told him to make sure of my death before sending the letters to my mother and another.[42] I have given him my watch and money also to keep for me or to send home. I am not fearful of death, and I may be one of the number. My trust is in God, for he doeth all things well. If we make the attack I feel sure we shall win.

Before Petersburg Saturday April 1st 1865—Still ready for the move with orders to be ready to attack at a moment's notice. The enemy evidently are expecting some move on our part, for their pickets are on the alert and heavy firing is kept up. My men are very quiet, and I feel confident that they will sustain the good name of the 2nd R.I. Vols. The strain upon our nerves is great, and I feel that the sooner the suspense is ended the better. We get no news at all, but every officer looks anxious. I have had my officers meet, and I have talked the situation over with them and urged them to do their duty. It was unnecessary with such men, but as I am on the best of terms with them all I felt that a word of encouragement could do no harm. Many of them I have promoted from the ranks and feel for a boy of twenty-three a *fatherly* interest in them.

Inside the Rebel lines at Petersburg, Sunday evening April 2nd 1865—Thank God Petersburg has fallen or at least must be evacuated tonight. Last night the Regimental commanders were ordered to Brigade Headquarters, and we received our final orders. We were told that we *must* succeed, as to fail would endanger the whole Army. It was a solemn gathering, and as I left Gen. Edwards took me by the hand and said: "God bless you, Colonel. Give them tomorrow morning what *Paddy* gave the drum, a good beating." I returned to my camp and had the officers assemble and again tried to impress upon their minds the gravity of the situation. About 10 P.M. all our Batteries in the Sixth Corps front opened on the enemy. The noise was terrific, and the shriek of the shot and shell gave us an idea of what we might expect in the morning. Battery "E" 1st R.I.L.A. occupying Fort Wardsworth on the left of our camp was hard at work. Shortly after our Batteries opened our Brigade left camp. The men were instructed to place their cups and pans inside their haversacks and under no circumstances to speak aloud or light a match. In silence we marched to Fort Fisher about four miles distant and passed through the fort and formed in front. The 6th Corps was in line of echelon by Divisions with the 1st Divisions in which we serve on the right and somewhat to the rear. Towards morning a dense fog settled down upon the field, and we could not see twenty yards in any direction. Our orders were to move at the sound of the bugle, silently but straight to the front. While waiting the enemy opened on us from the picket line, and Corporal Mills of my color guard was killed.[43] A detachment from the 37th Mass. Vols. with axes were to precede the line and cut away the abatis. I had ordered my men to load their muskets before leaving camp, and I now went along the line and had them take off the caps from the guns, as the officers were to lead in front, and I did not want them shot by our own men. The 2nd R.I. was in the second line of our Brigade. While waiting for the signal a mule belonging to the Brigade Pioneer Corps and loaded with picks and shovels broke loose and made for the front. The entrenching tools rattled at such a rate that the Rebels thought that something was up and opened a terrible fire. But for this accident I think the surprise would have been complete. When the signal sounded the entire Corps, notwithstanding the orders to keep silent, sent up a mighty cheer and then dashed forward into the fog. As I was in the 2nd line I could not see my position very well and so moved to the right. The 2nd R.I. Vols. first struck the Rebel picket line who fired in our faces, and we went over them without firing a shot. In fact as my men had no caps on their guns we could not fire. It worked just as I had planned. The Rebels in the rifle pits threw down their guns and surrendered. They shouted "Don't fire, Yanks!" and I ordered them to go to the rear, which they did on the run. I hastily reformed my line in the rifle pits when Corporal Maurice O. Hearn called for "Three cheers for Colonel Rhodes!" and they were given before I could interfere. This cheering gave the enemy an idea of our position, and they opened four guns from a redoubt on my left and two guns from one on my right. I shouted "Forward!" and on we went in between the two redoubts. As we struck the enemy's abatis I happened to be on the right flank of the Regiment, and discovering an opening left for wagons to go through the wood I gave the proper commands which caused the Regiment to go through by the flank and then come into line in front of the two gun Batteries. The first I knew I fell into the ditch with a number of my men after me. The Rebels fired their cannon and muskets over our heads, and then we crawled up the rope and onto the parapet of their works, stepping right among their muskets as they were aimed over the work. It was done so quick that the Rebels had no chance to fire again but dropped their guns and ran. As the 2nd R.I. reached the parapet I gave the order to prime and then fire, and we sent a volley into their huts which were in rear of the line of works. My Acting Adjutant 1st Lieut. Frank S. Halliday shot a gunner at one of the cannon. The Rebels ran one gun out of the rear of the fort, but we were upon them so quick that they left it. Halliday then turned the gun upon the enemy and fired several rounds into their works. As they rallied to charge upon it Corporal William Railton put in a cartridge, but not having a shot filled the gun to the muzzle with stones and fired it right in the faces of the Rebels who were charging upon us. The gun burst but did not hurt any of my men, but broke up the Rebels who retreated. Not seeing any of our Brigade I hastily formed my line and followed down through the camps. My orders were to find the Boydton Plank Road and then halt. I soon reached the road and halted. In a few moments I saw a Regiment in line advancing from the direction of the works we had captured. Not knowing who they might have been I deployed a skirmish line and soon found that it was the 49th Penn. of our Brigade Lt. Col. Hickman commanding. We remained here for a short time, and then by order received through a staff officer we marched back to the Rebel works. Here I met Gen. Wheaton who congratulated me most heartily upon the work done by the 2nd R.I. We claim that we were the first troops that reached the Rebel line and that we placed the first flag upon the Rebel works. The 6th Corps now formed a line at right angles with the enemy's works and marched towards Hatcher's Run, but after marching perhaps three miles we faced about and marched towards Petersburg until we struck their interior line. Here we were under fire all day, and at dark we could look down one of the main streets of the city. Lt. John K. Dorrance was severely wounded and fifteen enlisted men were killed and wounded. After dark the officers assembled and we joined with gratefull hearts in singing "Praise God From Whom All Blessings Flow." Hurrah for the Union! It will soon be restored, thank God.

Monday April 3rd 1865—This morning Gen. Edwards sent the 37th Mass. Vols. into Petersburg and found that the enemy had evacuated during the night. Great is the rejoicing. The Mayor of the city surrendered the town to Gen. Edwards. The Army then started in pursuit of the Rebels in the direction of Lynchburg. We heard today that Richmond has been evacuated and is in flames. Well, let it burn, we do not want it. We are after Lee, and we are going to have him. I have been recommended for a Brevet as Colonel for gallant conduct at the storming of Petersburg. Hurrah!

Tuesday April 4th 1865—Still following the demoralized Army. The road is filled with broken wagons and the things thrown away in the flight of the Rebels. I do not know just where we are but do not care, for Grant is at the head and we shall come out all right.

Wednesday April 5th 1865—Still plodding along following up Lee. Every step we see proof of the demoralized condition of Lee's troops. We shall catch him if we keep on, and when we do the war will end. He has often followed us, and we him, but this is the last time. At night we joined Sheridan's Cavalry at Jetersville.

Friday April 7th 1865—Yesterday the old 6th Corps had a grand fight and won a victory that must help to bring the war to a close. Thank God that I am alive. My heart is sad to think of the brave officers and men that died yesterday. So near the end and yet men must die. Yesterday the 2nd R.I. happened to lead the 6th Corps and of course had to furnish the details for guards left at houses and other places on the road. I have about four hundred men in the Regiment, but details were so heavy that only about two hundred men and eleven officers were left. In the afternoon as we came out of the woods into an opening I heard firing off to our right and front. I saw Gen. Sheridan, Gen. Wright, Gen. Wheaton and Gen. Edwards sitting on horses and talking earnestly. Gen. Edwards held up his hand as a sign for me to halt, and I gave the command to the Regiment in my rear. He then invited me to join the party. I rode up and saluted and was told that in our front was a small stream called Sailor's [Sayler's] Creek and that on the opposite side Gen. Ewell's Rebel Corps was guarding Lee's wagon train, and that our Cavalry had cut them off and we were to attack. As I rode back to the regiment Captain Charles W. Gleason stepped up and said:

"Colonel, are we to fight again?" I answered: "Yes." "Well," said he, "This will be the last battle if we win, and then you and I can go home. God bless you, Colonel." I replied: "God bless you, Captain. I hope to meet you after the battle." Poor Gleason, he was shot through the head a few minutes after and killed. He was a gallant fellow, and I thought the world of him. I had taken him from the ranks and made him a 2nd Lieutenant, 1st Lieutenant, Brevet Captain and Captain. The Corps line of battle was formed faced to the rear which brought me upon the extreme left flank of the line. Our Brigade of six Regiments was in three lines, and the 2nd R.I. came in the *third* line. Before we had moved far I was ordered to take position on the left of the second line and finally on the left of the first line, which brought me to the extreme flank of the Corps. I spoke to the Brigade commander about it, and he told me that a squadron of Cavalry would protect my flank. The line moved down a hill, and seeing a river in front I dismounted and sent my horse to the rear behind a barn. The Rebels opened upon us soon as we reached the river, but we jumped in with the water up to our waists and soon reached the opposite side. Here we formed and advanced up a slight hill

Lieut. William H. Perry   *2nd Lieut. George B. Peck*

towards a piece of wood, the Rebels retreating from our front. When within about fifty yards of the woods a Rebel officer stepped out and shouted: "Rise up, fire!" A long line of Rebels fired right into our faces and then charged through our line and getting between us and the river. The fight was fierce, and here poor Captain Gleason fell, as did also First Lieut. William H. Perry. Capt. Jeffrey and First Lieut. Halliday and 2nd Lieut. George B. Peck were wounded as well as several enlisted men. I found that the Rebels had our state color, but quickly faced the Regiment to the rear, and we charged them and breaking their line recrossed the stream. Gen. Edwards had become separated from the Brigade, and I, being the senior officer present, was ordered by General Wheaton to take command and recross. I sent for my horse and after reforming the line, we again crossed the stream and drove the enemy from the woods capturing the wagon train. Sergeant Cameron of the 5th Wisconsin Regiment of our Brigade captured Gen. Ewell, while Commodore Tucker and other naval officers surrendered. We had in our Regiment about fifty Rebel officers prisoners. We set fire to the wagons which appeared to be loaded with potatoes and sorgham molasses, which our boys enjoyed. We followed until after dark and then halted. Gen. Wheaton ordered me to advance our Brigade line which I did in the bright moonlight. The 2nd R.I. lost forty-four killed and wounded. About 10 o'clock I laid down to sleep but was soon awakened by Gen. Edwards who had found us and relieved me from the command of the Brigade. The 2nd R.I. as usual behaved splendidly. Today we have been guarding our wagon train and still following up Lee's Army.

Saturday April 8/65—We left the wagon train last night and joined our Brigade. I have fifty men less than when I left Petersburg on the 2nd. Some are dead, and some are wounded. God help them and bring us peace.

Still on, on, with the cannon booming in our front showing that Lee is not far away and perhaps may be at bay.

Sunday April 9/65, Near Appomattox Court House, Va.—Glory to God in the highest. Peace on earth, good will to men! Thank God Lee has surrendered, and the war will soon end. How can I record the events of this day? This morning we started at an early hour still following the sound of an occasional cannon shot. I found a Rebel Captain from North Carolina by the roadside, and finding him to be a Mason I had him go with my Provost Guard. About 11 A.M. we halted in a field facing the woods and stacked arms. Rumors of intended surrender were heard, but we did not feel sure. I took the Rebel Captain over to Gen. Edward's Headquarters, and we lunched with him. The Captain insisted that Lee would surrender and begged that we would not send him to the rear. Some time in the afternoon we heard loud cheering at the front, and soon Major General Meade commanding the Army of the Potomac rode like mad down the road with hat off shouting: "The war is over, and we are going home!" Such a scene only happens once in centuries. The Batteries began to fire blank cartridges, while the Infantry fired their muskets in the air. The men threw their knapsacks and canteens into the air and howled like mad.

General Wheaton and a party of officers rode to our Regiment and actually gave three cheers for the 2nd R.I. which were returned with a will. I cried and laughed by turns. I never was so happy in my life.

The Rebels are half starved, and our men have divided their rations with them. The 2nd R.I. had three days' rations and after dividing their rations with the Rebels will have to make a day and a half's rations last for three days. But we did it cheerfully. Well I have seen the end of the Rebellion. I was in the first battle fought by the dear old Army of the Potomac, and I was in the last. I thank God for all his blessings to me and that my life has been spared to see this glorious day. Hurrah, Hurrah, Hurrah!

Monday April 10th 1865 Appomattox C.H.—It seemed queer to sleep last night without fearing an attack, but the Rebels are now all under guard. I have talked with some of them and find that they are as glad as we that the war is over. They all seem surprised at our kind treatment of them, and I think General Grant's way of managing affairs will help on the peace that must come. I do not know just what is going on at the front, as no one is allowed to visit the Rebel camps, but I am satisfied. I have seen all the Rebels I want to see for my life time. I understand that we are to move tomorrow, to what point I cannot say.

Tuesday April 11/65—We left camp near Appomattox Court House this morning with the 6th Corps and after marching 20 miles are now on the road to Burkesville, if anybody knows where or what it is. The marching is fair, and the men are in good spirits.

Wednesday April 12/65—We have made a good march today and expect to arrive at Burkesville tomorrow. I understand that it is an important rail road junction. The natives that we meet on the road appear to be dazed and do not seem to comprehend that Lee has surrendered.

Thursday April 13/65—We arrived this day at Burkesville which is at the junction of the Richmond and Danville and Lynchburg R.R.

Frederick Miller, Esq. of Providence is with me on a visit and right glad am I to see him, as I was a clerk in his office when I enlisted in the 2nd R.I. Vols. Of course everything is new and strange to him, and he is enjoying the life.

As we marched through Farmville I heard some one call: "Colonel, Colonel," and as I did not answer, as Colonels are plenty, I heard "Elisha" called. I looked towards the hotel steps and saw Mr. Miller standing with a valise in his hand. I rode up to him, and dismounting my orderly I had him mount and ride on with me. He will remain a few days, as he is on duty with the Christian Commission.

Burkesville, Va., Friday April 14/65—My camp is in a fine piece of pine wood, and we are enjoying the rest. A mail arrived last evening and gave great satisfaction to all. The past two weeks has been the most severe of any of my campaigning, but I am well and tough as a knot.

Burkesville, Va., Saturday April 15/65—We are having a rainy day, but as the trains have arrived I have my tent pitched and so feel quite comfortable. Mr. Miller is reading to pass away the time.

Bad news has just arrived. Corporal Thomas Parker has just told Mr. Miller that President Lincoln was dead, murdered. I sent for Parker and told him not to repeat the story, but in a short time a staff officer rode up and told me the sad sad news. He handed me a circular from General Meade announcing the terrible fact and giving the particulars as far as is known. It seems that a man by the name of Booth shot him with a pistol while at the theatre last night. The circular stated that an attempt upon the life of Secretary Seward had also been made and that General Grant who had started for New York had been sent for. I called Mr. Miller from the tent and read to him the dispatch after which the Regiment was formed, and the Adjutant read the dispatch to the officers and men. The sad news was received in grief and silence, for we all feel that we have lost a personal friend. We saw President Lincoln only a day or two before we captured Petersburg. We often would see him when he visited the Army, and he was always received with cheers. What does this murder mean, and who is responsible? The soldiers feel that the leaders of the Rebellion are responsible, and I fear that if Lee's Army had not surrendered that they would have fared hard at our hands. My men after listening to the dispatch turned and went to their Company streets in silence. We cannot realize the fact that our President is dead. May God help his family and our distracted country. I trust that good will come out of even this sad calamity.

Burkesville, Va. Sunday April 16th 1865—This has been a sad Sunday in camp, for the news of the death of President Lincoln seems to paralyze every one. We can only talk it over and speculate on what will be done next. The soldiers are wild with rage to think that this great and good man who did so much for our land should be stricken down in the hour of victory.

Burkesville, Va. Monday April 17/65—Mr. Frederick Miller left camp today for home. I was sorry to part with him, for I have enjoyed his society very much. Everything was new and strange to him. I think he now has a very good idea of Army life. I hear that my Adjutant Brevet Captain Thorndike J. Smith is on his way to the Regiment. I shall be glad to see him, for I need his services very much. It is rumored that our Corps is to be sent to North Carolina, but of the truth of this I cannot say. This is a bad place for supplies, as the railroad is old and in bad condition making the running of trains slow and uncertain. Some think that our Corps will be ordered to Richmond or Petersburg. It seems good to feel that the fighting is over and that we are not liable to be called out nights. The more I think of the matter the more I rejoice that I saw the first and last battle of the Army of the Potomac. I rode down to Burkesville Station today but did not stay long as there was nothing to see but the depot and a few houses. This is not a first class town.

Burkesville, Va. Tuesday April 18/65—I have received a fine present from Lieut. William H. Bullock of my Regiment who has just returned from Rhode Island. It is a silver shield with the sixth Corps cross in the centre in red enamel, while my name, rank and Regiment surround the cross. It was made by Gorham Co. in Providence.

Burkesville, Va. Wednesday April 19/65—The flags of the Army are at half mast and draped in black while minute guns were fired today in honor of our dead President. We cannot realize yet that he is dead. All hearts are sad, and the grand old Army of the Potomac is in mourning for the nation's loss. Lincoln was truly the soldiers' friend and will never be forgotten by them.

Burkesville, Va. Friday April 21/65—No news today and nothing to write about. I spend my time in official duties and drill and do some riding about the country. The people seem to be good natured and I believe are glad the war is over. The officers are already talking about the Regiment going home. Well, now that the war is virtually over this will suit me. I reckon I shall feel proud riding up Westminster Street in command of a Regiment that four years ago I marched down the same street as a private. Last night we received a rumor that the Rebel General Johnston had surrendered to General Sherman. All the camps were illuminated, and the men paraded with torches making a fine display. If this news be true the war may well be considered as at an end, for the enemy can never raise other Armies.

Burkesville April 22/65 Saturday—We are under orders to be ready to move at a moment's notice, and the rumor is that Johnston has not surrendered, and we are going to help Sherman capture him. Well, I thought we were all through with our fighting, but here goes. The old Sixth Corps is full of fight yet. I suppose we shall march today or tomorrow.

Sunday April 23/65, Keyesville, Va.—We left camp at Burkesville this morning and marched to this little place about twenty miles by the road. It is said that we are bound to Danville, Va. on the border of North Carolina. We have had a good march today, and I have rather enjoyed it. I think the men prefer the march to the camp life. The country that we passed through is fine and seems to improve as we go south.

Monday April 24/65—This morning we continued our march and are now encamped on the bank of a river which the people call the Staunton River. The country is still fine, and we are making good time.

Halifax Court House, Va., Tuesday April 25/65—This morning we crossed the river on a pontoon bridge that the engineers laid during the night and continued on our way through a place called Laurel Hill to this town. Halifax Court House is a quiet little settlement on a hill. The people received us very cooly and seem to be bitter against the Yankees. We took possession of the town and planted the Stars and Stripes upon the Court House. This is probably the first U.S. flag seen in this part of Virginia for several years. Yesterday the citizens held a meeting here and denounced the Union, but we did not find any of the parties when we arrived.

Brooklyn, Va. Wednesday April 26/65—We left Halifax Court House this morning and made a good march to this little hamlet. The Negroes are wild with delight, for they know now that they are free. We are fast nearing Danville and will reach there tomorrow.

Danville, Va. Thursday April 27/65—We reached this city this afternoon and crossed the Dan River on the bridge. The Rebels had tried to destroy it and had cut some timbers, but our Cavalry reached the river in time to save the bridge. The people looked at us with disgust in their faces as we marched through the streets with drums beating and colors flying. I did not see a smiling face except among the slaves, who of course were glad to see us. "We have been waiting for you!" was shouted to us many times. The railroad yard was full of locomotives when we arrived. I suppose Uncle Sam will claim them as his own.

Danville April 28/65 Friday—My Regiment is in camp just outside of the city, very near to the North Carolina line. In fact we are not quite sure which state we are in. Danville is quite a little city, but I have not had time yet to look it over. The weather is fine and just like June in R.I. We have just received news that Johnston has at last surrendered and all our Batteries are firing salutes. This is good news, and the war is certainly over. But I will wait, for it has ended so many times that I am a little doubtful. At any rate we shall not probably march any further south. On our march to Danville we saw many Negroes. The roads were full of them laughing and grinning. Of course we told them that they were free, but their masters would not believe it. At one place the overseer ordered the Negroes to go to work, and they refused. Some of them came over to my camp for advice. When they returned they offered to work if paid for their labor. I do not know how the matter ended.

Danville Saturday April 29/65—We have looked the city over today, and I have come to the conclusion that Virginia cities do not suit me. I made a purchase of some good cigars however that did suit. They are the first I have seen for some time.

Danville, Va. Sunday April 30/65—This has been a busy day and not much like Sunday. My Regiment was mustered for pay by Lt. Col. Hickman of the 49th Penn. Vols., and I had to muster the 5th Wisconsin Vols. It took so much time that I did not go to the city to church as I intended. Major William C. Gray of the 119th Penn. Vols. has been spending the evening with me. Yesterday I took a look at the buildings in the city used for Yankee prisoners. Well, I do not want to be confined in either of them. There are six large brick tobacco warehouses lately used for this purpose. No more prisoners for you to abuse, Johnny Reb. The city is full of paroled Rebel officers who walk the streets with ladies and sometimes are rude to our officers and men. But we can afford to humor them, for we are the victors. Our people are somewhat angry that these Rebel officers are allowed to walk about in uniform. Not that we have any ill will towards them, but because we feel that they ought to be a little more modest. If we go for a ride we are sure to meet a party of them riding also. One lady made the remark that she could look at our troops, but the sight of the Stars and Stripes made her angry. But she afterwards stated that the Yankees behaved better in the streets of Danville than the Confederate troops had done. In speaking to some ladies they said that they had been in the habit of carrying revolvers when the Confederates occupied the town, but now felt safe with the Yankees. It sounded pleasant this morning to hear the bells ringing for church. It reminded me of home. But for the muster I should have attended church. We have had no mail for some time.

Danville, Va. Monday May 1st 1865—We have just been informed that a mail for the North will leave today, as the trains are running on the railroad to Richmond. My camp is not a very pleasant one, but as we shall probably remain here but a short time it does not matter much. We are in the midst of a thicket of brush and were obliged to cut out the young trees in order to make streets for the Companies. We are not doing much in the way of drills at present.

Tuesday May 2/65—It is rumored that we are to move, and I hope it is true for I have seen all of this section of Virginia that I care to. I have looked the city all over and been as far into the country as I felt it safe to do without a large escort. Now that the war is over I feel that I should like to become a citizen again, although I like a soldier's life.

Wednesday May 3/65—This morning orders were received to move by railroad to Burkesville, and I am told that our troops or our Corps is to be distributed along the Southside Rail Road as guards. We left our camp in the brush without regrets and marched to the depot where we are waiting for the cars. There is some trouble with the telegraph wires, and as I could get no news of a train that is coming this way, I refused, much to the disgust of the Quartermaster in charge of the railroad, to embark my men. Our boys found a storehouse filled with corn meal and bacon near the depot and have transferred a good share to the cars. As it belonged to the Rebel government and not to private parties, I took good care not to see any of the movement.

Burkesville May 3rd 1865 10:30 P.M.—We have just arrived after a tedious ride from Danville, but it was better than marching. The conductor gave me the use of his car or caboose which had a kitchen attached, so I fared quite well. The railroad is old and made of scrap iron, so that we were obliged to run slow. On arrival here I found Brevet Captain Thorndike J. Smith, my Adjutant, who reported for duty from leave of absence on account of wounds. I also found a new Company of 80 recruits in command of Capt. Joseph Pollard. They came a little late for active service, but they will make good my losses in the last battles. Well, I am tired and weary, so here goes for a nap under a tree. I have just had some *mush* and sorgham molasses sent to me by one of the men. The mush is made from stolen meal, but it tastes good.

Wellsville, May 5/65—Yesterday we left Burkesville and made a short march and went into camp for the night. This morning we started again and reached this place which is twenty miles from Burkesville. I believe the place where we stopped last night is called Black and White. The 2nd R.I., 49th Penn and 119th Penn. are stationed here. The town does not amount to anything, there being only a little cluster of houses with a railroad depot. The country here is fine—the best that I have seen in Virginia. Many planters who have been wealthy are living here. I do not know just what we are to do, but probably patrol the railroad and keep the country quiet, as it is reported that small bands of guerillas are still roaming about. Brigade Headquarters has been established at a railroad station called Wilson about four miles from here towards Petersburg. The people seem to be well disposed, and several have called upon me and invited me to the hospitality of their houses.

Wellsville Saturday May 6th 1865—This morning as I was sitting under a fly in front of my tent clad in flannel shirt and pants, an old gentleman with a cane under his arm rode up and greeted me pleasantly. I called an orderly to hold the horse, and the gentleman dismounted and came under the fly. He said he was looking for the commanding officer of the troops. I arose and told him that I was in command. He replied: "No, I want to see the Colonel." "Well," I said, "I am the Colonel. What can I do for you?" He said; "You are a Colonel? Why you are nothing but a boy." I told him that I could not help being young. He replied that he was surprised that the U.S. should send a boy to take charge of their affairs. I then told him that I did not propose to discuss my age or the policy of the U.S. with him, but that if he had any business with me he should attend to it, otherwise I would excuse him from stopping longer. The old gentleman immediately changed his tactics and introduced himself as Dr. Shore, a planter living near. He was having trouble with his ex-slaves and appealed to me to settle the matter, which I did. He invited me to dine with him tomorrow and suggested that coffee, tea, and sugar were scarce articles at his home.

General Sherman's Army commenced to march by this station early this morning. His troops are on the way from North Carolina to Washington. They look tough and hearty but without much style. My men have new uniforms and white gloves, and my camp was overrun with Sherman's men who thought we were green troops and undertook to help themselves. When they found that we had been in service for nearly four years they treated us better and gave us a round of cheers. I had however to post guards to keep them out of my camp.

Wellsville May 7th 1865 Sunday—We have had a delightful day, warm and pleasant. After the morning's work was finished I, with a part of the staff, rode over to Dr. Shore's house for dinner. The ride was about three miles through the woods and very pleasant. The Doctor was the richest man in this county, I am told, (This is Nottoway County) and did own one hundred and thirty slaves, but with the exception of a few very old and a few very young they have all skipped for the North and liberty. We found him a true southern gentleman and very hospitable, while the ladies were very kind and pleasant. The dinner was enjoyed by we soldier people and was well served. After dinner a servant passed pipes with long reed stems to each of us. The people are really kind to us and try to make our life here pleasant. They send me flowers from their gardens, and I in turn furnish them with little luxuries which they have been deprived of for many a long month. Tea and coffee are in great demand among the people here. Dr. Shore has sent to Danville for his daughter who has been there at school. When she reaches our station I shall send an escort with her to her home.

Wellsville, Va., Monday May 8th 1865—Today I sent Co. "F" Capt. John A. Jeffrey to a station on the railroad called "Black and White" where he is to remain on guard. The other Captains of the Regiment take turns patrolling the railroad. The service is not hard, and I think both officers and men enjoy the duty. I spend my time listening to statements of disputes between whites and blacks and trying to settle their affairs. I am Judge, Jury, and almost Executioner. Most of the people have taken the Oath of Allegiance to the U.S. and are trying to be loyal. But with some of them it is evidently hard work, and the old spirit of rebellion shows itself quite often. I try to be patient with them and help them in their troubles.

Wellsville Tuesday May 9th 1865—Dr. Shore's daughter (they call her Miss Epsey) with her governess arrived today from Danville, and my tent is full of trunks and other baggage waiting to be sent over to the Doctor's house. We have fine headquarters with the tents pitched on three sides of a square and opening into an arbor. All the field and staff officers appeared today in straw hats made by ladies in this vicinity. Not a very soldierly headgear, but very comfortable in the hot sun. This beats all the soldiering that I have ever performed. But then it is a time of peace now, and we are making up for the years of hardship that we have passed through. We are having plenty of vegetables now and enjoy them very much. This is a fine section of Virginia and very fertile.

Wellsville, Wednesday May 10/65—All quiet in camp and very little to do. We have a great many country people, white as well as black, who walk about the tents and look at the Yankees with open eyes and ask innumerable questions. It is rumored that the Army of the Potomac is to be mustered out of service, but we hear nothing about the old Sixth Corps. Perhaps we are to remain until everything has quieted down. I am ready to go home now that our work is done, but at the same time I am willing to stay if I am needed. I suppose some troops must be kept for guard duty.

Wellsville, Friday May 12/65—One year ago I was at the Battle of Spottsylvania amid blood and carnage. But God was gracious to me and spared my life. How different the scene today. Here all is peace, and the war is over.

Yesterday accompanied by Surgeon Wm. F. Smith and Adjutant Thorndike J. Smith I dined with a lawyer named James at his place called "Woodlawn." We had a good dinner and a good time. We then called upon Dr. Shore at the "Aerie" and intended to return to camp in the evening, but a violent thunderstorm came up, and we thought it wise to remain over night. We found a party of ladies at the "Aerie" who entertained us with piano music and singing. One young lady who was decidedly rebellious sang a song with a chorus beginning: "Farewell forever, the Stars and the Stripes" and ending with something about "Thirteen bright stars and the palmetto tree." I suggested that a Yankee named Sherman had cut down the palmetto tree.[44] She was quite indignant, but being a visitor our host could not control her sentiments. Dr. Shore has taken the Oath of Allegiance to the U.S., and his daughter told me that they were glad to have the protection of the U.S. troops. The rain poured in torrents, and the thunder was loud and deep. I have a guard stationed here, and during the evening the sentinel at the barn fired his musket at a man who approached and would not halt. I took my pistol and went out but did not find anyone except the guard. The country is full of horse thieves, and we have to watch our horses. We finally went upstairs to bed, and as a precaution we placed a bureau against the door, but we felt ashamed of it this morning when we came down and found a fire in the sitting room and a nice breakfast waiting for us. At the same time this country is not safe for Union soldiers away from camp, as many Rebel soldiers are loafing about. We had a hard ride to camp, as many trees had fallen across the road and the rain had made deep gullies. We found the camp rather wet, but the sun made it all right.

This life reminds me of *Uncle Tom's Cabin.* Many of the ex-slaves are at work, and this gives us a chance to watch plantation life. I cannot say that I admire it very much, for it seems to be a lazy sort of living. The ladies dress in old styles but seem to be educated.

Wellsville Saturday May 13/65—Today I gave a dinner for a party of citizens in return for the hospitable manner in which they have treated me. The party seemed to enjoy a Yankee dinner, and we did our best to give a fine spread and make them welcome. They were very curious about our troops and paid attention to all that they saw.

Wellsville, Va. Sunday, May 14/65—As we have no church to attend I have spent the day making calls. I rode over to Wilson's Station and called at Brigade Headquarters and then made a call upon some ladies at a plantation near. It is quite amusing to meet many men who seem to be ignorant of the war. That is, they do not want to admit that they served in the Rebel Army. Many think that they are liable to arrest and trial for the part they have taken. I ask them all sorts of questions just for fun.

Wellsville, Monday, May 15/65—Today we have orders to be ready to move, so I have called in my guards and detachments and have made my farewell calls. I have many invitations to return and make visits after I become a citizen. Well, I am glad that I have succeeded in getting the good will of these people.

Wilson's Station, Va. Tuesday, May 16/65—We left our camp at Wellsville this morning and marched to this place where we joined our old Brigade. We are to march to Richmond where we are to have a chance to see the city and wait for orders. The march will be by easy stages, as there is no hurry, and I think we shall enjoy it.

Wilson's Station, Wednesday, May 17/65—We are waiting for

orders to start upon our march to Richmond. The weather is good, and we just enjoy soldiering under such pleasant circumstances, The road to Richmond will take us through the country that is now historic, and we shall get an idea of the inside of the late southern confederacy.

Near Petersburg, Va., Thursday May 18th 1865—We left camp at Wilson's Station and took the road to Richmond making easy marches.

Friday May 19/65—At last I have been through Petersburg. This morning we commenced our march through the city. Petersburg is a fine little city, and it was hard to realize as we tramped its peaceful streets that we had been nearly a year getting into it. The city shows the effect of Yankee shot and shell. The stores are open and mostly kept by men from the North. The buildings near the railroad are badly damaged by the fire from the Union Batteries. The people came out to see us pass but did not make any audible comment. Well, I was glad to see the place that had caused us so much bloodshed.

Near Manchester, Va. Saturday May 20/65—We arrived at this place which is opposite Richmond on the James River at 9 o'clock this morning. On the march we passed near the Rebel Fort Darling and saw a good many other forts. Around this the south side of the city there appear to be four lines of strong works. This afternoon Surgeon Smith, Adjutant Smith and myself rode into Richmond. We passed through Manchester, which is a small town and much dilapidated, and crossed the James River on a pontoon bridge. The first thing that I noticed was a brick building with a large sign: "Libby Prison." We rode down, dismounted, and went in. It made my blood boil to remember that in this hole so many of our brave boys died from starvation. We then took a look at Castle Thunder, another prison, and found it nothing but a brick building once used as a storehouse. From here we rode to the Spottswood Hotel and then to the Ballard House. We then took a look at the Capitol which sheltered the Rebel Congress and whose walls heard much treasonable talk. The Capitol stands in a fine park in which is a famous statue of Washington. Jefferson, Mason, Clay, and Patrick Henry stand guard over it. Here under the eye of Washington treason was plotted and traitors made their plans. The court house was destroyed by fire with a good part of the business portion of the city. It was the work of the Rebel General Ewell. Near the Capitol stands a fine granite building once used as the Rebel Treasury Department, but now as the First National Bank of Richmond. This building was draped in mourning in memory of President Lincoln. Riding up Franklin Street we passed many fine residences with ladies at the windows accompanied by ex Rebel officers. Just before dark we returned to camp well pleased with our first visit to Richmond.

Near Manchester Sunday May 21/65—After the usual inspection I rode into Richmond intending to attend church but found that the churches were not open in the afternoon. I went into the park and listened to a band that was playing. Many ladies were walking in the park, some escorted by Union and some by Rebel officers. One fourth of our men are allowed to visit Richmond daily, and in this way all of the soldiers will have a chance to see the late Rebel Capital. I think that this is right for the boys have earned the right to see the city captured by their valor.

Near Manchester, Va. Monday May 22/65—Last night we had a terrible storm of wind and rain. My tent blew down, and I got wet. We managed by the help of the guard to pitch the tent again, but I was too wet to sleep. Fortunately the sun came out this morning and made us comfortable. Adjutant Smith and myself rode into Richmond for dinner and found some strawberries and cream.

Near Manchester, Va. Tuesday May 23/65—I have remained in camp today making preparations for our march to Washington which will begin tomorrow and for the review as we pass through Richmond. The road is a long one, and the weather is very hot, but we are going towards home.

Hanover Court House, Va. Wednesday May 24/65—We left Manchester this morning and marched through Richmond passing in review before Major General Halleck, U.S.A. The people looked on with indifference, but a party of colored children sang "John Brown" to us as we marched along. We are camped near the battlefield of 1862, and it brings many sad memories to our minds. Then we were bound for Richmond; now we are bound for Home Sweet Home.

Camp 20 miles south of Fredericksburg, Saturday May 27/65—Here we are so far on our journey, but the mud is so deep from recent rains and we have had to stop for awhile. Reveille is sounded at 3:30 A.M. and we leave camp at 5 A.M. and march until 2 P.M. and then go into camp. We like this, as it gives us a chance to see the country.

Near Fredericksburg, Va., Monday May 29/65—We left camp this morning, the sun having dried up the mud, and are now encamped on the old battlefield of Fredericksburg. How well I remember the dark days of December 1862 and May 1863 when we buried so many of our brave boys on these fields. Thank God it is all over, and tonight we sleep without *pickets.*

Tuesday May 30/65—This morning we marched through the streets of Fredericksburg and found the old town quite in ruin. It seemed queer to march down the street where in 1863 (May 3) we dodged the Rebel Shell. We made about 17 miles today and have a pleasant camp for the night. I like to march without any enemy near much better than where we were looking for him or he for us.

Camp near Fairfax Court House, Va., Thursday June 1st 1865—We left camp this morning and crossed Wolf Run Shoals, and not for the first time either. Here we are at the spot where we camped when we went to Bull Run. At that time I hardly thought that I should ever be in command of the 2nd R.I. Vols.

Hall's Hill, Va., opposite Washington, Friday June 2nd 1865—We arrived here today and have pitched our camp. I think I have made my last long march as a soldier. It is singular that we made our last march today over the same road that we made our first march on in going to Bull Run. We left Fairfax Court House this morning and made about fifteen miles today. The march from Richmond has been rather a hard one, but it is over at last. An order has been received directing the muster out of men whose time will expire before Oct. 1/65. This will take about one hundred men out of my Regiment but will leave a good command.

Hall's Hill Saturday June 3/65—We are having a good rest after our long march, and the men enjoy it.

Hall's Hill Sunday June 4/65—Sunday again and my camp is full of visitors. A party of R.I. people made me a call, and I had a dress parade for their benefit. They seemed to enjoy the parade by the veteran Rhode Island troops.

Hall's Hill, Va. Monday June 5/65—Four years ago today I enlisted as a boy in the Army. I was proud to be a Corporal and prouder still to be a soldier. Today as I look back I cannot realize that I have seen the beginning and the end of the great Civil War. But such is the fact, and I devoutly thank God for it. On these anniversaries I always sit down and think over the events of the past and derive much satisfaction.

Hall's Hill Tuesday June 6/65—Our camp is not a very pleasant one, but if we remain long it will be changed. This morning the 119th Penn. Vols. Col Hickman of our Brigade left for home. We paraded and saluted as they passed. It made me feel homesick to see them leave, but our turn will come some day. We are making preparations for the review of the 6th Corps which will take place next Thursday. All the men of our Brigade have been furnished with new uniforms, and we expect to make a fine show. Although so near Washington, yet I see very little of it.

June 7th 1865—Still at work getting ready for the review. The 2nd R.I. will look well. Made a visit to Washington and the Capitol.

Thursday June 8/65—The day has come and gone, and the review is over. We left camp just at daylight and marched to Long Bridge where we crossed and the Corps was massed on Maryland Avenue and other streets. At 9 o'clock the march began. President Johnson with other dignitaries was seated upon a platform in front of the White House. They received us very kindly, but the people with the exception of the ladies who waved their handkerchiefs were very quiet. We expected to meet with a warm reception, as the 6th Corps saved Washington in 1864, but evidently reviews are played out with Washington people. The city was fearfully hot, and the men suffered much. I sent the Regiment to camp by way of Georgetown and Aqueduct Bridge, and I remained in the city to dine with friends. I returned to camp this evening. The 2nd R.I. looked well in their new clothes and white gloves.

Friday June 9/65—This morning I paid my respects to Mrs. Gen. Edwards who is staying with her husband, our Brigade Commander, in camp. In the evening I called upon General Wheaton. General Meade is to go to Philadelphia to command the Department of the Atlantic.

Sunday June 11/65—It is rumored now that the 2nd R.I.V. is to remain in service and may be made a part of the Regular Army. Well, all right, I think this would suit me. After inspection today I made some calls, but have spent most of the day in my tent.

Saturday June 17/65—Last night Col. Thomas S. Allen commanding 5th Wisconsin of our Brigade gave a grand supper to the field and staff officers of our Brigade. The 5th is to go home in a few days. General Wheaton and General Edwards were present. The camp was illuminated and presented a fine appearance. The officers of the 5th presented Colonel Allen with an elegant 6th Corps badge. Speeches kept us busy until eleven o'clock.

June 19/65 Monday—General Wheaton thinks that the 2nd R.I.V. will remain in service for a long time yet. Co. "E" Captain James A. Bowen was mustered out of service today and will leave for home tomorrow.

Tuesday June 20/65—Co. "E" left camp for R.I. today. Capt. Bowen was the senior Captain, and this leaves Captain Stephen Thurber as senior Captain. My Regiment is reduced by the muster out of Co. "E" but is still as large as most of the Regiments remaining in the field.

Thursday June 22/65—Today Colonel Benedict and wife, Mr. Manly and Miss Emilie Marie came out from Washington and spent the day in camp. They brought ice cream, cake, pies, lemons etc. and we had a fine time. They returned to the city this evening. Mrs. Benedict brought me a lot of bedding for my tent. I have now two wall tents floored and arranged very finely. The 37th Mass. Vols. left for home today, and the 2nd R.I. escorted them towards the city. General Edwards has been mustered out of service, and as I am senior officer I have taken command of the Brigade by order of General Wheaton.

Friday June 30/65—The week has passed as usual—drill and inspections etc. Today I mustered the Regiment for pay. The Army of the Potomac has ceased to exist. Our Corps has been reduced to a Division as has all the other Corps. Immediately after the 4th of July the Army is to march to the Monocacy River near the Baltimore & Ohio R.R. in Maryland and go into camp. General Horatio G. Wright is to command the Army and Gen. Wheaton a Brigade. I do not know whether my Regiment will be placed in Wheaton's or Hamlbin's Brigade. Either will suit me. I am going to R.I. in one week to be married and return with my wife to camp. I have all my furniture made and everything in readiness for housekeeping. Lt. Col. Clendennin of Wheaton's staff is to remain in service and Mrs. Clendennin will be with him. Our camp will be about forty miles from Washington and being on the line of railroad will be quite handy for us. Just how long we shall remain in service I cannot say, but it will probably be for a year. Some of the officers want to stay while others prefer to go home. I am indifferent, but determined to see the end of the 2nd R.I.V. or die in service.

Hall's Hill, Va. Saturday July 1st 1865—We are hard at work getting ready to move to our new camp in Maryland. We are at present in the 3rd Brigade commanded by Gen. Joseph E. Hamblin who has relieved me from command. We expect to be transferred to the 1st Brigade commanded by Gen. Truman Seymour.

Hall's Hill, Va. Sunday July 2/65—Today I rode into Georgetown and called upon James F. Benedict and family. They are very kind to me, and it seems like going home to visit them. I have applied for a leave of absence and shall leave for home just as soon as I can get my Regiment into the new camp in Maryland.

Hall's Hill, Va. Monday July 3/65—We are making great preparations for the celebration of the 4th tomorrow. I have ordered *Taps* postponed tonight until 10 o'clock, and the men are having a fine time parading about and shouting. I called at the War Department in Washington to see about the muster out of my Regiment. They told me that we should probably remain in service at least one year, so we have settled down for a life in the Army in time of peace. Well, all right, if my plans work well I can stand it. I shall give a dinner party tomorrow to the officers and friends in Washington and Georgetown. If the weather is fine we shall have a good time and try to give the men an enjoyable day. I like to please my men whenever I can, for it makes them more content with a soldier's life.

Hall's Hill Tuesday July 4th 1865—Another Independence Day in the Army and this has been my fifth. The first we passed at Camp Clark near Washington, the second at Harrison's Landing, the third at Gettysburg, Pa., the fourth at Petersburg, and today we are back at Washington with our work finished. We have had a fine time today with a large party of ladies and gentlemen from Washington who with the officers of the 2nd R.I. dined at my headquarters. We managed to make a fine spread. The Sergeant Major, Benoni Sweet, amused the party by a tight rope walking exhibition. The day has been fun.

Wednesday July 5/65—I have passed most of the day in Washington dancing attendance upon the War Department. Some time ago an order was issued from the War. Dept. consolidating the men of the 4th & 7th R.I. Vols. with the 2nd R.I. Vols. The order was in some way lost, and the men did not report. Today I had the matter arranged and shall expect these men in a few days.

Thursday July 6th 1865—We expect to move to our new camp in Maryland next Monday, and I shall leave for home as soon as I can place the Regiment in their new camp.

Friday July 7/65—No news as we are busy getting our accumulated traps packed up ready to move. Since peace was declared I allow the men to have more things, and want to save them for them for future use.

Hall's Hill, Va. Saturday July 8/65—Well here we go. Instead of Maryland it is Rhode Island, so I reckon I will give up the idea of a ten days' leave from the Army and take one for life.

Last night I received an order to prepare the Rolls for the muster out of the 2nd R.I. Of course there was great rejoicing in camp, and everybody is happy at the prospect of home and friends. It will take some days to make out all the papers, but we shall start for R.I. within a week I think.

Sunday July 9th 1865—Although I want to go home, yet as I think of the separation from comrades some of whom I have known for more than four years, I cannot help feeling sad. I trust I entered the Army with pure motives and from love of country. I have tried to keep myself from evil ways and believe that I have never forgotten that I am a Christian. Thank God no spiritous liquors have ever passed my lips as a beverage, and I feel that I can go home to my family as pure as when I left them as a boy of 19 years. I have been successful in my Army life simply because I have always been ready and willing to do my duty. I thank God that I have had an opportunity of serving my country freeing the slaves and restoring the Union.

Monday July 10/65—The time draws near.

Tuesday July 11/65—My men are wild with joy, and many plans are being made.

Wednesday July 12/65—The Rolls are finished, and we are to be mustered out of service tomorrow. I have written my last letter from the Army today.

July 13/65 Thursday—Today the 2nd R.I. paraded and were mustered out of service from the day when disbanded in Providence. I am arranging the transportation and shall start tomorrow or next day.

July 14/65 Friday—We are waiting waiting, but tomorrow we shall probably start. Goodbyes have been said to the few left behind. Most of the troops have already gone home, but a very few are left.

Saturday July 15/65—Goodbye camp at Hall's Hill. Goodbye Virginia. Goodbye Army, dear old Army of the Potomac. Tattered and torn, you are crowned with the victor's laurels at last. We are to leave at 9 o'clock A.M. today.

New York Sunday July 16th 1865—We arrived here this morning after a day and night on the road. The 58th Mass. Vols. came on the train. I put the 2nd R.I. into the park at Castle Garden and closed the gate. I propose to take my Regiment home in good condition. I have telegraphed to Governor James Y. Smith, and he has authorized me to charter a steamer.

On board steamer July 16/65—I left Castle Garden about 4 o'clock and made a fine march up Broadway past the *Herald* office, our men giving the *Herald* three cheers. I then embarked on the steamer for New Haven, which is the only point I could get transportation to. The 58th

Mass Vols. Lt. Col. John C. Whittier[?] is on board this same boat.

New Haven, Conn. Monday morning 6 o'clock July 17—We arrived this morning in a rain storm. I got breakfast at the New Haven House, and the men ate from their haversacks under the coal sheds on the wharf. I have just procured a train of cars to take the Regiment to New London.

Groton, Conn. 3 P.M.—We arrived at New London about noon, and I was surprised to be called out of the car by a committee from the City Council who announced that a collation was waiting for our men in the street near the depot. We gladly accepted and were waited upon by the pretty girls of New London. The dinner was fine and much enjoyed by our men. We then crossed to this place by the ferry and will take cars soon. I have telegraphed to Providence to have horses ready for myself and staff. My horse Katie started with us, but I do not know where she is now.

Providence, R.I. Tuesday July 18/65—Here we are at "Home Sweet Home." We left Groton last night about 4 o'clock, but the train was slow, and we did not reach Providence until midnight. Here I found a Militia Company commanded by a Col. Bennett waiting for us, but as it was so late I declined an escort or to parade. I marched the men into a hall where they partook of a collation and then sent the Regiment to the barracks of the Veteran Reserve Corps on the Cove lands to sleep. I found much to my joy that the car containing my horse Katie had been attached to our train, and mounting I rode home and then sent her to a stable by my orderly Zack Chase. This morning my staff reported at my mother's, and I rode down to Exchange Place where the Adjutant formed the Regiment in line. I marched them to the Cove lands, and after forming line gave my last commands: "Order arms. Parade rest." I then briefly addressed the officers and men and gave them furloughs to report when notice was given through the papers. I cautioned them to behave like men and soldiers and to wear their uniforms until finally discharged. The officers gathered about me, and we said our farewells. The men gave "Nine cheers for the Colonel" and then broke ranks, and I took every man by the hand and said goodbye. My eyes were full of tears, and I felt sad, for I knew these men, and they had always stood by me. Some of them I had served with in the ranks and felt a warm affection for them all. I have present and absent 18 officers and 438 enlisted men, nearly all of whom were present. Major Henry H. Young is absent serving on Gen. Sheridan's staff and one officer absent wounded. I then rode to the Governor's office and reported my return home.

Providence, R.I. Friday July 28th 1865—Today the 2nd R.I. was paid off and discharged. The Regiment met at 9 A.M. and without arms and marched to a building[45] on South Main Street where they received their money and final discharge papers. About noon the Paymaster told me that I was the only man left in the Regiment and that he would be ready to pay me at 2 P.M. I went home, took off my uniform, and put on a suit of citizen's clothes for the first time in over four years. I then went down to the office and received my pay and discharge. As I came out of the building I found the Regiment, yes my Regiment, drawn up on the sidewalk, and again I took each man by the hand. It was sad, yet joyful, for the war is over and we are at home. No more suffering, no more scenes of carnage and death. Thank God it is over and that the Union is restored. And so at last I am a simple citizen. Well, I am content, but should my country call again I am ready to respond. The Governor has given me a commission as Colonel for gallant conduct during the war. But what are honors now, compared to the delights of peace and home. Four years and fifty-eight days I served my country, and now I am content to be a civilian. I am proud of my old Regiment and shall ever think of my comrades with pleasure.

Elisha H. Rhodes, Colonel, 2nd RI Volunteers

AN ALPHABETICAL LIST OF THE BATTLES (WITH DATES) ENGAGED IN BY THE SECOND RHODE ISLAND REGIMENT

*ANTIETAM, ALSO KNOWN AS SHARPSBURG
   MARYLAND, SEPT. 16-17, 1862
APPOMATTOX COURT HOUSE
   VIRGINIA, APRIL 9, 1865
BULL RUN (FIRST), ALSO KNOWN AS MANASSAS
   VIRGINIA, JULY 21, 1861
COLD HARBOR
   VIRGINIA, MAY 31-JUNE 12, 1864
FORT STEADMAN
   VIRGINIA, MARCH 25, 1865
FORT STEVENS
   D.C., JULY 12, 1864
FREDERICKSBURG
   VIRGINIA, DEC. 11-16, 1862
GETTYSBURG
   PENNSYLVANIA, JULY 1-3, 1863
HATCHER'S RUN
   VIRGINIA, FEB. 5-7, 1865
MALVERN HILL .
   VIRGINIA, JULY 1 & AUG. 5, 1862

MINE RUN
   VIRGINIA, NOV. 26-28, 1863
OPEQUON (WINCHESTER)
   VIRGINIA, SEPT. 19, 1864
PETERSBURG
   JUNE 10-12, 1862 & DEC. 4-APRIL 3, 1865
SAYLERS CREEK
   VIRGINIA, APRIL 6, 1865
SALEM HEIGHTS
   VIRGINIA, MAY 3-4, 1863
SEVEN PINES
   VIRGINIA, MAY 31-JUNE 1, 1862
SPOTTSYLVANIA
   VIRGINIA, MAY 8-12, 1864
WILDERNESS
   VIRGINIA, MAY 8-21, 1864
WILLIAMSBURG
   VIRGINIA, MAY 5, JULY 11, 1862
YORKTOWN
   VIRGINIA, APRIL 5-MAY 3, 1862

Second Rhode Island witnessed, but took no action in main battle.

EPILOGUE

Frederick Miller Rhodes, Jr., born in 1899, remembers his grandfather.

"I don't think that Grandpa owned a house. He and Grandma used to board on Benefit Street and out at Fruit Hill, and sometimes they stayed with Aunt Alice (Mrs. Howard P. Chase) at Fruit Hill. They also used to visit us at Lime Rock at our summer house. When I was a little boy I would climb into bed with Grandma and Grandpa before they got up, and he would tell me tall yarns about a young soldier he called "Johnny Mud" who was in the Civil War.

I used to parade with him. Sometimes he was the Chief Marshal. On Memorial Day we would go to the old armory on Benefit Street where Prescott Post of the G.A.R. met and march downtown and through Providence, and I would march along with him. There would be flower wagons laden with flowers for the cemeteries. We used to take the trolley out to Swan Point Cemetery where the flowers were placed on the graves of the veterans.

Grandpa took my older brother, Elisha, and me on trips when we each turned thirteen years old. We had our choice of going by boat or else by train to Philadelphia, Baltimore, etc. Elisha went with him by train, but I chose to go by boat. By the time Jack (younger brother James) was thirteen Grandpa had died, so he missed his trip.

Grandpa and I went from Providence to Norfolk, Virginia, and I think the name of the boat was the POWHATAN. We visited Fortress Monroe and took the train to Williamsburg. We stayed overnight in an old wooden hotel (probably where Chowning's Tavern has been reconstructed). There were wooden stairs up the side of the building for a fire escape. At dinner we had a very tough chicken.

"George!" called Grandpa. "Come here a minute."

"Yassuh?" answered the waiter. (Grandpa called all the colored men "George")

"In '62 I passed through here with the army, and this same chicken was sitting on the Court House steps," said Grandpa.

We visited several battlefields along the coast: Yorktown, Fredericksburg, and Seven Pines. We stayed in Washington two or three days. We rode out to Mount Vernon by trolley from Washington, and we had hot chocolate and gingerbread in the kitchen. We took the night boat from Washington down the Potomac River to Norfolk and then the Merchant and Miners line boat back to Providence. Grandpa knew the captain, and we sat at the head table. He always met people that he knew. An old army chum and his son were traveling on the same boat. We had soft shell crabs and watermelon for supper.

Grandpa used to take me over to Fort Adams in Newport, R.I. when the garrison was still there. A lot of men used to salute him. He always carried himself with a military bearing and wore a lapel pin, which was probably for the Army of the Potomac. Grandpa was a good speaker and was always making speeches at banquets and reunions for the G.A.R., the Masons, or at the dedication of monuments. There were trees planted in his honor on the Rhode Island State House lawn and at Roger Williams Park on Arbor Day, and there is a window at the Central Baptist Church in Providence in his memory."

Frederick Miller Rhodes, Jr. — Spring, 1985

SECTION NOTES

[1]Mathews house.

[2]Surgeon James Harris remained on the battlefield after the retreat began in order to care for the wounded and dying. John Russell Bartlett, *Memoirs of Rhode Island Officers Who Were Engaged in the Service of Their Country During the Great Rebellion of the South* (Providence: Sidney S. Rider & Brother, 1867), p.125.

[3]Secessionists, or Secessioners.

[4]S. James Smith of Company "I."

[5]The First Rhode Island Detached Militia commanded by Col. Ambrose E. Burnside, was composed of ten companies of infantry and a battery of artillery, and served for only three months in response to President Lincoln's proclamation for raising an army of 75,000 men on April 15, 1861. The Second Rhode Island Regiment was raised in response to a call by Lincoln on May 3, 1861 for troops to serve for three years.

[6]*National Cyclopedia of American Biography* (New York: James T. White & Co., 1893), v.3, p.428: "On December 16, 1861, a resolution, introduced by Mr. Wilkinson, called for the expulsion of Mr. Bright on the ground of disloyalty, although the committee on the judiciary had reported adversely by a vote of five to two. The charge was based upon a letter written by Mr. Bright March 1, 1861 and addressed to 'His Excellency Jefferson Davis, President of the Confederate States.' This recommended to Mr. Davis's notice a friend, Mr. Thomas B. Lincoln of Texas who, as the letter stated, 'visits your capital mainly to dispose of what he regards as a great improvement in fire-arms.'

Charles Sumner, supported by other senators, maintained that Mr. Bright was a traitor, who was directly giving aid and comfort to the public enemies, war having actually begun . . ." There was a vote of 32 to 14 in favor of expulsion.

[7]"Copperhead" became a lable of scorn for all Northerners who sympathized with the South, were "soft" on slavery, or protested against keeping the South in the Union by fighting. Some were radical Democrats who said that the Confederacy would be restored to the Union if the Abolitionists would leave the slavery issue alone. General McClellan was favored by the Democrats, but he was no politician. When Congress passed the 1863 Draft Act many infuriated people formed secret societies such as the "Sons of Liberty," "Order of the American Knights," "Knights of the Golden Circle," "Order of the Star," and had rituals as secret signals. They were responsible for some of the draft riots and agitation against the war. Many broadsides and cartoons were printed and distributed against the Copperhead movement. Whether the term originated with copper pennies or copperhead snakes is unclear. There is an interesting account of the arrest of Clement L. Vallandingham, a Copperhead leader, by General Ambrose Burnside as written by Frederic S. Klein, "The Great Copperhead Conspiracy," *Civil War Times Illustrated*, v. 4, no. 3 (June 1965), pp. 21-26. For a longer history see Wood Gray, *The Hidden Civil War: the Story of the Copperheads* (New York: Viking Press, 1942) 314pp.

[8]Henry Wilson, A Senator from Massachusetts was Chairman of the Committee on Military Affairs during the war. In 1861 he raised a regiment from Massachusetts and accompanied it to the front as its colonel and was on General McClellan's staff. In 1873 he became Vice-president under U.S. Grant.

[9]The soldier was Private George W. Wilcox from Mendon, Mass., and Co. "I," Second Rhode Island Volunteers. Augustus Woodbury, *The Second Rhode Island Regiment: a Narrative of Military Operations in Which the Regiment Was Engaged From the Beginning to the End of the War for the Union* (Providence: Valpey, Angell & Co.,

1875) pp. 70, 414.

[10]For an account of the gruesome work see Virgil Carrington Jones, "The Dead Behead Easily," *Gray Ghosts and Rebel Raiders* (New York: Henry Holt and Co., 1956), pp.66-73 and his notes on pp. 379-381.

[11]Edwin W. Stone, Rhode Island in the Rebellion (Providence: George H. Whitney, 1864), p. 294: "It is a remarkable fact in the history of this regiment, that from the first battle of Bull Run to that of Chancellorsville, it has met the same rebel regiments on picket, and been opposed to the same on the field. So frequently had they met, that many of the men, on both sides, formed a familiar acquaintance. On the first picket service after a hard battle, the secesh would inquire, with apparent interest, after the Federals present. The scrupulous regard paid by the 2nd Rhode Island to the order against picket firing, secured the respect and entire confidence of these opponents, and when the former took their posts, the latter would leave their rifle pits to which they had resorted for cover, stack arms, and enter into friendly conversation. From the beginning the regiment has supported an honorable reputation for respecting private property in proximity to its encampments."

[12]Hiram Berdan commanded the 1st U.S. Sharpshooters.

[13]Admiral David G. Farragut captured New Orleans on April 28, 1862.

[14]This plantation belonged to Major General William H.F. Lee and was used by the Lee family.

[15]In an article in the *Providence Sunday Journal* May 24, 1914 in the fifth section Providence Civil War veterans recalled their "worst meal" experiences during the war. Elisha Rhodes said: "I saw over in a clump of bushes a little old grist mill. The thought struck me that perhaps I might find some flour or meal, but to my great disappointment everything appeared to have been swept up clean and carried away.

I was terribly hungry, for we had all been on very short allowances. About to leave the mill, I observed that the upper stone had been raised for the purpose of 'pecking' it, and that in the grooves of the nether stone there was quite a collection of flour and dust.

Hastening to the woods I secured a sprig of spruce which, used as a brush, produced a good handfull of the gritty flour. This I put in a cup, wet down to a paste and spread on a piece of board which I placed in front of a fire that it might dry out and bake.

Quite pleased with my good fortune, I was watching that little cake brown up, when a voice broke in upon my joyous meditations. 'Sergeant-Major, where did you get that meal? If you have more of that johnnycake than you think you need, I would like a piece of it, for I'm very hungry.'

It was Col. Wheaton who was addressing me. When the cake was sufficiently baked I halved it with Col. Wheaton, who agreed with me that, saltless though it was and full of grit, it was something delicious.

We had been without salt, bread, or anything save hard, tasteless meat, when a gunboat came up the Pamunkey River with a lot of hardtack aboard. This was to be apportioned to the commands and regularly issued to the men. The men did their own issuing. They fell upon those boxes of hardtack like of drove of famished wolves. Instantly the boxes were broken open and the men began a ravenous feast. I think that was the time when the hardtack was really pie to famishing soldiers."

[16]Professor T.S.C. Lowe's ballon's usual height was 1,000 feet. When lower than 300 feet it was within range of Confederate guns. See *Battles and Leaders of the Civil War* (New York: Century, 1884-1888), v. 2, p. 321.

[17]Mary Custis Lee, who was a granddaughter of Martha Washington, after fleeing

her mansion "Arlington House" near Washington, D.C. had been living at her "second home" at White House, where Martha and George Washington were married. When Joseph E. Johnston drew back his forces before McClellan's advance she didn't get away quickly enough and was left behind the lines. Dr. Macon arranged for her safe passage. McClellan used the house as a hospital and assured protection of it, but when the Union army abandoned the White House Landing as a supply base on June 28, 1862 the White House was burned. Harnett T. Kane, *The Lady of Arlington* (New York: Doubleday, 1954).

[18]Harrison's Landing was the location of the famous Byrd family's manor house Westover and also Berkeley Hundred, also called Bermuda Hundred. Berkeley Hundred was patented in 1618 and claims the first celebration of Thanksgiving in what is now the United States. This historic house was the birthplace of Robert E. Lee's mother, Anne Hill Carter Lee, as well as the home of a signer of the Declaration of Independence and of two Presidents of the United States: Benjamin Harrison and William Henry Harrison. During the time of its occupancy by General McClellan "Taps" was composed here, and the house was used as a hospital and a signal station in July 1862. Within hours of the arrival of the Federal troops the plains spreading from the house to the river had all been reduced to paste by men's boots, horses' hoofs, and wagon wheels, causing the wheat fields, corn fields, vegetable gardens and flower gardens to all disappear. Most of the trees and fences and furniture were burned for camp fires. One of the original trees, a huge poplar, which shaded the cooks' stove still stands and shades the house. Berkeley house and plantation has been restored and is now open to the public as a museum. Clifford Dowdey, *The Great Plantation: a Profile of Berkeley Hundred and Plantation Virginia from Jamestown to Appomattox* (New York: Rinehart & Co., 1957) pp. 312-313.

[19]Rhode Islandism for "gambrel"

[20]His commission was back-dated to read July 24, 1862.

[21]General Pope fought at Second Bull Run on August 29th and 30th and retreated toward Washington until supported by the Army of the Potomac. At Chantilly the union of these two forces resisted Lee who moved through the mountain passes to the Shenandoah Valley.

Stonewall Jackson led the Confederates into Frederick, Maryland. McClellan took over command from Pope. The Battle of South Mountain was fought on September 14th, a victory for the North.

[22]At Antietam on September 17, 1862, the single bloodiest day of the war, McClellan lost 12,410 killed, wounded or captured, and Lee 10,700. In the long run however it proved to be a victory for the North in that it halted Lee's invasion and drove him out of Maryland, defended Washington, D.C., strenghtened the organization of the Union Army, and established Union control of the Potomac from Washington to Williamsport. Lee's forces were greatly weakened. Lee had intended to keep the Union forces from launching a major offensive in Virginia, and in this he succeeded, but at a terrible price. Tilberg, Frederick, *Antietam National Battlefield Site, Maryland* (Washington, D.C.: U.S. National Park Service Historical Handbook Series No. 31, 1960), p. 47.

[23]Michael Fay of Providence died September 27, 1862 at Downsville, Md.

[24]Good camp discipline and sanitation resulted in less illness in this regiment than in many others.

[25]Woodbury, *op. cit.,* pp. 121-122: "The army lay at Warrenton and it its neighborhood from the 9th to the 15th. Meanwhile, the authorities at Washington were deliberating

upon General Burnside's proposed plan of operations. It was sent to Washington on the 10th, was discussed by Generals Burnside and Halleck, at a personal interview at Warrenton, on the night of the 12th and a part of the day of the 13th, and was approved by President Lincoln on the 14th. 'The plan, in brief, was to demonstrate toward Culpepper, and then to make a rapid march to Falmouth, to cross the Rappahannock upon pontoons at that place, to seize Fredericksburg and the heights beyond, and to establish a temporary base of supplies at Acquia Creek. The movement beyond Fredericksburg was to be a matter for subsequent consideration. But it was in Burnside's mind to push immediately on toward Richmond upon the roads leading through Spottsylvania Court House, Bowling Green and the villages beyond; have supplies waiting at York river, then cross the Peninsula rapidly to the James River, and, with that for a base, march directly upon the city of his destination." [Quote of plan from Woodbury, *Burnside and the Ninth Army Corps,* pp. 182, 256.]

[26]The pontoons coming by land from Washington didn't arrive until November 25th because of mud on the roads. The pontoons coming by water came on the 18th, but there were no wagons to move them. While Burnside was being delayed by the weather and mud Longstreet moved the Confederate troops into Fredericksburg and made strong fortifications on the heights. Woodbury. *Second Rhode Island Regiment.* pp. 122-123.

[27]Burnside could have forded across the Rappahannock River on the 17th before the rain raised the river, but he waited for the pontoons. He delayed even after the bridges were laid and then gave unclear and incomplete battle orders to Sumner, Hooker and Franklin. Burnside lacked confidence in himself and some of his officers lacked confidence in his plan of attack. His vacillation resulted in his losing the element of surprise, the ever-strenghtening of the Confederates already good defensive position, and the demoralization of his troops in the miserable weather. When the Confederate line behind the stone wall at Marye's Heights proved to be impregnable, Burnside, despite the obvious failure of his plan, refused to change his orders. 6,000 Confederates held off 40,000 Union soldiers because of a good defensive terrain and the superior leadership of General Robert E. Lee.

Probably the best tactic employed by Burnside at Fredericksburg was his rapid and silent escape across the river during a noisy, stormy night. For an excellent analysis of the Battle of Fredericksburg see the special issue of *Civil War Times Illustrated,* v. 4, no. 8, (December 1965).

[28]One of the difficulties with the state volunteer troops was the political favoritism of the governors in appointing as officers people with political power but no practical military experience. In this case several veterans who were qualified and seasoned by fire should have been promoted. The rifles with greater accuracy permitted a new kind of warfare which made much of the old military tactics obsolete, so the war need no longer be fought "by the book."

[29]Governor Sprague, who had haughtily refused any advancements among whom he considered insubordinate officers of the Second Rhode Island because of their petition to him, became a U.S. Senator on March 4, 1863, and the newly sworn-in Governor Cozzens acceded to Colonel Roger's request for promotions from within the regiment.

[30]Laurence Kelley and John H. Flier.

[31]General Pickett's elite troops charged for one mile across an open field to the Union line which was behind a stone wall with artillery and muskets, and breached the Union line at a clump of trees. After fierce combat during which the Union soldiers closed in around the Confederates, Lee sent another column which was driven back. This disaster to Lee's

army has become known as the "high water mark" of the rebellion as the tide ran out for the Confederacy after this defeat.

[32]Mechanics and artisans of all kinds were to be found in the ranks of every volunteer regiment. Private George A. Bush of Bristol, R.I. and Co. "G" collected a lot of tin cans, melted the solder, and from the tin shaped a pair of candle holders which were placed on either side of the pulpit. Chaplain Beugless was wounded at the Battle of the Wilderness on May 5, 1864 and was mustered out of service June 17, 1864 when the regiment, enlisted for three years, reached the end of its service. Chaplain Beugless then entered the U.S. Navy, being appointed Chaplain July 2, 1864. He remained in the service until his death at Nagasaki, Japan on July 31, 1887. In 1888 Mrs. Beugless sent a letter to Elisha H. Rhodes saying that she was sending him the candlesticks for his collection of war relics.

[33]The North had a problem as to the status of the Negroes who escaped from the South. When they were proven fugitive slaves, sometimes they were returned to their masters. If they were not returned they had no status. General Benjamin F. Butler at Fortress Monroe, when confronted by a slave named Luke, called him a *contraband of war,* and the name stuck. The ex-slaves became the property of the U.S. Government. In July of 1862 Congress passed a confiscation act which proclaimed these people "forever free." Lincoln's Emancipation Proclamation did not take legal effect until January 1, 1863.

[34]Built in Liverpool, England the *C.S.S. Alabama* ranged the seas and in eleven months captured 69 Northern prizes valued at $6,500,000 before she was sunk by the *U.S.S. Kearsage* off the coast of Cherbourg, France on June 19, 1864.

[35]He had become a Mason at Pawtuxet, R.I. on March 29, 1864 at Harmony Lodge No. 9, F. & A.M. while home on leave.

[36]John Singleton Mosby and his Rangers knew all of the highways and byways of Loudoun, Prince William, Fauquier and Fairfax Counties in Virginia and could appear and disappear like magic. The local residents fed, protected, and supported him as guerillas. Mosby began as a scout for J.E.B. Stuart, but soon he had an outfit of his own, the 43d Battalion of Virginia Partisan Rangers. His daring and intelligent exploits added much of value to the Confederate army and contributed much to the romance of the South, and were explored in a television series called "Gray Ghost." See "An Appraisal of John S. Mosby," *Civil War Times Illustrated* v. 4, no. 7 (November 1965), pp. 4-7, 49-54 and John S. Mosby, "A Bit of Partisan Service," in *Battles and Leaders of the Civil War. op. cit.,* v. 3, pp. 148-151.

[37]General Sheridan had been away at Washington on official business when General Early with reinforcements attacked near Winchester on October 19th. When Sheridan reached Winchester that morning he met soldiers retreating from the battle. He then made the famous "Sheridan's Ride," gathering the troops, shouting and swinging his hat and rallying his troops to drive Early all the way to New Market after defeating him at Cedar Creek. Early lost "90 pieces of artillery with ammunition, 40 flags, 19,000 small arms, with ammunition and equipments, 3,500 horses, 7,500 unwounded prisoners, and probably in killed and wounded at least 15,000 more." Woodbury. *The Second Rhode Island Regiment, op. cit.,* p. 307.

The dramatic battle virtually finished the Confederate army's use of the Shenandoah Valley as a source of food and supplies as Sheridan captured and destroyed "1,200 barns, 435,000 bushels of wheat, 77,176 bushels of corn, 20,000 bushels of oats, 20,397 tons of hay, 10,918 beeves, 12,000 sheep, 15,000 swine, and 12,000 pounds of bacon and ham." *Ibid.,* p. 315.

The horse ridden by Sheridan is now in the Smithsonian Museum on exhibit.

[38]General Sherman marched from Atlanta and entered Savannah on December 21, 1864, and sent a dispatch to President Lincoln presenting to him the city of Savannah as a "Christmas gift." The Library of Congress has the letter from Lincoln to Sherman thanking him for this present.

[39]For an account of true cases of insanity see Dr. Byron Stinson, " 'Battle Fatigue' and how it was treated in the C.W.," *Civil War Times Illustrated* v. 4, no. 7, (November 1965), pp. 40-44.

[40]Major Henry Harrison Young, a small, handsome, intelligent, and courageous man, was detached from Co. "B" of the Second Rhode Island Infantry on April 30, 1863 and went into dangerous Secret Service work on Sheridan's Cavalry staff, becoming Chief of Scouts over about 60 well-disciplined men. They dressed in Confederate uniforms and mingled with the Confederate soldiers and citizens, causing much confusion, passing mis-information, gathering intelligence for Sheridan, and capturing Confederate soldiers and officers. After the war he went on a secret mission for the United States to support President Benito Juarez against Archduke Maximilian. He was recognized by a band of Mexican rancheros and ex-Confederates sympathetic to the cause of Maximilian and killed at the age of 25 in 1867, although his body was never recovered and for years his family hoped that he had escaped. See Richard P. Weinert, "The South Had Mosby; the Union: Maj. Henry Young," *Civil War Times Illustrated.* v. 3, no. 1 (April 1964), pp. 38-42. and also Jacob H. Martin, *The Campaign Life of Lt. Col. Henry Harrison Young, Aid-De-Camp to General Sheridan and Chief of His Scouts* (Providence: Sidney S. Rider, 1882). and General Oliver Edwards, "Sheridan's Chief of Scouts: Col. Henry Young's Daring Career," *The Springfield* [Mass.] *Weekly Republican.* Friday, February 11, 1887. p. 4.

[41]The Union League was formed to counter-act the Copperhead organizations. their object was "To preserve Liberty and Union of these United States; to maintain the Constitution thereof, and that of this State, and the supremacy of the laws of the United States, to sustain the existing Administration in putting down the enemies of the Government, and thwarting the design of traitors and disloyalists, and to protect, strengthen and defend all loyal men, without regard to sect, condition, or party." National Council of the Union League of America. *Ritual.* 1863, p. 4. The ritual placed a charge upon its members which included the Holy Bible, the Flag, the Constitution, the Declaration of Independence, and Washington's Farewell Address. Questions and answers and oaths against Secession and other matters make up the rest of the ritual.

[42]"Another" probably refers to Miss Caroline Pearce Hunt, whom he married, and whose letters apparently have not been preserved.

[43]Corporal Alexander Mills was a Canadian who served with the 12th R.I. from October 1862-July 1863, and he joined as a private in Co. "E," 2d R.I.V. on September 15, 1864.

[44]The palmetto tree is native to the south and is the state emblem for South Carolina, the site of Fort Sumter and the first attack of the war.

[45]This was the Fall River Iron Works Building.

ACKNOWLEDGMENTS

I wish to express my appreciation to Andrew and Penelope Mowbray and staff of Andrew Mowbray, Incorporated—Publishers, for recognizing this book as being worthy of publication at a time when other publishers were uninterested, for their fine job of publishing the first edition, and for their generosity and cooperation with the transfer of publication to the Orion Books edition.

I am much indebted to Ken Burns and staff of Florentine Films for making Elisha Hunt Rhodes famous almost one hundred fifty years after his birth, and for their wise choice of quotations from *All for the Union* in assembling their wonderful documentary film *The Civil War.* Without them this book would have sold out relatively unnoticed.

The following gentlemen I wish to thank for their kind words and assistance regarding this book: Geoffrey C. Ward, David McCullough, Stephen W. Sears, and James McPherson. Special thanks go to Stephen Topping of Orion Books for guiding this edition through the myriad details leading to publication.

Please note the following errata:

On page 185 the name should read James Q. Rice of 2nd Conn. Heavy Artillery.

On page 238 the name of the plantation of Dr. Henry Edwin Shore (1800–1867) was called "The Acre," because the plantation was laid out in acres with one acre for the yard. (See Turner, W. R. *Old Homes and Families in Nottoway.* Blackstone, Va.: Nottoway Publishing Co., 1932. pp. 78–80.)

MP 12X